V - 31.- k

Inv.-Nr. 33106

Inv.-Nr. 33106

Geographisches Institut
der Universität Kiel
ausgesonderte Dublette

Geographisches Institut
der Universität Kiel
Neue Universität

Work and Leisure

NATIONAL
ATLAS
OF
SWEDEN

Work and Leisure

SPECIAL EDITOR

Kurt Viking Abrahamsson

THEME MANAGER

Department of Geography
Umeå University

The National Atlas of Sweden

SNA Publishing will publish between 1990 and 1996 a government-financed National Atlas of Sweden. The first national atlas, *Atlas över Sverige*, was published in 1953–71 by *Svenska Sällskapet för Antropologi och Geografi, SSAG* (the Swedish Society for Anthropology and Geography). The new national atlas describes Sweden in seventeen volumes, each of which deals with a separate theme. The organisations responsible for this new national atlas are *Lantmäteriverket, LMV* (the National Land Survey of Sweden), *SSAG* and *Statistiska centralbyrån, SCB* (Statistics Sweden). The whole project is under the supervision of a board consisting of the chairman, Sture Norberg and Thomas Mann (LMV), Staffan Helmfrid and Åke Sundborg (SSAG), Frithiof Billström and Gösta Guteland (SCB) and Leif Wastenson (SNA). To assist the board and the editors there is a scientific advisory group of three permanent members: Professor Staffan Helmfrid (Chairman), Professor Erik Bylund and Professor Anders Rapp. A theme manager is responsible for compiling the manuscript for each individual volume. The National Atlas of Sweden is to be published in book form both in Swedish and in English, and in a computer-based version for use in personal computers.

The English edition of the National Atlas of Sweden is published under the auspices of the *Royal Swedish Academy of Sciences* by the National Committee of Geography with financial support from *Knut och Alice Wallenbergs Stiftelse* and *Marcus och Amalia Wallenbergs Stiftelse*.

The whole work comprises the following volumes (in order of publication):

MAPS AND MAPPING
THE FORESTS
THE POPULATION
THE ENVIRONMENT
AGRICULTURE
THE INFRASTRUCTURE
SEA AND COAST
CULTURAL LIFE, RECREATION AND TOURISM
SWEDEN IN THE WORLD
WORK AND LEISURE
CULTURAL HERITAGE AND PRESERVATION
GEOLOGY
LANDSCAPE AND SETTLEMENTS
CLIMATE, LAKES AND RIVERS
MANUFACTURING, SERVICE AND TRADE
GEOGRAPHY OF PLANTS AND ANIMALS
THE GEOGRAPHY OF SWEDEN

CHIEF EDITOR	Leif Wastenson
EDITORS	Staffan Helmfrid, Scientific Editor
	Märta Syrén, Editor of *Work and Leisure*
	Ulla Arnberg, Editor
	Margareta Elg, Editor
PRODUCTION	LM Maps, Kiruna
SPECIAL EDITOR	Kurt Viking Abrahamsson
TRANSLATOR	Michael Knight
GRAPHIC DESIGN	Håkan Lindström
LAYOUT	Typoform/Gunnel Eriksson, Stockholm
REPRODUCTION	LM Repro, Luleå
COMPOSITION	Bokstaven Text & Bild AB, Göteborg
DISTRIBUTION	Almqvist & Wiksell International, Stockholm
COVER ILLUSTRATION	Jan-Peter Lahall/Great Shots

First edition
© SNA
Printed in Italy 1993

ISBN 91-87760-04-5 (All volumes)

ISBN 91-87760-22-3 (Work and Leisure)

Contents

Our Time on Earth   6
EINAR HOLM

Time and Space 7
Use of Time at Home and Away 7
The External Framework 8
Attitudes towards Work and Leisure 8
Work and Leisure in Time and Space 9

In the Old Days   10
NILS ARELL

Perceptions of Time 10
Time for Work 12
Pay for One's Pains 13
Reindeer Nomadism and Farming in Lappland 14
Mobility and Migrational Work 16
The Working Year in Peasant Society 17
The Coastal Population 18
The Transformation of Manufacturing 19
Leisure Time and Social Life 20

Transformation of Everyday Life   22
KAJSA ELLEGÅRD, BO LENNTORP

Everyday Life in Sweden Today 24
The Bergs in the Big City 24
The Bergs in Smalltown 26
Different Fates—the Same Roots 26
Various Kinds of Household 27
Projects in Life 28
Dominant Projects in Life's Stages 28
The Working Days of the Year 29
Touchdown in Time—Three Snapshots 30
Opportunities in Everyday Life 36
Constraints on Everyday Life 37
Everyday Resources 38

Work   40
LARS-ERIK BORGEGÅRD, URBAN FRANSSON, LARS LUNDIN

The Concept of Work 40
Occupations and Specialisation 42
Education 44
Gainful Employment 46
Intensiveness of Economic Activity 50
Full-time—Part-time 52
Manufacturing Industry and the Public Sector 54
Employment in the Service Sector 59
The Information Society 59
Local Labour Markets 60

From Local to Regional Labour Markets 70
Working Locally 72
Localisation of Workplaces 74
Mobility on the Labour Market 76
Immigration and the Labour Market 78
Unemployment 80
Absence Due to Illness 82
Pay 84
Measuring and Evaluating Time and Work 86
Organisation of Work 88
Regional Policies 90
New Structural Problems—Mobilisation 92
Europe—a Threat and a Promise 93

Leisure   94
NILS ARELL

Aspects of Leisure Time 94
Leisure Time? 95

BRUNO JANSSON

Leisure Time Activities 98
Sedentary Leisure 99
Television's Dominance 100
Young People's Sports 102
Study Circles 104
Religious Activities 105
Hunting and Fishing 106
Long Holiday Trips 108
Cinema, Theatre and Sports Events 112
Home-Loving Swedes Make Many Journeys 112
Holidays—something to save up 113

KURT VIKING ABRAHAMNSSON

Recreational Areas 114
Snowmobiling in the Mountains 114
Leisure Time on the Norrland Coast 115
Torup—Recreation for Townsfolk 116
Summer Cottages in Småland 117
Roam along the Finnskogen Trail—Country Traditions along the Border 118
Bunkers, Rough and Greens—Our New Landscape on Öland 119

The Future   120
EINAR HOLM

Our Time on Earth

"There goes the bus! Now I'll be late for work again! Peter's got the car to take the kids to the day nursery. So I go home and dig my bike out of the store room and get to the nursery just in time to catch him before he goes off to have the car tested. We drive to my office instead. The morning traffic is pretty thick—cars inching forward. What started as being a quarter of an hour late is now a whole hour's delay for Peter, while he waits for a new time for the car test. When he finally gets to work, there's a long line of people waiting outside his door. He picks me up after work, we fetch the TV set from the other side of town and then go on to the day nursery. I get the kids dressed—they're feeling pretty tired—and leave with the last of the staff, wheeling my bike back home and dragging two protesting kids behind me. In the meantime Peter does the food shopping. When we are all back home, it's too late to cook a proper meal before our elder daughter has to be taken to her riding lesson and I start my keep-fit class."

Why is there never enough time? This book will describe how we manage our daily lives in Sweden today. How do we work and how do we combine work and all our leisure activities? This will be a geographical picture of the role of work and leisure in our lives—activities, changes and location: a picture of people's work and play through the day, the week, the year and a lifetime. The social, economic and cultural geography of our society will be seen through the individual's eyes.

Time and Space

The way people use time and space is shaped by what they want to do and are able to do, by their wishes and situation in life and by environmental constraints. Closest to them are the family, the TV set, the home, the neighbours and the nearby streets. A little farther off are the schools, shops, workplaces and local authority offices. Even farther away, in Sweden and in the world, are private and public organisations which shape our local living conditions but also provide new opportunities for life at home and away. All of this is embedded in our vulnerable natural environment.

This book describes the conflicts between people's different wishes with regard to work and leisure, and the variety of workplaces and service and leisure facilities which are available in different parts of Sweden. What do we do, where do we do it and how often and for how long do we do it? Time will often be used as a measure of how we work and how we use our free time.

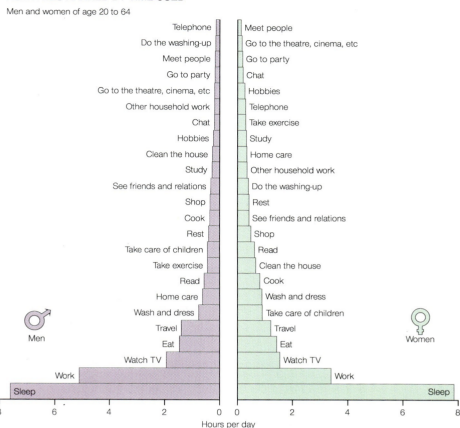

The diagram reveals both similarities and differences between the lives of men and women. The similarities are increasing, apparently as a result of women working more outside the home.

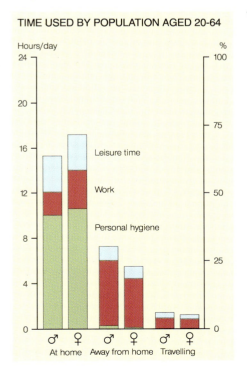

We spend most of our time at home, not only to sleep.

Use of Time at Home and Away

A number of maps show where we work in Sweden and where we spend time on various leisure activities. Many of these activities are important for the individual, even though they may not take up very much of his or her time. If, however, one looks at the length of time spent at various places, home is the most important place on earth. The difference between home and away is the most significant geographical form of categorisation.

People of working age spend on average two thirds of all their time at home. They sleep, eat, rest, wash and get dressed mostly at home. This kind of obligatory personal care takes up two thirds of the time at home. Of the remaining time, women use half and men a third to look after children and things, to tidy up, wash up and do other sorts of housework. More than half of the rest of the time, just over three hours a day, is spent watching television. Free time does not usually come in a lump, but is on average divided up into five or six short periods which come before or after other more fixed activities.

About a quarter of all time is spent by people of working age at various places outside the home. The most important ones are workplaces, shops, leisure centres and other people's homes in the neighbourhood, that is, places easily reached within the day. Work and shopping are the most time-consuming activities; less than a fifth of the time outside the home is used for pure leisure activities.

Moving from the home to these various places in the neighbourhood requires many short journeys and a few long ones. More than five per cent of time is taken up by journeys between places, on average one hour and twenty minutes per day. What makes it possible nowadays to go to more places, sometimes miles apart, is the fact that the speed of travel has increased enormously; it is not due to an increase in travelling time.

Motor traffic is the most decisive factor in this increase in travel range. The development of various means of transport and transport routes has led to the present scattered pattern of dwellings, shops, workplaces and leisure centres. We shall show how work, dwelling and leisure activities are localised in regions and city dis-

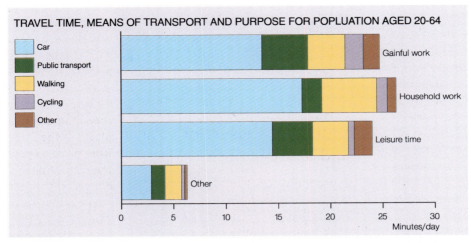

The car is our most frequently used means of transport, not least in connection with work in the home.

tricts and how distances between various activities lead to commuting and other travelling.

The External Framework

Our time on earth is short—this is true both of the individual and of the human race. Mankind has lived on earth for only the last fraction of its history, something like the last twenty seconds of a whole day. Settlement and activity in the area that corresponds to Sweden today occupies even less time—a fraction of a second at the most. We have already used up two thirds of the 15,000 years or so during which our land is inhabitable between the latest and the next ice age. Reckoning on 35 generations per thousand years, our descendants will, within only 175 generations, be back in an environment which our ancestors immigrated into about 300 generations ago. This date may, however, be altered somewhat by the greenhouse effect.

We have greater cause for concern about mankind's own influence on the conditions governing life. This could be as disastrous as an approaching ice age, and within just a few generations. The more immediate problem is to control global threats like reductions of the ozone layer, the greenhouse effect, destruction of the soil and lack of ground water. At the same time poor countries need continuous, resource-preserving economic growth and controlled growth of population. The solution to these problems is as important for our great-grandchildren's work and leisure in Sweden as all our efforts to improve the economy and the environment within our country's borders.

Attitudes towards Work and Leisure

Ways of looking at work and leisure vary according to country, epoch, culture and individual. Leisure is, at least as a concept, a more recent invention than "honest" and necessary work. Most of us would agree that employment, what we do to earn money, is "work". It is more difficult to assess attitudes towards unpaid work in the home and the distinction between work at home and work "at work", as well as that between work in the home and leisure activities.

From one point of view work is a necessary means for getting desired production. The value of work lies in its result, whereas the work process itself is a necessary evil. Free time, on the other hand, is used for voluntarily chosen activities which have a value in themselves. If we apply this criterion, work in the home is also work—though unpaid. The distinction between reproductive and productive, paid and unpaid and taxed and untaxed work is a flexible and arbitrary one.

It is often a matter of chance whether identical tasks are performed as work in the home or as paid work. Children are looked after at home or at a day nursery. Lunch is prepared at home or at a restaurant. The house is painted by a firm that pays tax or by a friend who, instead of payment, gets a helping hand with his lawn. Self-subsistence and an informal barter economy used to be the commonest ways in Sweden of organising work and benefiting from the division of labour, just as it still is in many countries in the world today.

A calculation made by the Swedish Consumer's Association shows that one hour of work in the home today pays for goods and services to the value of 46 Skr. All production at home in one year would then correspond to purchases worth 313 billion Skr or 24 per cent of the gross national product for 1990.

If, instead of thinking of the value of work for other people, one emphasises its value for feelings of affiliation and self-realisation, it becomes even more difficult to draw a meaningful line between free time, personal care and work in the home. Is it free time to sit at home in the evening, working out solutions to problems that have to be dealt with tomorrow at work? Or personal care if one does the same thing in bed? Is it work to discuss the ice-hockey match at work while wait-

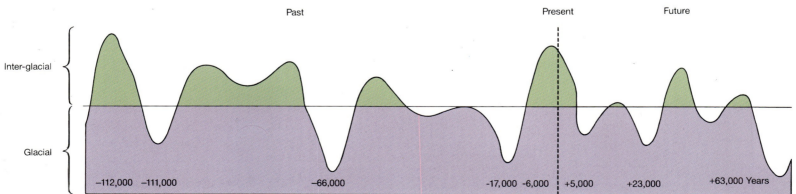

ing for the next job to come up?

It is historical and cultural chance that decides what work is paid work, what is informal exchanged work and what is unpaid work in the home. Likewise, payment for work is based on social conventions and power structures. Pay is not merely reimbursement for work which most people do not want to do—and would not do if there was not a demand for it in households or on the market. It is also used to signify power relations, responsibility, complexity and perceived significance. That is why impoverishing, dangerous work performed in isolation is often paid less than stimulating, safe work performed in a social setting.

The way in which work and leisure are separated in this book is also typical of our time and age. Our division is based mainly on a system chosen for Statistics Sweden's time-utilisation studies for 1985/86 and 1990/91. The data in this introduction is a summary of the latter study.

One fifth of our time, for people aged 20 to 64, is spent working for pay, on average 27 hours a week for women and 41 hours a week for men. If time for work in the home is included, the total working time for men and women becomes virtually the same: just over 60 hours a week, or 36 per cent of the week's 168 hours. On top of this there are 70 hours for sleep and personal care and a little more than two hours for education. This leaves 34 hours of "freer time", which is as much as for paid work, 20 per cent of our time. Spread over a whole lifetime, paid work occupies less than ten per cent of our time.

Work and Leisure in Time and Space

In the following chapters our use of time and space will be the central issue. Changes in attitudes towards work, leisure, time and space will be described from a historical point of view, as will the amount of time and space used by various work and leisure activities.

This time perspective and geography will be linked together in a "time-geographic perspective", in which the population's use of time will be described at both the macro and the micro level. A number of cases will exemplify how life can turn out for the individual and how the lives and behaviour of the multitude of individuals together create an overall pattern of activities for the whole population.

Various stages and situations in life often result in typical and fairly inevitable daily and weekly routines, if everyday life is to function properly. In the short term we are tied by social and more formal contracts with our family, friends, employers and the state. Many activities are dependent on other things being completed; others have to be performed at certain times, at certain places, together with certain other people. Every activity requires a certain amount of space, which cannot usually be used for any other purpose at the same time. Nobody can be at two different places at the same time—moving from place to place takes time. Contracts, routines, co-ordination, the indivisibility of people and things, physical inertia and space requirements reduce the number of options here and now quite drastically. We shall take a look at the patterns of life that are in fact feasible in present-day Sweden, in contrast to what people believe is possible when they see the enormous potential range of work and leisure activities available.

One chapter describes work in Sweden today. In addition there is a comprehensive picture of the population's work input and the organisation of work in space and time. Various leisure activities are described in a similar fashion. Where and when we can do different things in our free time makes up part of Sweden's organisational structure. For this reason special attention is paid to the development of more work-like, organised leisure. Finally, we give examples of the ways in which various leisure landscapes are formed and utilised—for instance, the way in which yesterday's industrial landscapes can live on as tomorrow's leisure landscapes.

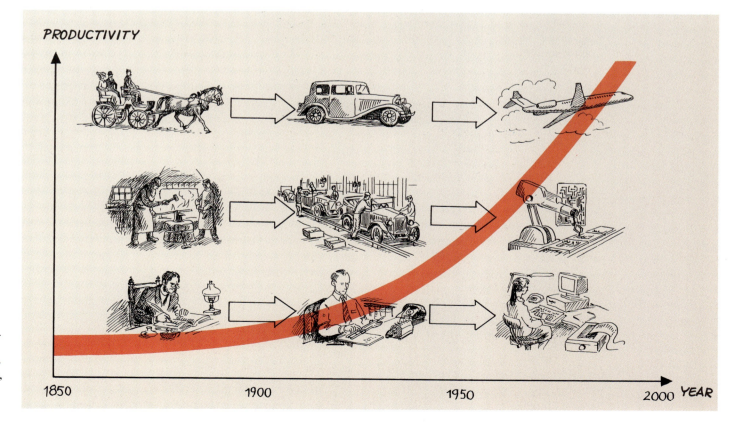

The most important factor in social development is the increasingly rapid growth in productivity, production per hour of work, thanks to technological progress.

In the Old Days

Vital information could be transmitted from island to island in the archipelagoes at the speed of light. "Beware of breakers at sea" or "Russians on the way!".

Summoning sticks were sent from farm to farm to call people to village meetings, search parties, fires or other urgent matters. The same could be done acoustically and rapidly by blowing ox horns or bronze lures, or by beating large drums.

The well-known sound of church bells reminded parishioners in a village which their church was. The limits of a parish were defined by the area from which churchgoers came. There was a close feeling of community.

The shape and area of a town are set by local conditions and restrictions which describe "time-space", determined by the means of transport available. Practical factors limited the size of pre-industrial towns to what was within "walking distance", which favoured a round shape. All parts of the town could easily be visited on foot. In later times new forms of transport led to star-shaped growth.

The French economic historian Fernand Braudel once suggested that we should make a hypothetical call on Voltaire and have a long talk with him. We would be able to manage a conversation without too much difficulty in communicating with each other. In Braudel's opinion 18th-century man was very like ourselves today as far as attitudes to life were concerned. Their mental attitudes and passions were close enough to our own to make mutual comprehension possible. But if we were to stay on for a few days, all the details of daily life would create a great many problems, such as lighting at night-time, heating, transportation, food, personal hygiene, illnesses, medicine, news reports... How representative of his time was the enlightened Voltaire and his daily routine?

"Good to have it, a pity it's necessary" was the general opinion of perfume in the 18th century, at the court of King Gustav III in Sweden. A clue of some kind, perhaps?

A century is not a particularly long time, really. It is only a hop, skip and jump back in time from today's subsidised football practice for eight-year-olds to yesterday's child labour in the smithy or the match factory: father, grandfather, great grandfather. But there is a world of differences between them.

It is, of course, difficult to apply the customs and values of our own time to yesterday's conditions—but it costs nothing to make the comparison. For us it is natural to think of the 24 hours of the day as divided between our own private time and the time taken up by various obligations, of which work is for most people the most time-consuming. But if one goes back a few generations, how much time was there left over for oneself after working for one's daily bread? How did people use this time? The historical section which follows will deal with mobility in working life. Even if the old peasant society was on the whole static, its members had to make a living wherever they could find it.

Perceptions of Time

Man has always had a perception of time; he has questioned the nature of time, the best way to make use of it, how to make time pass or last long enough. Time had to be measured.

The Middle Ages have been described as "islands of time in a sea of timelessness"; there were sundials on the church walls, mechanical clocks governed by the sun. Each place had its own local time. The strict rituals of the Catholic church demanded a more accurate division of the day (it was not the Christian church that invented the seven-day week, but it found it convenient for its fundamental purposes) and town routines began to be regulated. Bells tolled when the town gates were opened or closed, and so on. Did this affect people's perception of time? Hardly. The ringing of bells reminded them of days of rest and red-letter days. For some the tolling of bells marked the end of life. The concept of past, present and future was diffuse and fatalistic. There was little cause to expect anything else in the immediate future than what had just passed. As it was, so had it always been and always would be. Monks and other men who needed to measure short periods of time used an hourglass. And the hourglass was something Death the Reaper carried, too.

Peasant society had an innate, natural rhythm, oscillating between absolutes: life and death, light and darkness, heat and cold, work and

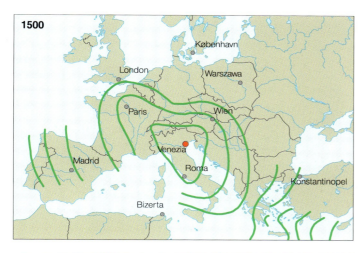

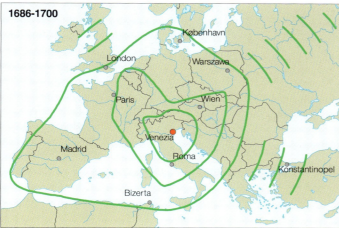

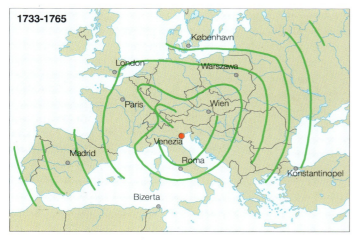

(K1)

A LETTER TO VENICE

Poor roads and low speeds, that is how we think of travelling in olden times. Transport technology developed slowly. Napoleon travelled no faster than Julius Caesar. We can see this from the maps, which show how long it took for a message to reach Venice. By horse, coach, boat or runner it was at best possible to travel 100 km in 24 hours. Higher speeds were rare and a luxury. The big towns attracted fresh news because they paid for high speed. Distance meant money.

The isochrones on the maps show the time in weeks it took for a letter to reach Venice. In the early 16th century it took three weeks from Antwerp and over a month from Copenhagen. It was no faster in the 18th century.

rest, working day and holiday. It was a cyclical time, like a wheel that slowly turned in harmony with the working year and nature's seasons, a time with clear differences in living conditions and narrow limits for survival. The geographical dimension is evident in countries that stretch a long way from north to south in northern latitudes, like Sweden. Usually the snow still lies deep on the ground in the north when it is time for spring ploughing on the southern plains. For us Northerners it is natural to associate light with warmth, darkness with cold. In contrast to this cyclical time came middle-class clock time, industrial time, linear time, national mean time. The factory hooter became the symbol of authority, the signal by which factory and mill owners controlled their workers. Yet certain sectors of the economy remain dependent on the old cyclical routines. Christmas shopping is a particularly good example of this.

"Why all the hurry, lad? You'll get to your grave in time, you know." Those were the words that greeted the Swedish writer Wilhelm Moberg when his father, a conscript soldier from Algutsboda parish in Småland, noticed his son's nervous restlessness when he visited the family home. Moberg says: "Nobody in my childhood was ever in a hurry. They did a lot of hard work, but they were never rushed." Moberg's father certainly thought there was no point in filling every minute of the day with some sort of activity. But if you didn't do what had to be done, poverty and misery were waiting round the corner — in the worst case starvation and death. Peasant society was task-oriented. Work was done when it had to be done, regardless of how long it took. Time had to match the job to be done. Besides, nobody saw any point in using all time as productive time, unless the product was needed. Intensive periods of work were followed by idleness, a pattern which can still be traced among those who work in the "free" professions today. Is this a natural, human rhythm of work? Who needs instant coffee?

Our watches show what the time is, either analogically with hands, or digitally with figures. If you want to teach a child the spatial dimension of time, the connection between time and the way the earth turns, you would do well to choose an analogue watch, which is one step in a long tradition of measuring time, cyclical time. In contrast a digital watch mesmerises the eye with a line of figures which gives no point of reference, linear time.

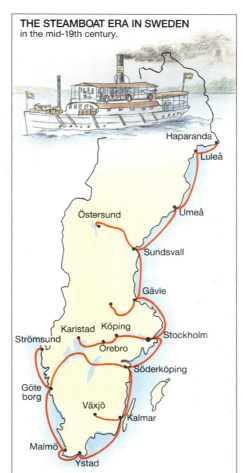

THE STEAMBOAT ERA IN SWEDEN in the mid-19th century.

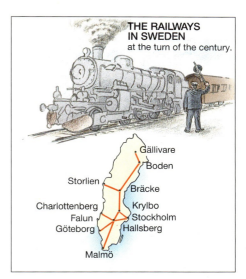

THE RAILWAYS IN SWEDEN at the turn of the century.

AVIATION IN SWEDEN today.

0   1   2 Days

Time for Work

In our culture we carry a heavy burden of traditional moral attitudes towards work. The message in J O Wallin's hymn is not to be misunderstood:

*No crust of bread to us will come
But God will care to grant us,
And he who does not care to work
Shall not expect to eat it.
And this, the message
From the Lord,
Must never be forgotten.*

Karl Marx would probably have agreed. In one fundamental respect it was, of course, vital that people used their time effectively enough to support themselves. The whole capacity of the household had to be utilised. In pre-industrial society, the traditional peasant society, the question of the time needed for a certain piece of work was less important than the result. Was it good enough? People did not think in terms of working time and free time; the one melted into the other. Work which was done together was often followed by feasting and festivities that were enjoyed together. There was a good deal of moving about, which was very time-consuming. People invested in the time it took to travel in order to make an, often temporary, living. They would ski 200 kilometres to get to a lumber camp, walk some 300 kilometres from Mora to a building site in Stockholm or row 60 kilometres with a catch of herring from Möja into Stockholm.

Dividing time into categories, apart from working days and holidays, came with the Industrial Revolution. The distinction between work and leisure was for a long time unclear and arbitrary. The problem was not defined, and people were not so particular about working conditions. An 11 to 12-hour working day, somewhat shorter on Saturdays, with an hour's break for food, was usual in 19th-century industry and craft work. A 70-hour working week was normal. Expressing working hours as a certain number of hours on the job does not, however, tell you how well the time was utilised. A worker in the 1890s writes: "Our dream of an eight-hour working day came true, but what a change in the pace of work! It used to be considered sucking up to the foremen to start work before they arrived, and half an hour could pass before work started. Now (1950) you start work as soon as the hooter goes and it goes on at the same fast pace till the end of the day."

A hundred years ago six billion hours of work were done per year in Sweden. Since then the population has doubled and the standard of living has risen enormously. Yet we do no more than 6.5 billion hours of work. What is accomplished per hour, however, is quite different from the results of work in the 1880s.

The way in which the stages of life are portrayed is tied to time and space. The phases of life change as society changes. The 19th-century picture of the life cycle shows a middle-class society in which man is at the height of his powers at the age of 50. At the same time people in other social classes could be physically worn out before they were 40. Nowadays children are allowed to be full-time children for the first 15 years of their life, and their youth, their time for education, usually continues well into their twenties. In earlier times confirmation was seen as the longed-for ticket to the adult world when you could get a job and expect to be paid. You were grown up at an early age and went on working, to put it bluntly, until you died.

Jean François Millet (1814–1875), the painter of working life. This painting is called The Angelus and depicts the peasants' peaceful devotions and rest after a day of arduous work in the fields. The landscape is bathed in twilight and one can almost hear the bell of the distant church ringing out across the fields.

This chart describes life from the cradle to the grave in ten-year steps. Painting from Dalarna by Jufwas Anders Ersson.

Stigbergsgatan in Södermalm, Stockholm, is an example of a housing environment at the end of the 19th century. The photograph was taken in 1890. People lived on top of each other. The buildings were cold and damp, lacking water and drains. Rats and other vermin caused great prob-

Pay for One's Pains

The following list gives a picture of work, income and expenditure in Södermalm, Stockholm, in 1906–07.

Industrial work was to be had at some hundred factories, like Bergsund's and Ludvigsberg's Engineering Works, the Great Docks at Tegelviken, the München Brewery, Nürnberg, Neumüller, Barnängen's Technical Works, the Tanto Sugar Mill, Stockholm's Cotton Spinning and Weaving Mill at Barnängen, Wicander's Cork Factory, Liljeholmen's Candle Factory at Danvikstull, Hellgren's Tobacco Factory in Götgatan and the Swedish Bottlecap Factory in Tjärhovsgatan.

In addition there were:
- 1 sour milk factory
- 2 cardboard box factories
- 3 fruit juice factories
- 5 ersats coffee factories
- 3 iron-bed factories
- 6 sausage factories
- 3 shoe factories
- 13 foundries
- 2 yeast factories
- 1 margarine factory
- 4 soap factories
- 1 cotton wool factory

Many people were engaged in crafts of various kinds: tin smithying, book and brush binding, dyeing, saddlery, lace-making, dress-making and coach-building.

WAGES IN A NUMBER OF OCCUPATIONS

Men (age)	Skr/year
Brewery worker (48) at München Brewery	1,290
Dock worker (30)	1,000
Textile worker (53) at Barnängen	1,090
Mechanic (54) at Bergsund	766
Brewery manager (50)	17,500
Wholesale merchant (48)	6,200
Insurance clerk (44)	4,300

Women (age)	Skr/year
Dressmaker (32) at Nordiska Kompaniet	830
Bookbinder (22)	740
Cigarette worker (42)	720
Washerwoman (22) at a wash-house	740

EXPENDITURE (%) FOR MOST FAMILIES

Food and drink	50%
Housing (rent, heating, light)	20%
Clothes and footwear	10%
Union dues and insurance	5%
Taxes	4%

The remaining 11% had to cover washing, cleaning, repairs, furniture and kitchen equipment, tools, health and hygiene, school fees for children, travel, books and newspapers and entertainment.

A "LESS WELL-OFF" FAMILY'S ANNUAL BUDGET

Income	Skr/year
Husband	1,208:35
Wife	12:35
Lodger	310
Benefit	106
Other (loans, gifts etc.)	34:95
Total	1,671:65

Expenditure	Skr/year
Rent	424:41
Heating and lighting	71:58
Food and drink	782:84
Clothes	102:60
Insurance and union dues	67
Health	41:38
Taxes	66:92
Other	145:26
Total	1,701,99
Annual deficit	30:34

These figures are from 1 October 1907 for one year and were given by a shoe-factory worker (aged 33) with a wife (aged 29) and two young children, and four lodgers (2 men, 2 women), one of whom had full board, and the others lodging with morning coffee only. The apartment had two rooms and a kitchen.

From a report from The Committee for Workers' Insurance, 1885: "Sanitary conditions in the major town industry—mechanical engineering—were known to be poor. Long working hours and excessive overtime led to chronic gastric catarrh, air filled with soot and iron particles to pulmonary catarrh and eye injuries, the continual manhandling of iron to skin afflictions and the hard work performed by children to periostitis."

Child labour was common in workshops and factories and was identified as a social problem towards the end of the century. Apprentices were taken on at an early age. Apprenticeship was long for many occupations. This was one aspect of the problem. The other was purely economic. Match and textile factories, for example, based their production for many years on cheap labour, on teenagers who worked for a few years doing simple tasks for a low wage and were then forced to leave when they were 20. Mechanisation made it more difficult to handle the machinery. Children were made redundant in certain processes and were replaced by adult men.

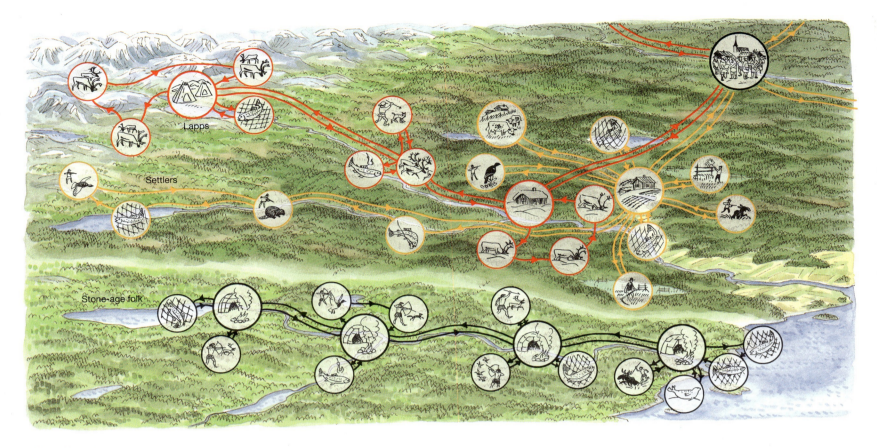

A hypothetical resource landscape showing lines of migration.

MOBILITY AND ADAPTATION

Time, space, distance, accessibility and use of resources are concepts that are closely connected with mobility. Survival demands some kind of adaptation, trimming one's sails according to the wind. If the conditions for survival do not exist at one place, people are forced to move elsewhere. Mobility increases one's possibilities of utilising the resources in an area; one can choose between different ways of making a living, thereby creating greater security and stability in the household. The opportunities for combining resources improve.

Mobility widens one's frames of reference. One gains knowledge and can make comparisons between the opportunities and conditions provided by different kinds of environments. More options become available. In this historical section we pay special attention to mobility in industry.

NOMADS IN ANCIENT AND MODERN TIMES

The cultural form developed by the food collectors and hunters who first settled in Sweden was similar in some respects to the nomadism of modern Lapp reindeer farmers. The people who followed the melting inland glacial ice were reindeer hunters. They lived along the coast and shores of lakes. It is possible to see similar parallels between the later colonisers of inland Norrland and the earliest farming cultures, with hunting, fishing and primitive agriculture as a base. These settlers had no absolutely fixed home; they would often spend long periods away on hunting and fishing expeditions, collecting winter fodder or visiting markets.

The economy of the early Stone Age was based on hunting, fishing and collecting anything that was edible. This extensive utilisation of resources required a migratory life and vast areas of land. A system evolved of moving from one base to another, with climatic conditions and animal habits giving a seasonal rhythm to this nomadic economy.

The crofts on the hillsides were the old form of the forest districts' half-nomadism. The crofts in Dalarna, for example, are known to have existed since the Middle Ages and were a living feature of the culture until the mid-twentieth century. These crofts came into being as a result of overcrowding in the villages. A village would grow as a result of estate inheritance, and it became difficult to find enough grazing land round the village for the increasing number of cattle. The solution was to take the cattle, together with a few people from each household, to a forest pasture far from the farm. The croft which was established there might, in the course of time, become a permanent settlement and develop into a new village. Thus in some districts summer crofts played an important role in spreading settlements.

Reindeer Nomadism and Farming in Lappland

Reindeer nomadism provides an interesting example of the use of time and seasonal migration. The sketch maps here give a rough picture of two economies: nomadic reindeer farming and permanent farming. The data comes from the northeast corner of Sweden, where it meets the Norwegian and Finnish frontiers. On the right (south) edge of the map lies Lappland and on the left (north) edge part of the Norwegian frontier. The nomads' migratory routes between various seasonal pastures are shown, as well as the guest farms, that is, special farms where the nomad families stayed for part of the time they spent in the winter pastures. The nomads enter the map from the left, the north, on their return from the Norwegian summer pastures in the early autumn. If they move below the Lappland boundary during the winter, they leave the map for a while.

THE MID–18TH CENTURY

The settlers fetch winter fodder from natural meadowland, mires and the banks of streams. Hay is harvested in July, stooked in the field and taken to the farms as soon as the first snow falls. The amount of hay determined the number of cattle that could be fed over winter and was the decisive factor for the survival of the settlement. According to the government settlers

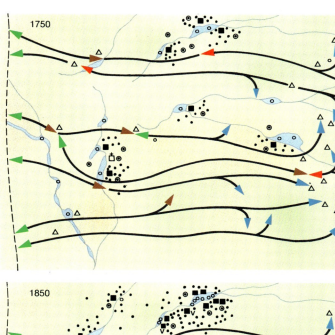

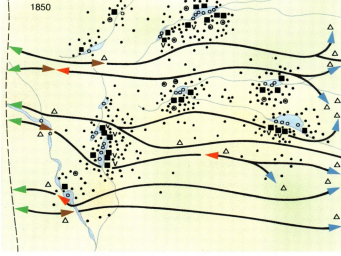

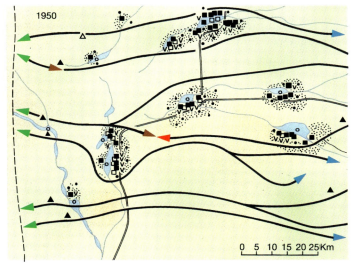

The reindeer farming year, 1750, 1850 and 1950

If the 1750 migrations in the diagram above are superimposed on southern Sweden, one clearly sees what long distances were covered.

- → Moving to winter pasture
- → Moving to autumn pasture
- → Moving to spring pasture
- → Moving to summer pasture
- ▫ Other husbandry
- ▪ Settlers, active farming
- ⁂ Hay meadows
- ⁖ Ploughed grassland
- ⌂ Church
- ○ Fishing
- ⊙ Hunting
- △ Temporary camp
- ▲ Permanent camp
- v Host

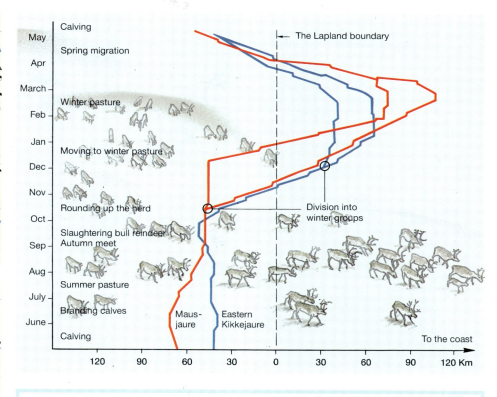

This diagram provides up-to-date examples of land use during the reindeer-farming year in two Lapp forest villages. This year starts in June and moves upwards along the vertical axis. The other axis shows how the Lapp village uses its land. The vertical line represents the boundary of the Lapp territory, from which the distances travelled are measured. Reindeer are allowed below the Lapp territory boundary between October 1st and April 30th. The legal effects of the boundary are illustrated graphically by showing how the line is cut by the lines for the autumn and spring migrations.

were supposed to work on their farms and devote their time to "useful cultivation" instead of wasting time on too much hunting and fishing.

The nomads cross the Swedish frontier on their way from their summer pastures during August-September. They stop here for a few weeks to round up the reindeer herds and slaughter the bull calves. In autumn and winter they try to keep close to a church or a market place, where the most important social events of the year take place. They have no permanent dwelling. Nomads and settlers exchange goods and services.

THE MID–19TH CENTURY

There are more farmsteads now, using more land, which requires more work. The farmers fish in the mountain lakes and are helped by the Lapps when they need to transport salt and barrels up to the farms in the spring and down again with salt fish in the autumn. The nomads' migratory patterns have not changed. The host farm system is fully developed. The settlers complain that the reindeer are spoiling their hay, the nomads that their fishing waters and hunting grounds are being exploited.

THE MID–20TH CENTURY

There are cultivated meadows now, making for more intensive land exploitation. Milk deliveries give cash income on a scale never known before. The district has formed links with the mining and service communities in the region. The reindeer farming households move over shorter distances. The families stay in their home in their home parish during the summer. They do not yet have their own permanent dwellings and rent rooms from the old host families. Since the 1970s farming has more or less ceased. The houses are used as second homes. The reindeer farmers have become residents and changed their migratory patterns. It is easier to get to the summer pastures along new roads, so the families can stay together again during the summer and part of the autumn. But the other migrations follow the old tracks. Hunting and fishing rights can lead to conflicts. When the reindeer-farming families got their own permanent dwellings, the host system and the old contact patterns were broken. People lived closer together physically, but were farther apart socially. The circle has not yet been closed.

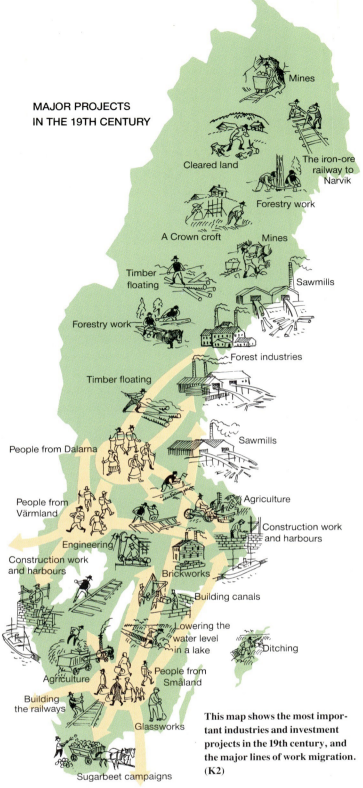

MAJOR PROJECTS IN THE 19TH CENTURY

This map shows the most important industries and investment projects in the 19th century, and the major lines of work migration. (K2)

Mobility and Migrational Work

Mobility in working life was particularly high during the 19th century, which need not contradict the general picture that peasant society was static. This mobility was above all caused by regional variations in industry, the seasonal distribution of work during the year and the way the economy was organised. The people who wanted work were not in the places were work was to be had. Pre-industrial society was unable to absorb the increase in population.

Sweden was a country in the process of change. Profound changes in agriculture led to an increase in the number of propertyless people. Half of the country's households were crofters, cottars and farm labourers paid in kind. They could not support themselves on their own land and were obliged to leave home in search of work. In fact it was a surplus of labour in the country districts that was the major social problem. It was easy enough to get work in the summer, but in the winter. . . ! For many countryfolk this was a time of unemployment, or even absolute destitution. Poverty was widespread, housing poor and infant mortality high. It was this large group of propertyless people who were called "the vagrants who live on potatoes and odd jobs". The authorities looked upon mobility, both geographical and occupational, with disapproving eyes. It was safest to have a fixed and stable population; jacks of all trades were difficult to keep under control. Regulations were introduced to reduce mobility and by-laws were passed to prevent people who were out of work from becoming a possible burden in the poorhouse.

What sort of work was there to be had? Country estates and large farms always needed extra workers for the summer. The consequences of the land reform were plenty of day work ploughing fields, digging ditches, herding cattle and building fences, for example. The new industrial society dug canals, built railways, created harbours, erected factories and houses. Of course there was work, but not enough of it, and it was not permanent. Even at the end of the 19th century a great deal of factory work was seasonal in, for example, sawmills, blast furnaces and brickworks. The work force often came from a long way away. Men came from all over the country to work in the Norrland sawmills. As the yearly rhythm of work became more regular, it was possible to stay over winter and in the next stage settle down for good. The same pattern could be observed in the iron mines and at many other places. People in search of a job moved from the south northwards to get forestry work, to State crofts and to newly cleared land in the State forests. From forest and farming districts all over Sweden a stream of job-seekers poured into towns and industrial areas. Many of them escaped by saving enough money to buy a single ticket to America.

Migratory work affected the whole of the country and in Dalarna it had a long tradition. During the summer people walked to Bergslagen, Mälardalen and first and foremost Stockholm in search of work. In the late 19th century they also went to the sawmills in the north. They usually took heavy construction jobs, often at building sites. In Stockholm the girls

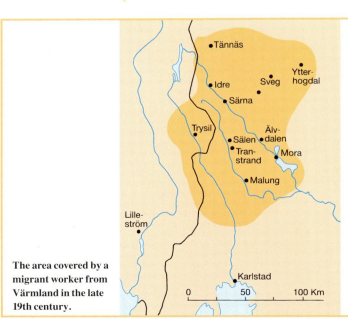

The area covered by a migrant worker from Värmland in the late 19th century.

KARL BJÖRKMAN, A MIGRANT WORKER FROM VÄRMLAND (BORN 1860)

"I started working in the forests at 14, and was considered a man at 15, after my confirmation. Got a job felling trees west of the Klarälven for the winter, and then timber floating in May and June. Our little forest croft didn't need much work and there wasn't any work in the local forests, so I had to move off again." This pattern was repeated year after year. Felling trees far from home, floating timber, harvesting hay in the meadows and then off again in the autumn. "One autumn we decided to go to Lillherrdal and packed our bags with food for the journey, 200 kilometres on foot through the forests. Three of us the same age went together. One was going to haul the timber out by horse and we would fell for him. We lived in a hut by a stream. Another year we walked 350 kilometres for a badly-paid job in the forests at Tännäs. We had to build our own hut when we got there."

They lived on fatty pork, porridge, pancakes and coffee. Work and leisure ran together. Their clothes had to dry on them. Get up at four or five o'clock to use the light. "In 1890 I was made foreman for timber floating on the river and had a steady income – three months' floating and then forest work again." Karl Björkman spent many years travelling far and wide. He was probably typical of a large number of Värmland lumberjacks.

Mortar and brick carriers worked like a human conveyor belt, carrying their hods up and down the swaying scaffolding to the bricklayers on the job. Construction work was seasonal. Work was done in the summer and autumn and left standing during the winter. Then the carpenters took over. Workers on all the construction sites in Stockholm in the 1880s and 1890s – here the Royal Opera House – came from many parts of Sweden. The mortar carriers were often girls from Dalarna, the construction workers often came from Mälardalen or Dalarna, too.

from Dalarna were well-known as rowing "dames", until they were driven off the market by the steamboats. The men from Dalarna were well organised; they walked and worked in teams and kept together in their leisure time as well.

The propertyless population increased seven times over in Småland between 1760 and 1860. There was quite simply not enough fertile land and many people were forced to go out looking for work. In the mid-nineteenth century many new jobs were created when canals were constructed, lakes were drained, ditches were dug and railways were built. People took jobs building apartment houses in Stockholm and at the brickworks round Lake Mälaren. At times there was even a stream of workers from Småland to Denmark and Germany. Many women worked on the sugarbeet fields on the central plains.

In Värmland people learnt to be foresters at an early age and often worked in the Norwegian forests.

The Working Year in Peasant Society

In the working year around 1900 in the village of Kamsjö in the parish of Degerfors in Västerbotten County, the whole family worked, everyone with his particular task. The women were responsible for the house and the cowsheds; much of their work was done in the kitchen in their "spare time". They carded, span and wove. The men made household equipment and tools. Their most important extra income came from the forest work which they did for the forest companies, when they were away from home for a few weeks and the women looked after the farm. This is thought to have made men's and women's roles less distinct. This division of work aimed at utilising the whole family's potential, to get as much as possible out of the land. As the number of different jobs increased, the importance of farming decreased and instead combined cash incomes grew. Instead of maximising yields from the land people started maximising the combined total of wages and farming. In the end a choice had to be made between, on the one hand, profitable side lines and paid work as a complement to farming and on the other hand, specialising in farming and forestry. These were difficult choices that many people were forced to make.

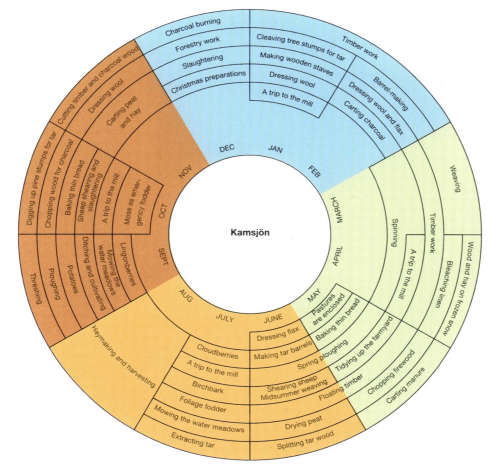

Some of the occupations in a farm household. Making barrels, cutting staves, midsummer weaving and reed cutting – each season had its specific tasks.

The Coastal Population

Sweden has a long coastline and a large coastal population that has made its living in many different ways, with fishing as an important occupation. When a money economy was introduced, the distinction between fishing and agriculture became clearer. We see here some typical developments along the west and east coasts. The examples are from Öckerö in Bohuslän and Runnö in Kalmarsund.

The importance of herring for the economy of Bohuslän is well known. During the latter part of the 18th century herring was of vital national importance, thanks to a growing market in Europe. The fish could be caught in seine nets close to land. Seine teams were formed, which followed the herring along the coast. Small communities grew up round salting houses and train-oil works and flourished during the fishing season. People made their way to them from far and near. When the big herrings disappeared from the coast in the early 19th century, there was a crisis. A vital industry was knocked out. The government tried to provide compensation by encouraging deep-sea fishing. The herring seasons of the 1870s were less critical and fishing had been modernised by that time. Catching areas and markets had expanded. Transporting fish in ice by rail, the canning industry and sales and processing in the home village created new potential. This development can be summarised in four phases: periodic herring fishing, trading in fresh fish, mechanisation of the fishing fleet and trawling.

Along the Baltic coast farming and fishing had a different role to play. The farmer-fishermen had "one boot in his boat and the other in his field"; they moved out to the skerries for part of the year to fish. Their varied occupations included hunting seal and seabirds, collecting eggs and eider down, building boats and shipping freight. Developments at Runnö in Kalmarsund are a good illustration of a common pattern of events along the Baltic coast. There was a long tradition of farming, but in the early 19th century fishing became more dominant. The fishing farmer became a farming fisherman. Spring and autumn fishing for cod and herring was particularly profitable. The farms were looked after by the womenfolk collectively. The cows were taken out to summer pasture on the islands, to which the women rowed for milking. Gathering winter fodder was a collective effort. It was fishing that demanded most work, but it also offered the greatest potential. The laws concerning fishing waters were obsolete, but the introduction of eel-fishing nets in the 1920s gave a new lease of life to Runnö. Investments and work input increased, as did incomes. The inhabitants of Runnö became fishermen, abandoning their old forms of work, apart from the traditional way of dividing up fishing areas. This development, from a variety of occupations to specialisation, did not mean the sort of change in migratory patterns that occurred on the west coast and may be summarised as: fishing farmer—farming fisherman—professional fisherman.

Herring could be caught with seine nets near the shore, 1906.

Herring catch before gutting, 1910.

The Transformation of Manufacturing

A great deal of manufacturing was done in rural districts. The workshops were small and served a local market. People learnt the trade on the job and got an overall picture of the manufacturing process by seeing all its stages. There was great mobility between workplaces, some of which could be categorised as journeyman travels. A workshop often had no permanent workforce but relied on "journeymen who came and went".

In the decades after 1870 industrial inventions led rapidly to the formation of a number of specialist industries. In 1912 65 per cent of industrial production was classified as special manufacturing, but the level of mechanisation remained low. The work of a mechanic was for many years close to that of a village blacksmith. Technological developments, however, resulted in tools and machinery that worked with a high degree of precision, which meant that it was possible to buy spare parts instead of rebuilding or replacing a damaged machine. Some of the mechanics were able to keep their jobs as instrument makers, but generally speaking construction work was transferred from the mechanic to a designer. The organisation of work was fundamentally changed. Here are the comments of a worker in 1871: "In the eighties each workshop had a master mechanic who was in charge of all operations. The foremen gave advice and help, which meant that we all worked together as a team."

The way work was organised meant that work and leisure were interwoven. The mill workers lived near the works and more or less only mixed with each other. The young workers lived in the workshops. During the breaks someone might come from the family with something to eat. But the new factories closed their gates when work started, so the workers were virtually locked in until the hooter went at the end of the day.

MTM AND THE LANCASHIRE PROCESS

One of the features of the development of modern society is the way working time has become more and more strictly controlled. Yet technologies from different eras and with very different attitudes towards time and its use were able to exist side by side during a transitional period. Around 1950 Swedish industry was introduced to the MTM method—a method for timing to the second every movement that a factory worker makes. The idea was to eliminate wasted time and to develop effective and standardised work routines. Every worker was to carry out all the items of work in exactly the same way. There was a good deal of controversy about this method, and at the same time the Lancashire process lived on in a number of Swedish ironworks. This method for producing iron came from the old style of iron production, before the modern ingot steel process. The Lancashire process demanded a very high level of skill from the workers. The smiths were self-taught, often having started work in the forge at the age of 13. This traditional craftmanship lived on alongside modern technical methods for almost a hundred years after the industrial revolution had come to Sweden.

Foundry at Bolinders Mechanical Engineering Works at Kungsklippan, Stockholm, 1893.

Foundry workers, 1899

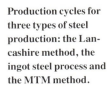

Production cycles for three types of steel production: the Lancashire method, the ingot steel process and the MTM method.

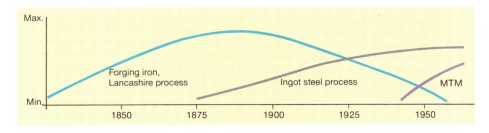

19

Playing croquet and quoits on holiday, 1895.

Summer visitors help bring in the hay harvest, 1903.

"Rosy-cheeked damsels and sun-tanned gentlemen handle their rackets like real Englishmen", 1906.

Leisure Time and Social Life

It was in the 19th century, in middle-class circles, within a narrow group of capitalists and senior managers, that a leisure time sector first developed. These people could afford to buy leisure time by letting a staff of servants take care of the house and the children. The middle-class style of living was characterised by clear ritualistic and formal features. It was necessary to know the social code. It was important to show one's class affinity in social life. The social and leisure activities that developed were gradually adopted by other groups in society.

Hasse Z's sketches of the Stockholm bourgeoisie in the archipelago at the turn of the century give a fairly good picture of their life style: "Stockholm used to be a dead city in the summertime. The middle class scattered pepper in their apartments, hung sheets over their crystal chandeliers to protect them from flies, covered up their plush furniture and took down their velvet curtains. Then they went out to the archipelago with their children and their pot plants and 219 pieces of luggage, sailed their yachts, preferably in a Royal Yachting Club uniform, fished, played croquet and saw to it that their daughters got engaged. In the evenings they sat on their verandas drinking chilled punch, but got up early to take up their fishing lines. If you were staying at Dalarö, Sandhamn or Furusund you belonged to "Society", socialised with actors and actresses, organised bazaars and took part in theatricals..."

Towards the end of the century new categories of people with plenty of spare time in the summer—teachers, university staff, artists and writers—began to find their way out to the outer islands, to Möja and Nämndö. They lived a simple and inexpensive life, fishing and sailing. They rented a cottage from an islander, who would move down into the basement or out to the fishing hut. In the words of Sten Selander Stockholmers in the early 20th century were in the hands of the Vaxholm Steamboat Company. They had no choice but to take their holidays on the islands to which the steamboats ran.

At the same time interest in the mountain districts as recreation areas began to grow in earnest. The pioneers were from the upper crust of society, often people with a university

A printer, J E Ringqvist, and his family on a Sunday outing, 1897.

Gardening on the allotment in spring, 1929

degree or senior army officers.

Starting in the Åre district, after the opening of the Östersund-Trondheim railway, tourist stations were opened all along the mountain ranges. The Swedish Touring Club (STF) took the initiative, opening a tourist station at Abisko as early as 1902, as soon as the railway line was completed.

Social life among working-class and artisan families was of a quite different kind. The dividing line between work and leisure was not fixed. Their homes were overcrowded and they were not well off. A lack of rooms where they could get together meant that they did not usually meet in their homes but rather outdoors, especially in the summertime.

That was when their finances were best, too. The idea of having holidays had not yet been invented, but it was possible to enjoy the warm part of the year in the evenings and on red-letter days. Accordion music, cards, beer and coffee laced with schnapps while you sat on the grass was a popular way of spending a Sunday. The highlight of summer was the Midsummer celebrations.

One movement which grew up in the early years of this century on a German model was allotment gardening. This lively description dated 1904 explains the aims: "Just imagine what pleasure and benefits these gardens give to those who are unable to spend the summer in the country. It is as if it was your own little garden, giving you a feeling of home and strengthening the family ties. The whole family can spend the evenings there from early spring to late autumn. The children can play there all through the summer instead of being on the streets, which are usually both physically and mentally unhealthy. . . "

These allotment gardens were supposed to be the working-class families' summer cottage, which could also provide them with welcome and useful contributions to the household. There was a lot of charity involved, and the driving spirits, Anna Lindhagen, for example, usually came from established circles in society.

Moving away from the countryside often meant moving from a croft to a city or a mill town, from a village with a church at its centre to a town with a Community Centre, temperance lodges and non-conformist chapels. The major popular movements were the non-conformist churches, the temperance societies and the labour movements, alongside the co-operative movement and sports clubs. These movements had emerged as a protest against social conditions and were based on shared values such as solidarity, comradeship, responsibility, democracy and education. Leisure time had to be made meaningful, so lectures, theatre performances and concerts were arranged, orchestras, choirs and sports clubs were formed and swimming baths and sports grounds were built. Team sports were given priority. A post of responsibility in a club or society gave an enhanced feeling of self-esteem and reduced class differences. Such activities were particularly evident in mill towns.

FRITHIOF ANDERSSON (B. 1875)

"People didn't worry too much about the problem of leisure time. They drank more liquor in the workshops than nowadays, and if you didn't feel like work you took a couple of days off. At the weekends it was Strömparterren and Djurgården that attracted most people, and in the winter Mosebacke with its athletic displays. The men trained in sheds and basements, dreaming of performing for their club at Mosebacke. Union work was also part of their leisure activities."

Transformation of Everyday Life

If we want to describe our everyday life, we have to see how the different activities in it hang together. The social sciences try to explain society and all its features, but usually in a very generalised way, placing work in one category and leisure in another. In everyday life, however, work and leisure activities are bound up with each other. So it is not surprising that social scientists often fail to see the connections. It is the constant stream of individual activities that shapes our environment, and, vice versa, we are influenced in our decisions by the resources, constraints and opportunities in our environment. This chapter will focus on the apparently trivial activities of everyday life, in order to allow us to see how social life hangs together, which after all is basically determined by a large number of such trivial events.

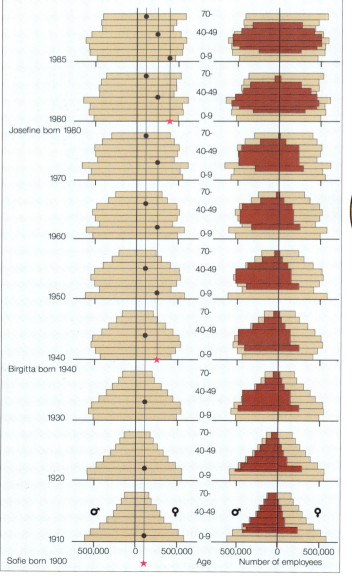

Population pyramids for Sweden, 1910–1985. The pyramids are linked to three persons' lives. The working population is in red.

THE LIFE OF A POPULATION

All of us who live in Sweden make up the present Swedish population. As people are born and die, immigrate or emigrate, the size and composition of the population changes. The distribution of ages and sexes may be described by means of population pyramids.

When the population is described in a series of population pyramids over a long period of time, some hundreds of years, the major changes in its composition become visible.

Developments may also be illustrated by concrete examples. We have chosen three ten-year-old girls from different generations to illustrate the changes in living conditions that took place for individuals and families in the 20th century. They are intended to be representative of their period. These examples show how everyday life changes through the various phases of life and how it is affected by the place where one lives and by developments in society and the economy. Individual lives are woven together in households and families and two of the girls come from the same family.

When Sofie, who was born in 1900, was ten years old, there were not very many people over 70 in the mill town where she lived. About as many men as women were as old as that. Sofie had a lot of playmates of her own age, but her little brother, Gustav, who was born in 1905, had even more friends of the same age. Sofie and Gustav had two elder brothers who had started working at the mill.

Sofie and Gustav's parents, Anna and Sven, were born in the hard times of the 1860s and 1870s. Many of their generation were already dead. Of the earlier generation only Sven's mother, Greta, was still alive.

Sven worked many long hard hours in a factory, as did almost all men after they had gone to elementary school for a few years, so Sofie and Gustav didn't see very much of their father. The only grown-up men they saw in the daytime were the men who delivered wood and coke, and the tailor who had his shop alongside their house.

Their mother Anna had her hands full with the housework. Sofie was good at looking after Gustav and the next-door neighbour's son while Anna did the washing and mending with her neighbour. Sometimes Anna gave a sigh when she thought of the village where most of her childhood friends still lived. It might have been better to have stayed there. But some had emigrated to the States, where a few of them had farms of their own. The family lived crowded together in a kitchen and one other small room, so she had to move the furniture around every morning and evening to make room for the beds in the evening and the kitchen table in the daytime.

Birgitta, who was born in 1940, didn't have many playmates of her own age when she was 10 in 1950, and no brothers or sisters of her own. But there were plenty of babies in the houses nearby.

There weren't many old people in Birgitta's life, but her grandpa and her granny were still alive. Every third Sunday the family went to have dinner with Granny. While Mummy was clearing the table and doing the washing-up, Granny and Birgitta played ludo.

Birgitta's mother stayed at home in the daytime and looked after the house. There was a lot of heavy housework to do, which took a lot of time. The pantry wasn't cold enough

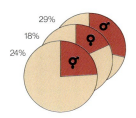

The adult population of Sweden (aged 20–64): time devoted to gainful employment.

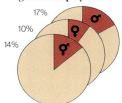

The whole population of Sweden: time devoted to gainful employment (the red sector) on a weekday in 1984/85. Population time for an average day was (8,358.139 persons times 24 hours) just over two million hours.

and the wash-house was across the yard. Birgitta often had to lend a hand. Birgitta's father worked in an office; dinner had to be on the table when he got home from work. They all had dinner together and then Dad read the newspaper. He usually asked Birgitta if she had done her homework. She almost always had because she liked studying and she didn't want to be a housewife like her mother, Sonja, and her mother's friends.

Josefine, who was born in 1980, was the first daughter of her mother Margareta but her father Bengt's third child. When Josefine was 10, she had a brother and a sister. Margareta thought it would good to be on maternal leave when Josefine started school, so she and Bengt planned the family so that the babies came when Josefine was 7 and 9. Her mother didn't want to be too old when she had her children, either. Margareta had already started a career when she had Josefine. She worked as a teacher and Bengt as a sales representative. He was often away on business.

There were lots of babies round Josefine, but not so many children of her own age. Josefine's grandparents were all alive, and so was her great-grandmother Sofie as well, but great-grandfather Tore had died in 1984. She used to go and see Great Grandma when she wanted to get away from her baby brother and sister a while. When she was there, she learnt how to make things herself and mend things, too. Great Grandma was very particular about not throwing things away that were broken. "Waste not, want not", she used to say. She told Josefine that when she was a young girl they had so little money that they just had to make do and mend. Josefine's mother Margareta always said: "We'll buy a new one" when something needed mending.

Margareta and Bengt thought it was fine that Josefine was such a big girl now, because that meant they could go to the theatre and the cinema as they had done before they had a family. Then Josefine helped Granny or Grandma Rut to look after the babies. Josefine had a happy life, but she was worried about the environment and war out in the world. Almost every day on television she could see how children in other parts of the world were suffering.

THE GENERATIONS' PATH THROUGH LIFE

The lives of our three ten-year-olds can be placed in a broader perspective. The population pyramids show clearly how people in each generation moved upwards through the years. They keep each other company in life and each year a few of each age group pass away. The small number of babies born in the 1930s and the large number in the 1940s appear particularly clearly in the population pyramids. The children born in the 1930s and 1940s have also greatly influenced social developments, the earlier generation through its small size and the later generation through its large numbers. The large generation of the forties also reached adult age just during the post-war period when Swedish industry, which had not been destroyed during the war, gave the Swedish economy a tremendous boost.

EMPLOYMENT

The descriptions of our ten-year-olds' everyday life also included the working fathers. The gainfully employed part of the population is marked in the population pyramids, and it is evident how more and more women went out into working life. At the beginning of the century it was only unmarried women and women without children that had a job.

In the 1960s even more Swedish women joined the labour market; in 1960 32 per cent of women had a job, in 1970 41 per cent. In 1985 women in Sweden worked outside the home more than ever before. On average 68 per cent of all women between the ages of 16 and 74 had a job. What is perhaps most surprising of all is that the group of women that worked most in the mid–1980s were those aged 35 to 44 whose children were at school (92%). Among Swedish men those who worked most were also married and aged 35 to 44 (98%).

During a weekday twenty-four hour period in 1985 Swedes of working age (20–64) devoted 24 per cent of their time to gainful employment. This figure includes those people who did not work at all.

In a historical perspective working people have on average devoted less and less time to their jobs. The explanation is that, thanks to better machinery and more efficient methods, it has been possible to shorten working hours in this century from generally speaking an unlimited number to eight hours a day five days a week—at the same time as pay has been raised.

OTHER ACTIVITIES, THE REST OF THE DAY

What does the working population in Sweden do during the rest of the day, and what do all those who have no job do? The data on employment covers a large part of the population aged 20 to 64, but if the way the *whole* population uses its time is to be reported, everybody must be included. Population time (= the number of persons in the whole population x the number of hours per day) gives the total time frame within which absolutely everything that is done has to be contained (including sleep).

During weekdays less than one fifth of the total population time is devoted to gainful employment. The time which is not used for gainful employment is devoted to very many different activities. Firstly, a great deal of time is taken up by human needs such as eating, sleeping and personal hygiene. Secondly, time is given to education. Thirdly, household work like cooking, mending, washing and child care takes time. The rest of the time is devoted to travelling, watching television, games, sports, reading newspapers, social intercourse and anything else one wants to and has time to do.

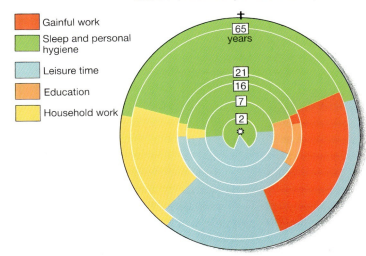

Use of time in the Swedish population, 1985 for age groups (shown as age rings) and important activities (illustrated by coloured sectors).

- Gainful work
- Sleep and personal hygiene
- Leisure time
- Education
- Household work

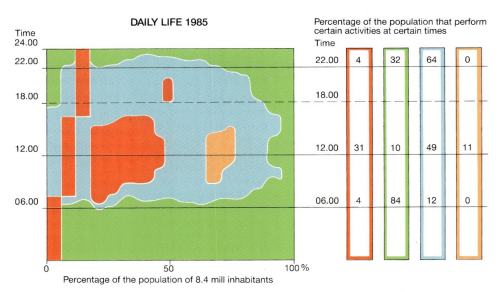

Distribution of population time among various activities during one whole weekday in 1985. The time axis shows the hour of the day. Few people work before 6 o'clock in the morning. Most people are asleep or attending to personal hygiene. During the daytime gainful employment and leisure are the dominant activities. A small section of the population work a three-shift system. The whole of the population of Sweden is shown along the vertical axis.

Everyday Life in Sweden Today

Life was rather different for Sofie, Birgitta and Josefine in our examples. Their experiences and values were coloured strongly by their everyday life.

Everyday life can be described in countless ways, but the passage of time is the same for everyone. We shall therefore use time as the basis for our continuing discussion. The starting point is the population time for Sweden in 1985 and how it was used for various activities during one whole day.

When Swedish population time is divided into four rough categories of activities, it appears that 42 per cent of the total time, is taken up by sleep and personal hygiene, 14 per cent by gainful employment, 2 per cent by education and 42 per cent by housework and leisure.

There are at every hour of the day always some people at work. Shift work means that sleep and other physiologically necessary activities are not uniformly distributed throughout the population during the 24 hours. There are also a number of pure night jobs, which are usually done as part-time work. These workers may include, for example, mothers of small children who work evenings.

Babies and people who are very ill spend all day and night sleeping or being attended to.

USE OF TIME BY HOUSEHOLDS

Households in Sweden differ greatly, and their use of time is affected by where they live, their occupations and incomes, whether they have children and how old they are, and how the community they live in is organised. For this reason it is necessary to be very cautious when generalising about the use of time.

About 40 per cent of all households with children have two children, and almost half of all children are in two-children families. Let us take a two-children family, the Bergs, to exemplify the use of time.

The Bergs in the Big City

Four people live in the Bergs' apartment in the big city: The father, Bengt, the mother, Margareta, their five-year-old daughter Josefine (whom we have already met as a ten-year-old) and Bengt's son from a previous marriage, Jonas, who is ten. Every other weekend the Bergs are visited by Patrik, Jonas's big brother, who lives the rest of the time with his mother, Lisbet, Bengt's ex-wife.

IN THE MORNING

Bengt is woken up at 6 a.m. by the alarm clock. He gets up, has breakfast and reads the morning paper. At half past six Margareta gets up and wakes up Josefine and Jonas. They have breakfast together.

TO WORK

Bengt starts work at 8.15. It takes him 45 minutes to get to the office, counting the bus journey and walking time, so he leaves home at 7.30. The family does not have a car because it is so expensive to rent a garage. Before Margareta starts work at the school where she is a teacher, she walks to the day nursery with Josefine and to the day centre with Jonas. They leave home at a quarter to eight. They only cycle when they are short of time; otherwise they walk because there is so much traffic. The day centre is very close to the school where Margareta works, so she takes Josefine to the day nursery first. Today Margareta starts work at half past nine. Jonas stays at the day centre until 10, when school starts. After school, at 3 o'clock, he goes back to the day centre. Margareta fetches him at 4 o'clock after she has finished marking her pupils' homework. On the way home they do the shopping at the corner shop.

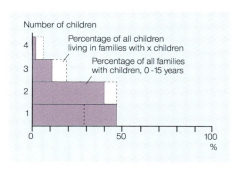

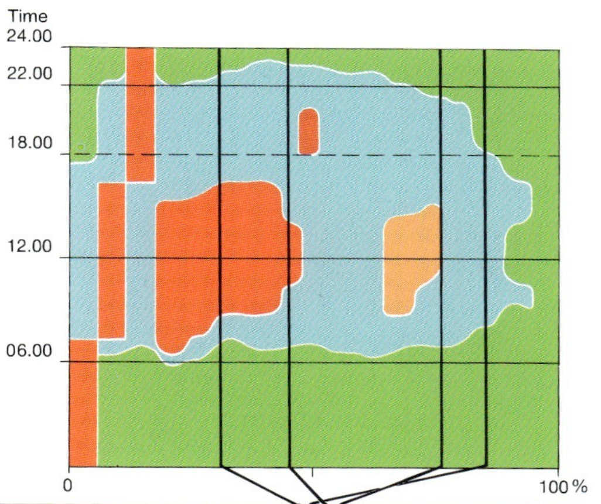

A weekday for a Swedish family with two children. We have chosen from the whole Swedish population a household consisting of two adults and two children. Both parents are at work during the daytime and one of the children is at school. The family lives in a large town, so school and workplaces are a long way from home. The middle diagram shows where and when each member of the household performs certain activities. The family is together at home until quarter to eight in the morning and after six in the evening.

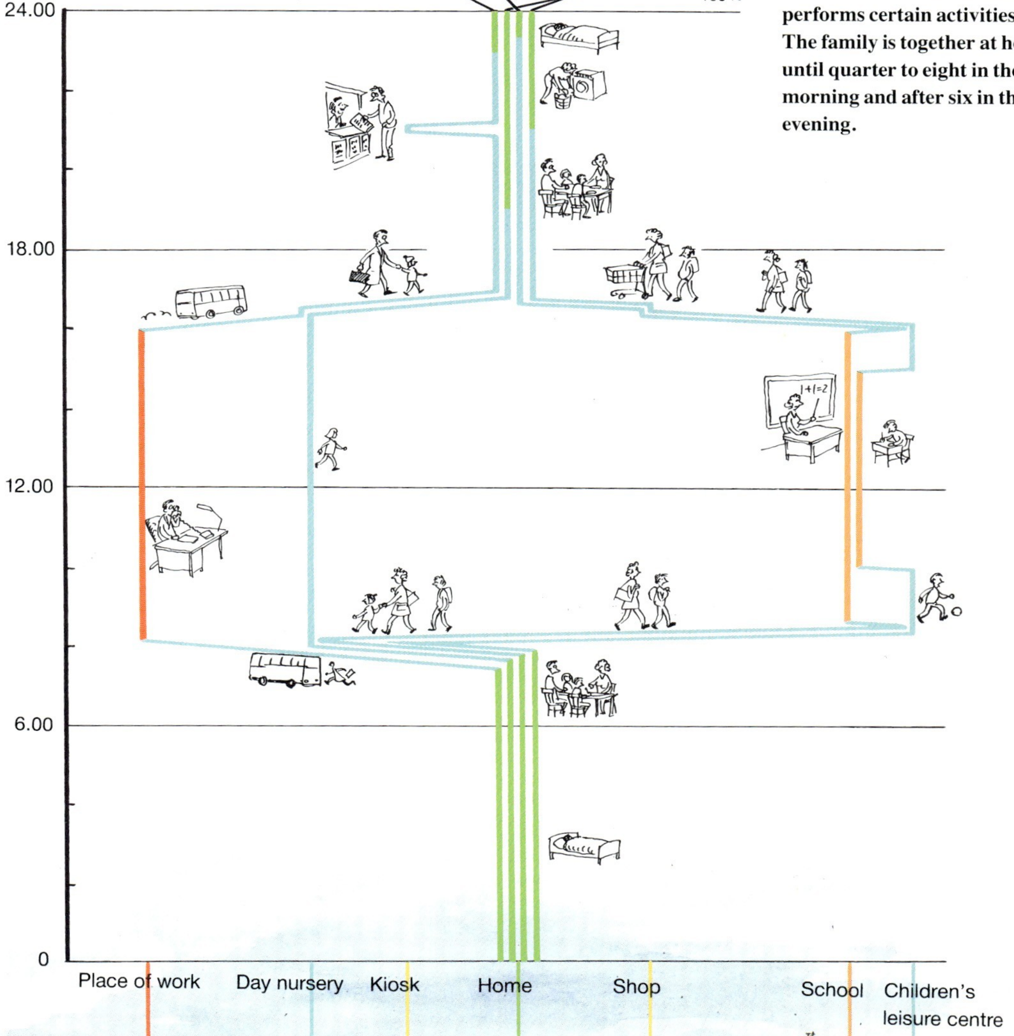

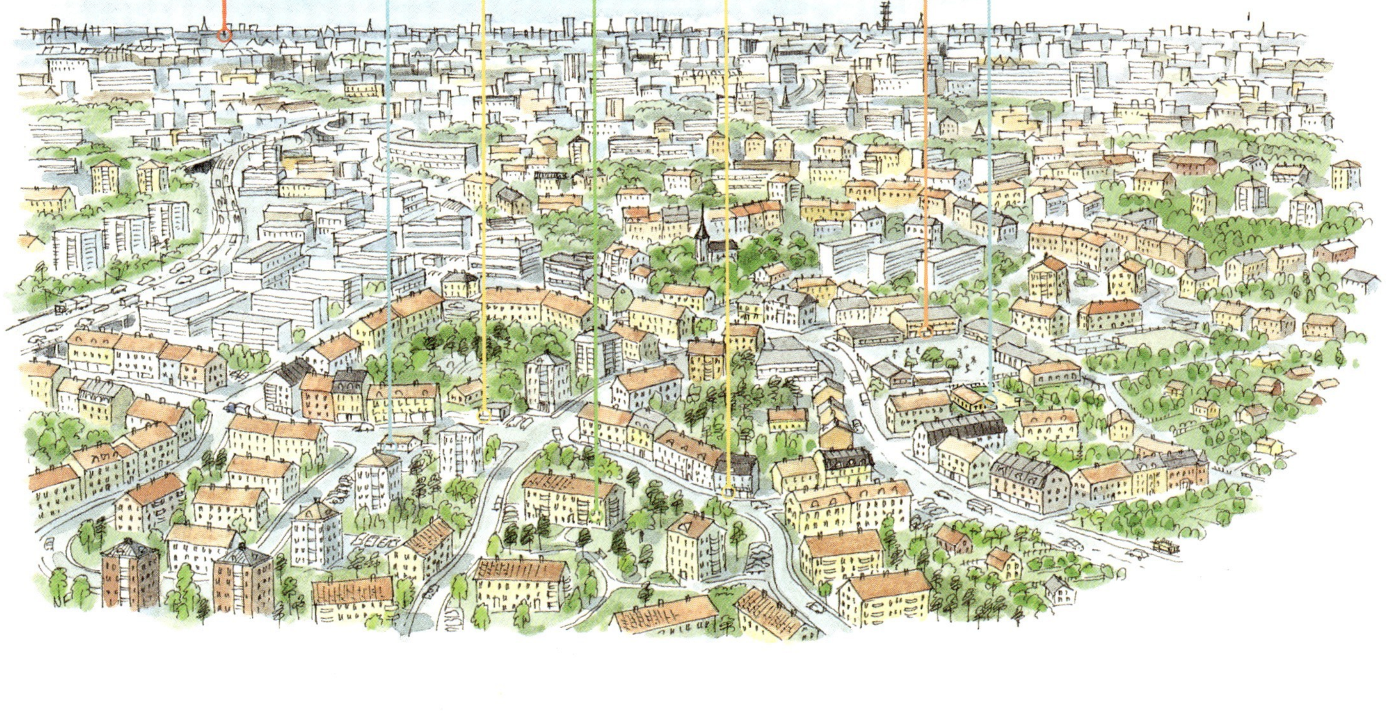

BACK HOME

As Bengt has been able to leave work earlier than usual today, he has fetched Josefine from the day nursery. Josefine likes this because he can't pick her up so often. The whole family have dinner together before the children's programmes begin on television. Margareta thinks it is best to eat at 6 o'clock on the dot. She doesn't want Josefine to watch the early news which comes just before the children's programmes. The news often shows frightening pictures and Margareta has noticed that they upset the children. At half past seven Margareta starts to put Josefine to bed. Bengt watches television and talks to Jonas. Jonas goes to bed at about nine, when Josefine has just fallen asleep. Bengt goes out and buys the evening paper and makes a cup of coffee for Margareta and himself. She has had an unusually long day because her pupils had a written test. This evening Bengt goes to bed at about half past ten, but Margareta has to do the washing in the basement laundry room until eleven, after which she also goes to bed—feeling very tired.

The Bergs in Smalltown

If we imagine that the Bergs live in a small town instead, we shall see that their daily life is somewhat different. Bengt is hardly ever at home on a weekday because he is out on a sales trip every week.

IN THE MORNING

On weekday mornings Margareta usually gets up at 6.30. She makes breakfast and wakes the children up. Her work at school begins at 9 o'clock, but she tries to be there half an hour earlier to prepare her lessons and do the odd chores. Jonas starts school at 9 o'clock.

TO WORK

Just after 8 o'clock Margareta takes Jonas and Josefine to Great Grandma's (Sofie, whom we have already met as a ten-year-old). Jonas stays with her together with Josefine until it's time to go to school just before nine. Josefine loves being at Great Grandma's and she has most fun when Jonas is at school. Then she can have Great Grandma all to herself. She already knows how to bake cakes almost all by herself. Margareta picks up the children at about 3 o'clock. Her grandmother is getting old now and the children don't always realise that they have to be quiet when she has her afternoon nap.

BACK HOME

When they are back at home they have afternoon tea. Then Jonas usually goes off to play with his friends. Sometimes Josefine goes to see a playmate in the afternoon and sometimes they come to play at Josefine's house. As Bengt is away travelling so much in the week, Margareta does all the housework. She does most of the housework during the week so that the whole family is free at the weekend and can have fun together. When Margareta has put the children to bed in the evening, she usually watches the late TV news. Apart from that she doesn't watch the telly much, far less than the two hours a day that the average Swede does. She has a lot of other things to do in the afternoons and evenings. One weekday evening a week Margareta's mother looks after the children, so that Margareta can meet some of her friends. They have kept in touch since schooldays and still have a lot of fun together.

Different Fates—the Same Roots

The biographies of two of our ten-year-olds come from the same family. Sofie, who was born in 1900, is the Great Grandma of Josefine, born in 1980. Sofie's daughter Ruth is Margareta's mother and Josefine's grandmother.

SOFIE AND TORE THROUGH LIFE'S STAGES

Tore was born in Chicago, USA, in 1898. His parents had emigrated separately from Sweden in the early 1890s, and they met in Chicago. Tore's father worked for a big engineering company and his mother worked on a construction site until Tore was born. By 1905 Tore's parents had had enough of life in the New World, so they returned to Sweden and their home district. There they gave Tore's uncle a hand on the small farm he had, but they didn't stay there long. About 1907 they moved to the nearby town. After leaving school in the town, Tore started work at a textile factory. After a few tough years he became a skilled weaver, looking after the machinery in the weaving room of a large mill.

STARTING A FAMILY

Tore met Sofie at a union meeting at the mill. Sofie was born in 1900 in a croft just outside the town. She worked in the spinning mill. Although she was only 19, she was already beginning to suffer from all the dust from the spinning machines. In 1925, at Whitsun, Tore and Sofie got married, and the following year their son Sune was born. Their daughter Rut came one year later. Sofie looked after the home and the children while Tore worked at the mill. During the Second World War Tore played an active part in the Home Guard. When the war was over, the family moved to a big city. The children were almost grown up and had started work. Tore got a job at a repair workshop in the big city thanks to his skills as a mechanic, while Sofie continued to stay

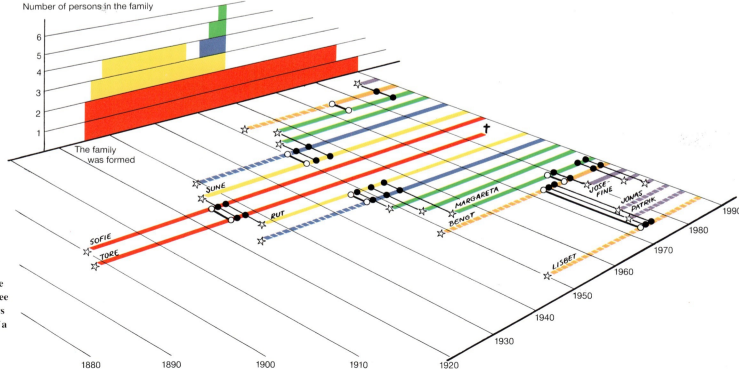

Generations and household size. Sofie and Tore's family tree over a hundred years show how the size of a household varies according to the life phase.

CHANGES IN THE SWEDISH POPULATION PYRAMID AND CHANGES IN FAMILY SIZE 1900-1985

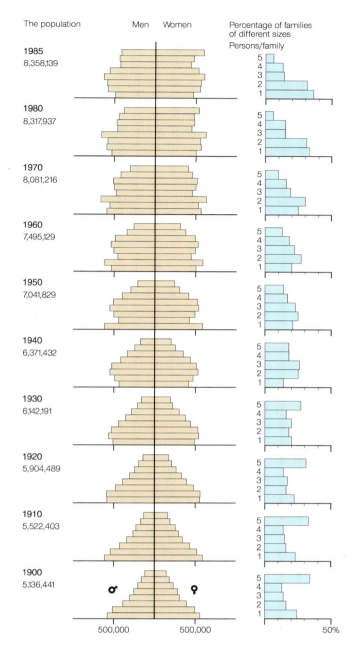

Changes in the Swedish population pyramid and household size between 1900 and 1985.

at home as she had done ever since Sune was born in 1926.

After only a couple of years in the big city, Tore and Sofie's lives changed when Rut married in 1947 and moved away from home. She had a son in 1948; after seven years of marriage she had three children.

THREE GENERATIONS IN THE SAME HOUSEHOLD

Sune studied to be an engineer and didn't get married until 1950. Four years later he had two children. Sune and his family still lived with Tore and Sofie because it was very difficult to get anywhere to live in the expanding big city.

So now Sofie had plenty on her hands. She helped with the grandchildren, knitting and sewing clothes for them. But with six people in the household, it was cooking that took up most of her time.

A SMALL HOUSEHOLD AGAIN

When finally Sune and his family moved to a newly built suburb in 1956, life in the flat was suddenly very quiet and peaceful. Tore and Sofie had had children and grandchildren in their home for 30 years, but now it was a small household of two. Tore retired in 1966.

The first great-grandchild was born in 1980. It was Rut's youngest daughter, Margareta, who had a little girl. She was called Josefine.

SOFIE LIVES ALONE

Tore died in 1984, the year before his son, Sune, had his first grandson. Sofie stayed on in the old flat after Tore's death, she wanted to live there as long as she could. She often says to herself that she has a good life, much better than many old people who are left alone out in the villages after their children have moved into town to get a job. It was much more common for children to move away from their parents in the villages in the 1960s than it was at the time when Tore and Sofie moved to the big city from their little mill town. Sofie thought it was good that they had been pioneers, because now she had children, grandchildren and great-grandchildren close to her.

Various Kinds of Household

HOUSEHOLDS WITH AND WITHOUT CHILDREN

In 1985 a fifth of all Swedish households had children; 40 per cent of these households with children had two children and 45 per cent one child. The most typical Swedish household in 1985, however, had no children. As many as 80 per cent of households had no children under the age of 18 at home.

The household structure of Sweden, 1985. Percentage of households according to the number of children under 18 still living at home.

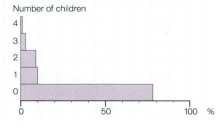

PERCENTAGE OF FAMILIES BY NUMBER OF CHILDREN AT HOME UNDER 18

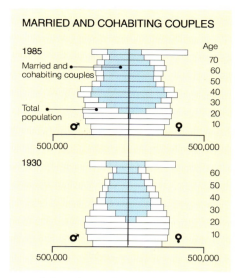

The whole of the population of Sweden and those married or co-habiting are shown by age and sex in the population pyramids for 1930 and 1985.

SMALL HOUSEHOLDS

The number of small households, especially those with only one person, has increased greatly. There are three commonly accepted explanations for this development:

1. The number of old people in the population has increased noticeably in the past 50 years. They almost always live in one or two-person households. Tore and Sofie's example is a good one, after their two children had moved away from home in the 1950s. The number of people over 65 who live together has increased during the past 50 years, among both men and women. A considerably larger proportion of elderly women live alone (60%) than of elderly men (30%). In contrast the proportion of cohabitants among young women is larger than among young men.

2. Nowadays young people are in a better position than before to set up a household of their own long before they start a family. This means that both the children and their parents who are left alone form small households. These two explanations are illustrated in a diagram showing how Tore and Sofie's household grew first larger and then smaller during the period 1925–1990.

3. In today's society many households break up. The generations that lived round the turn of the century lived their whole lives in one marriage. Nowadays many married couples and cohabitants split up after a few years. In 1985 over 20,000 marriages ended in divorce, compared with hardly 2,000 in 1930. After a marriage has broken up, small households are created until new relationships are formed.

Projects in Life

HUMAN RHYTHM

However different people may seem to be socially, they all have many common needs which control the ways in which they use time. The need for sleep is controlled by the rhythm of day and night. Meals fit in with the body's need for nutrition.

SURVIVAL

Every person's daily routine is more or less consciously divided up by sleeping and eating, or what we have called man's survival project. What form this takes depends partly on what one does between sleeping and eating, and this in turn depends on the technical and organisational resources one has at one's disposal.

IN AGRARIAN SOCIETY

In agrarian society almost all waking time was devoted to activities primarily aiming at survival. Life was a matter of getting food and warmth and keeping the house in order. The seasons and the weather were decisive factors: manuring, ploughing, sowing, harvesting, drying and threshing—each had its time. The light part of the year and the day were used by every member of the household for work. Everyone had his or her special responsibilities, children as well as grown-ups and old people, and all the tasks were equally important for the efficient working of the whole household. Almost all the work was performed at home, since everyone was working for the survival of the household. Leisure time in our sense of the word hardly existed at all. However, the church required everybody to rest from their usual labours on Sundays.

IN INDUSTRIAL AND SERVICE SOCIETY

In modern industrial and service society gainful employment is separated from work in the home. Some of the money earned from gainful employment is used to buy food and to pay the rent, etc. Gainful employment has its own rhythm regulated not by man's need for sleep and food but by production's demand for work. This means, for example, shift work. Shift work overrides the natural daily rhythm and disturbs social life.

Dominant Projects in Life's Stages

Looking at man's life as a whole, one sees that his everyday existence in various stages of life is dominated by specific activities, which we call projects. A baby's daily life is characterised by sleeping and eating. An infant's daily life allows plenty of time for playing, even though it may be channelled into strictly organised activities such as a day nursery. Teenagers get an education and middle-aged people go to work. As a pensioner one has plenty of free time again.

But regardless of the stage of life one studies, the survival projects of sleeping and eating are always present. Both infant play at the day nursery and at home and children's education at school and their many leisure time projects have to be fitted in between sleeping and eating. Many

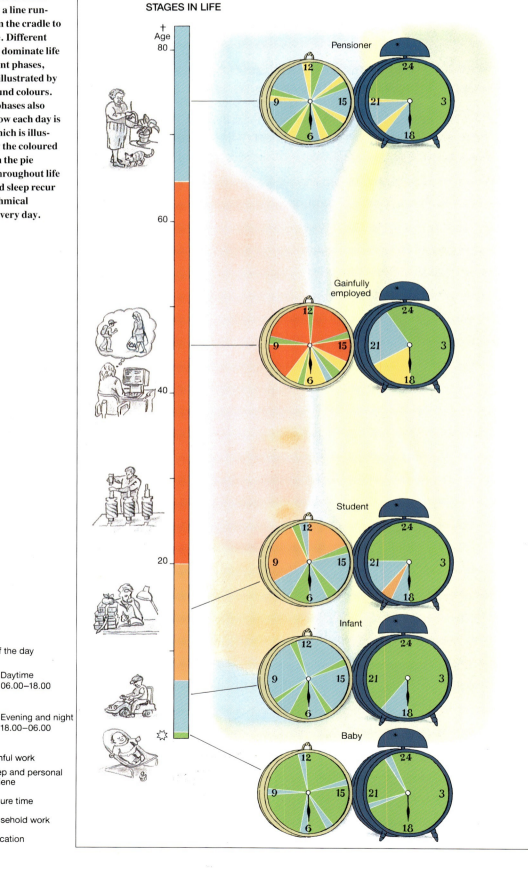

Life phases are illustrated by a line running from the cradle to the grave. Different activities dominate life in different phases, which is illustrated by background colours. The life phases also dictate how each day is spent, which is illustrated by the coloured sectors in the pie chart. Throughout life meals and sleep recur as a rhythmical pattern every day.

Division of the day
- Daytime 06.00–18.00
- Evening and night 18.00–06.00

- Gainful work
- Sleep and personal hygiene
- Leisure time
- Household work
- Education

schoolchildren go to a day centre or a child minder while their parents are at work. This, too, is a project that takes time in their schedule.

The people who are really busy, or tied up, are middle-aged working people. Apart from their jobs, many of them have to look after children and a home.

The Working Days of the Year

Of the 365 days of the year 1985 111 were Saturdays, Sundays and public holidays. A working person might have had 32 days of holiday and made up for another four day's work. If so, there would be 218 working days, 60 per cent of all the days in the year.

RARELY IN THE INDIVIDUAL'S LIFE — EVERY DAY IN THE COUNTRY AS A WHOLE

The natural needs and rhythm of life are important for what is done, but there are also one-time events that may be of decisive significance for the rest of life: birth, marriage, giving birth to a child and death.

EVERYDAY ROUTINES

During an ordinary day much will also happen, of course, that is of a far more routine character. Consuming fibre-rich bread, cigarettes and milk do not have immediate significance for the life conditions of the consumer himself or herself, but are of long-term importance for public health. Public health is the sum total of each and every individual's state of health.

Every Swedish household consumed on any ordinary day in 1985 one litre of milk. How has our consumption of milk, butter and cheese changed over a long period of time? The next few pages show how our consumption of these foods has developed over the past 100 years.

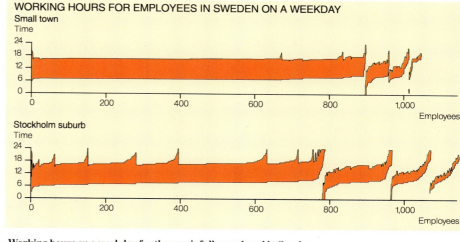

Working hours on a weekday for those gainfully employed in Sweden.

EVERYDAY EVENTS ILLUSTRATED BY CONSUMPTION. ONE DAY IN 1985:	
18,800,000	hours were used in gainful employment
4,400,000	letters were sent
31,000,000	cigarettes were smoked
121,000,000	kWh were consumed
53,680	nights were spent at hotels
40,610	people used domestic flights
150,000	kilos of crispbread were eaten
3,900,000	litres of milk were consumed

EVERY DAY SOME ROUTINE OR SPECIAL EVENT TOOK PLACE. ONE DAY IN 1985:	
270	lives began
100	marriages started
54	divorces went through
44	road accidents occurred
336	accidents at work occurred
1,831	jobs were announced
124	people were given redundancy notices
40	left the Church of Sweden
15	joined the Church of Sweden
82	moved to Greater Stockholm
40	moved to Greater Göteborg
27	moved to Greater Malmö
61	moved from Greater Stockholm
34	moved from Greater Göteborg
24	moved from Greater Malmö
258	lives ended

■ Gainful work
■ Sleep and personal hygiene
■ Leisure time

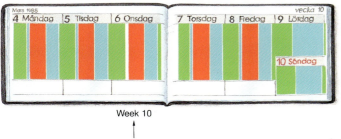

Week 10

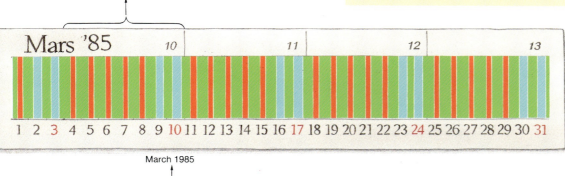

March 1985

DAIRIES, 1985
1:20 000 000

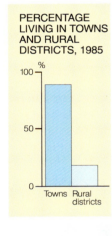

Approximately 50 dairies. (K3)

PERCENTAGE LIVING IN TOWNS AND RURAL DISTRICTS, 1985

Touchdown in Time — Three Snapshots

Our lives are shaped in part by how we manufacture, distribute and use goods and services. Industrialism has created an increasingly strict division between gainful employment, work at home and leisure time.

One of the driving forces behind early industrialism is the division of work into smaller and smaller units at the same time as specialisation increases. This has dramatically changed the nature of work in what, from a historical point of view, is a rather short time.

The achievements of technology have changed our lives greatly. Production is no longer a matter of craftsmanship, since mechanisation and in more recent years automation have made large-sized plants most profitable. This has led to a concentration and urbanisation of the workforce, which means that an increasingly large part of the population has moved to big towns. They are dependent on the modern way of producing goods and services for their livelihood.

These fundamental changes have, of course, dramatically influenced the ways in which people use their time. It is therefore impossible to separate the use of time from other fundamental features of social development.

These changes will be illustrated by capturing the development of society in three snapshots, which will give the historical features a more concrete form. One product which has been with us for a long time and plays an important role in our nutrition is milk. How has the transformation of society affected the production, distribution and consumption of milk? How does the way milk is transported from the cow's udder to our stomachs reflect changes in society?

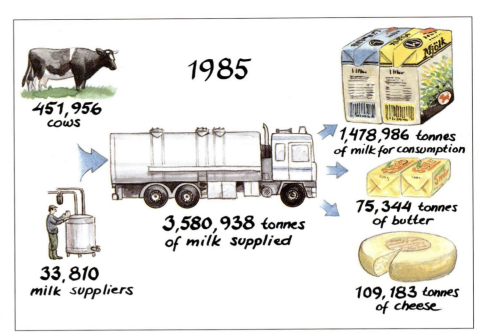

FROM UDDER TO STOMACH IN THE 1980S

The unbreakable glass is filled with milk straight from the fridge. There are two or three different sorts of milk there, with different fat contents in different coloured cartons. The best-before date reminds us that we bought it some days ago. It's time to fill up again from the shop. Nowadays we can buy almost every kind of regular goods that a household needs from one and the same store. In the mid–1980s there were almost 9,000

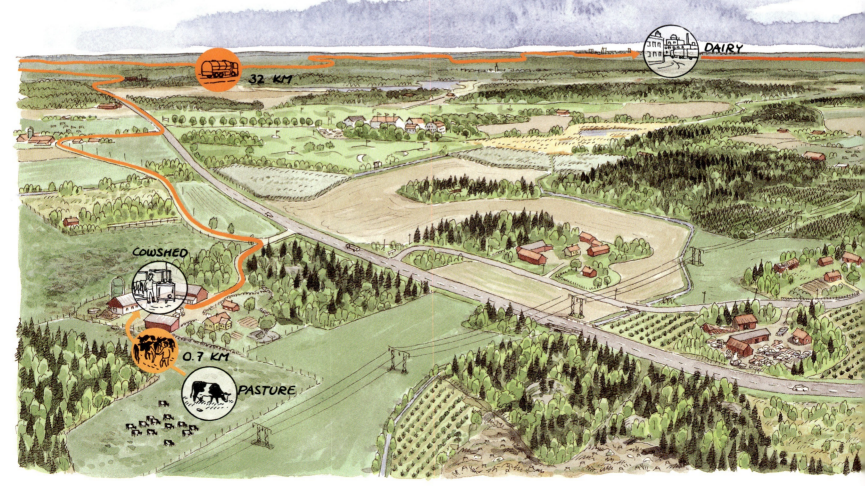

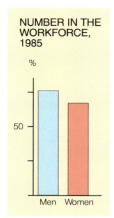

NUMBER IN THE WORKFORCE, 1985

WHAT A MILK CARTON TAKES FROM THE FOREST

= 38 grammes of wood

57,500 litre cartons

1 tonnes of paper

2.2 tonnes of wood

food stores in Sweden. Only 20 years earlier there were considerably more.

It is some time since the cows, whose milk is now blended in these cartons, were milked. It has stood for a few days in our fridge at home and one or two days before that it was in the shop and one further day was needed for distribution from the dairy.

Each dairy is a large workplace. All in all some 10,000 people work at about 50 dairies. Four thousand of them are specially trained dairymen. Everything is sparkling clean in the dairies; the law requires a high standard of hygiene. Each employee has his or her special function and his or her special skill. Working hours are strictly regulated from start to finish, including breaks, lunchtime and holidays.

The dairy workers' cars are parked in long lines outside the dairy; many of them travel for miles to get to work at the dairy and may have to use their cars to drop off and fetch their children from a day nursery on the way. The milk vans are on their way in to load up with about 3,000 litres of milk. They make their way past the tankers which have collected milk (maybe 13,000 litres in a load) from the surrounding farms. In the mid–1980s over 28,000 farms supplied milk to the dairies.

The tankers, equipped with cooling equipment, have just completed their collecting rounds, each of which covers quite a few miles and some twenty or so suppliers. Thanks to their cooling equipment they can drive long distances regardless of whether it is a hot summer's day or a frosty winter's morning. At each farm the milk is kept in a cooler, so it doesn't really matter when the tanker arrives.

But the installations are expensive. Besides the cooler, the costs of new milking machines and pipelines which are necessary for reasons of hygiene are heavy for the farmer. Many elderly suppliers have chosen to sell their herds at the prospect of having to invest in expensive equipment. This means that the number of cows per supplier has increased greatly. On average every supplier has 20 cows, but a fifth of the suppliers have considerably more, and they supply more than half of all the milk the dairies collect.

From five to eight days have elapsed from the moment the farmer puts the milking cups on the cows' udders until the moment we pour ourselves a glass of milk. The milk has been transported over long distances, gone through various processes such as standardisation, pasteurisation and homogenisation, been packaged, stored, transported, trans-

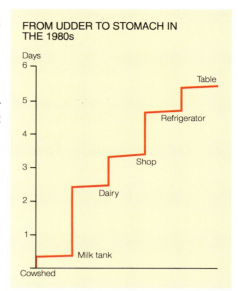

FROM UDDER TO STOMACH IN THE 1980s

ported again and stored again. When all the milk is gone, the carton is thrown away, to be transported to the municipal rubbish dump.

This description of the progress of milk from the cow's udder to our stomach reveals a good deal of the way in which our technologically well-developed society functions. Mass-production means fewer dairies and fewer suppliers. Work specialisation has created new occupations and has also made it possible to raise production per employee greatly. Transportation has become a very important part of bringing the material, more or less processed, to the consumer.

Transport routes for milk in the 1980s.

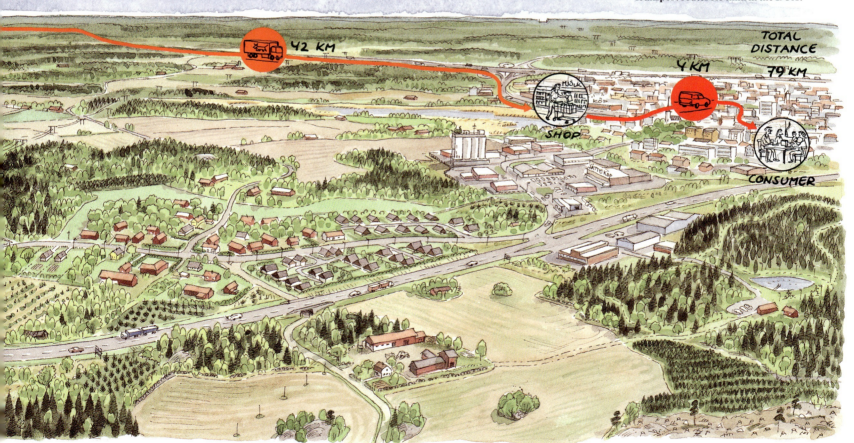

DAIRIES, 1930

1:20 000 000

Approximately 1,000 dairies. (K4)

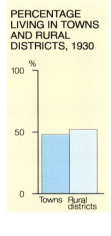

PERCENTAGE LIVING IN TOWNS AND RURAL DISTRICTS, 1930

BACK IN TIME — AROUND 1930

The way milk was taken from udder to stomach was quite different in the mid–1930s. The milk was poured into the glass from a pail which was kept in some cool place, or perhaps an icebox. Milk didn't keep fresh long in the summer months. If you didn't have cows of your own, you usually had to buy milk at least once a day. Refrigerators were a new invention, not to be found in many homes.

Carrying the empty, rattling pail in your hand, you would go to the local milk shop or the dairy. The milk was ladled up from large churns into your pail. You couldn't buy groceries in the milk shop, so in that respect shops were more specialised in those days than today. But there were not many milk shops left by the end of the 1950s.

Milk was carried from nearby dairies to the milk shops by horse and cart. This was a tough job involving much lifting and carrying every day. Behind nostalgic memories of the clatter of horses' hoofs on cobbles and the rattle of milk churns on the cart lay a hard reality for many workers.

In 1933 there were almost 1,500 dairies in Sweden — in other words, no mass-production. In principle, however, the processes at the dairies were

The dairy at Uppsala in 1935, before it was rebuilt, showing the first motorised van.

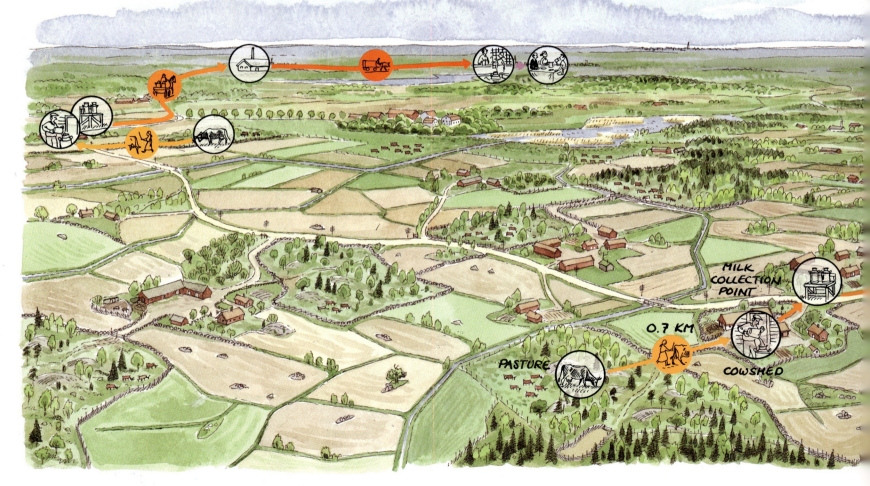

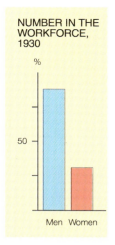

NUMBER IN THE WORKFORCE, 1930

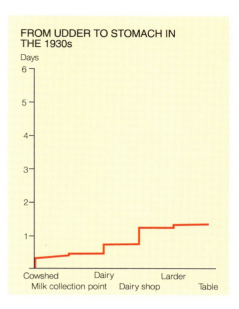

FROM UDDER TO STOMACH IN THE 1930s

the same as today. The number of dairies reached a peak in the late 20s and early 30s, after which new methods of production took over: the dairies became fewer and fewer and larger and larger.

Milk was produced on a large number of small farms, each farmer supplying on average less than 50 litres a day. The farmers usually delivered the milk themselves to the dairies once a day. Out in the country the farmcarts rattled along with milk from almost two million cows (more than four times as many as today). The dairies had started to employ lorries to pick up the milk.

Just when our industrial society was beginning to mature, the agrarian society stood at its peak. Living conditions varied enormously, not only between villages but perhaps even more so between town and country.

The number of people employed in industry exceeded the number employed in agriculture just after the middle of the 1930s. The countryside was full of fields and meadows, and new land was still being opened up.

Society in the 30s was on a small scale. Professionalisation had not developed very far; work required competence and allround skills from each and every person. At this time Sweden was a real mixture of an old agrarian society and a modern industrial society. The mill communities were in their special way a hybrid form of town and countryside, somewhere between industry and agriculture.

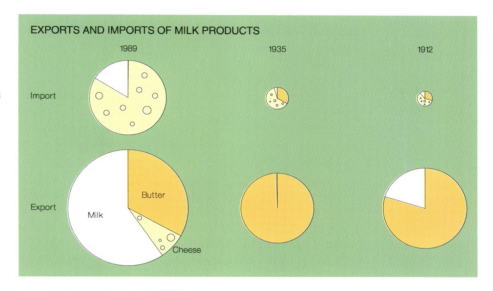

EXPORTS AND IMPORTS OF MILK PRODUCTS

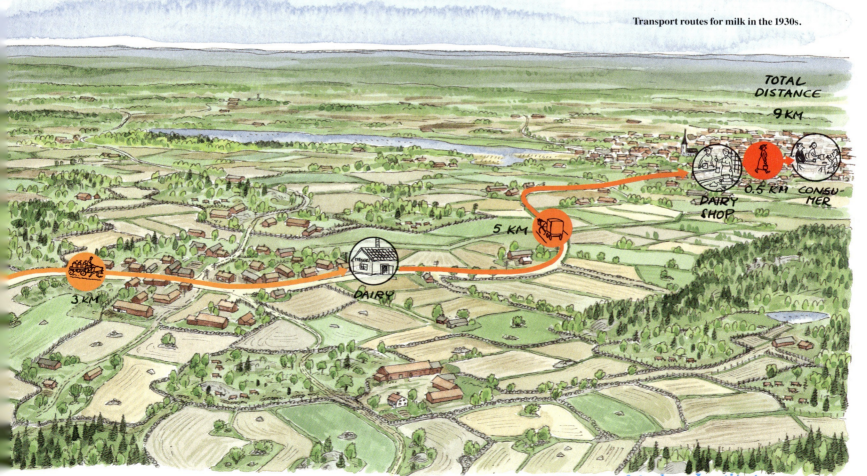

Transport routes for milk in the 1930s.

AT THE TURN OF THE CENTURY AND EARLIER

If we go even farther back in time, to the turn of the century, we meet yet another type of society with a completely different kind of life for the population. The way of life was much more affected by rural conditions. Most people made their living directly from farming. However, industry was growing fast and beginning to set its mark on small towns and cities. The population was divided into town dwellers and country folk, and life was quite different for these two groups.

There were plenty of dairies, almost 1,700. Milking was a craft and the milk had to be processed quickly. A few decades before the beginning of our century the most common kind of dairy was the estate farm dairy. It was the big country estates that created dairies in the modern sense of the word.

Just as with other industries, competent labour was imported from abroad, often in this case as dairymaids from Germany. Work specialisation had also begun to develop in this industry, as had happened previously in, for example, steel manufacturing. Changes came quickly, however, and by the end of the century the bulk-purchasing dairies, which had no cows of their own but bought all their milk, had gained a dominant position.

In many towns the newly-built dairy was a first sign of the transformation of wooden buildings into those of brick and stone. The town hall and dairy were often among the first stone buildings to be erected in a small town at the end of the 19th century.

In the mid–19th century almost all milk processing took place in the household. The way from udder to stomach was short and couldn't take long. Probably very little milk was consumed in towns, where people had to rely on farms which were still scattered within the expanding townships. It was the growing town populations that was a potential market for the growing dairy industry.

Changes were also encouraged by an expanding export market for dairy products. Urbanisation had progressed much further in other countries; England in particular was a mature industrial country with a strong demand for dairy products.

The demand for dairy products re-

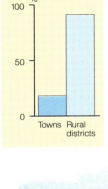

PERCENTAGE LIVING IN TOWNS AND RURAL DISTRICTS, 1850

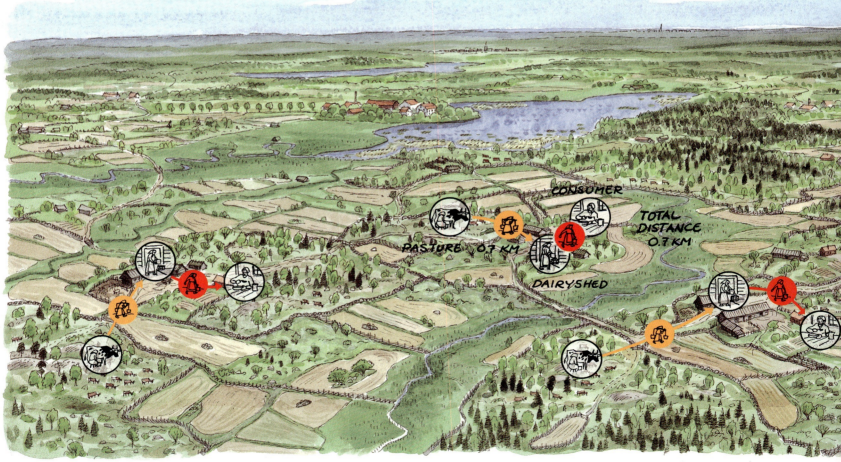

sulted in milk processing being taken away from the everyday life of the farm. It developed modern methods and gradually became more and more concentrated as time passed.

SUMMARY

Our three snapshots show how society has changed and transformed our lives. The same process could have been illustrated by examples from any other industry. Of course changes have been made at different speeds and with features particular to each industry, but the driving forces and shifts in direction have nevertheless been similar.

Production has been transformed from craftwork to industrial mass-production. Output per hour worked has increased many times over, thanks to technical inventions and training, and this has resulted in a geographical concentration of workplaces, with a consequent concentration of the population. Our dwelling patterns have changed; the majority of the population no longer live in the country but in towns.

Even in urban areas there has been a development towards a geographical separation of different activities. Workplaces and service industries have gathered in central areas or in areas well provided with transport services, while housing estates have spread far and wide. This means that people have to travel from their homes to their places of work and to make use of services. What used to be grown and processed on every farm is now dealt with industrially in many steps and at different places. This takes a long time and requires much transportation before the goods arrive in the shops. This change, supported and accelerated by technical progress, has created new occupations from the work that was previously done by one and the same person using simple equipment on the farm.

Modern technology has not only affected production but also helped to restructure distribution and consumption. Our example of the dairies shows that present-day cooling facilities have dramatically increased the time that milk can be stored on the farm. This has led to a decrease in the number of journeys to the dairy. An extended road network and the tankers' coolers have made it possible to transport milk less often and over greater distances. Thanks to these developments we consumers can now save a little of our shopping time, which gives us more leisure time — or perhaps more time to work.

Another factor which has encouraged change is Sweden's increasing

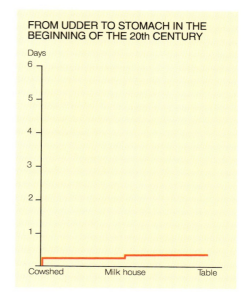

dependence on the world around us. For most people in the mid–19th century foreign countries seemed incredibly remote, and farmwork was not immediately affected by what was going on in Europe or in far-off America. It took a long time for events in the outside world to reach Sweden and be known — if they ever got to Sweden at all.

In the 19th century imports and exports began to grow. This was extremely important for the dairies. In the mid–19th century, when the estate dairies were developing, exports to England began, mainly in the form of butter. Initially only small quantities

Transport routes for milk in the 1850s.

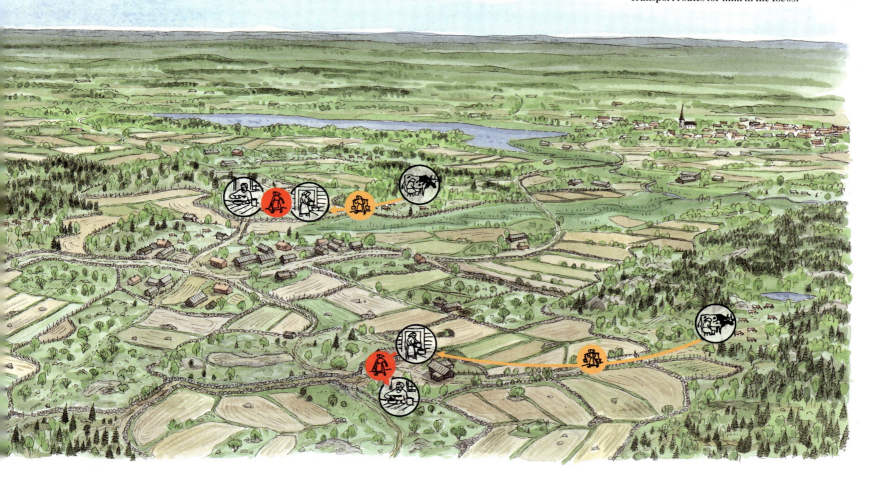

were involved, but by the 1880s the amount had increased to about 5,000 tons of butter. In the following ten years butter exports increased fourfold.

The agrarian society is characterised by vertical integration, which means that what people do is directly connected with and dependent on the earth and the climate.

The industrial and the service societies, on the other hand, are characterised by horizontal integration, which means that specialised activities are concentrated in different places throughout the country, which are tied together by the transportation of finished and semi-finished goods.

These snapshots from three different periods of time showing the transfer of milk from udder to stomach give a concentrated and concrete picture of some of the important features of Sweden's social development. Almost all the processes in the mid–19th century took place at the individual farms. During the 1930s town and country interacted more closely. Today's production pattern is characterised by dependence on and the flows between specialised parts of the milk production process. Both farmer and dairy are equally dependent on rapid, high-capacity transportation. The pictures also show clearly how the milk trade has become specialised and detached from the household, developing into employment in large industrial plants. What used to be one of many daily routine tasks on the farm has become a full-time job for a small number of specialists operating special capital-intensive equipment.

Opportunities in Everyday Life

Today's crowded streets full of cars, buses, cycles and pedestrians reveal that we spend a lot of time rushing between workplaces, shops and leisure centres. We have plenty of choices when we decide to do something. Quality, service and price affect our choice. We have to be able to move fast and frequently to be able to take advantage of these opportunities and make the best choice. We Swedes spend on average one hour twenty minutes every day travelling, and the average distance covered by each person is about 40 kilometres.

Our homes are full of technical equipment which makes life easier and even perhaps more enjoyable. More than 80 per cent of adult Swedes have access to a car in their household, which gives them many opportunities to travel. Workplaces are within driving distance, short or long, of home. With a car we can easily get to the hypermarket outside town, or quickly make our way to the theatre or bingo in the evening. Having a car makes it easier to pick up the children after a sports training session and to get out to the country cottage at the weekend. The shops' long opening hours mean that we can shop at almost any time we like on any day of the week. The corner shop, the kiosk or the petrol station with a grocery department make it easy to buy the evening paper and some milk.

Parts of our community never close. We expect many services to be available virtually all round the clock. It should always be possible to get into a hospital if there is an accident. We like getting the latest news on television and the radio. Passenger and goods trains should run through the night. Buses should provide services so that we can travel on them when we don't use our car.

Despite all these choices, everyday life for many people, as we have seen in the case of Bengt and Margareta's family, can be quite tricky. Each day brings a new jigsaw puzzle of activities to be fitted together to make life meaningful both for each individual member of the family and for the family as a whole. That is why Margareta does the housework on weekday evenings, so that the family are free when Bengt is at home at the weekends.

It is natural that the big city offers quite different possibilities from the small town. There are plenty of things to do in the big city at all times of the day and night. It is almost always possible to find a shop open or a film you'd like to see. But there are also crowds of people and queues. Children in a small town who are going to a training session can often make their own way there thanks to short distances and the fact that the traffic is less dangerous.

It is difficult to generalise about similarities and differences. There may be districts in the big city which are like a small town, which means that the family, in effect, can live quite detached from what otherwise characterises the big city.

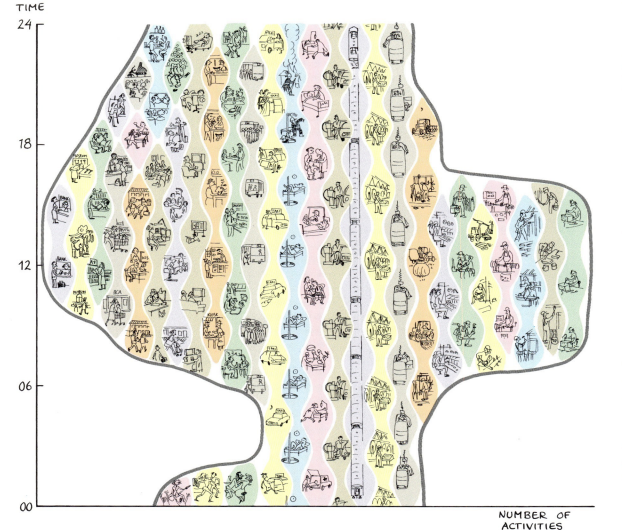

The day's options. In the daytime opportunities for work, education, services, consumption etc. increase; as evening approaches they decrease and in part change character. The more "entries", the more options to choose from. There are, however, many different kinds of constraints that reduce the individual's options.

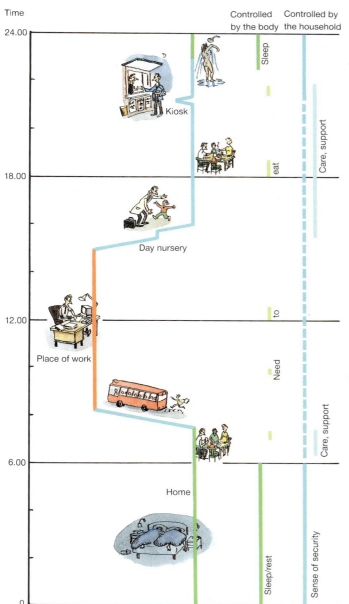

Free activities
Programmes and times for television, cinemas, clubs etc. Personal contacts and recreation.

Kiosks: Regulations for location, opening hours and range of goods.

Day nurseries: Regulations for leaving and fetching children, fees etc.

Gainful employment:

Working hours: Number, starting and finishing times, shifts, breaks, holidays, sick leave and parental leave.

Organisation of work: Assembly line, team work, machine-controlled etc.

Work environment: Noise, air pollution, safety etc.

Pay: Monthly salary, hourly wages, piece rates etc.

Transport: Road network, speed, parking, routes, regularity of service, bus stops etc.

Constraints on Everyday Life

We have many opportunities to utilise services and take part in social life, but they all demand time: time at home, time at work, time for shopping, time to watch television and in between time to move from one place to the other. But it is not just a question of time, of course. We cannot always get hold of a service when it best suits us. Other people decide about opening hours and time tables which control our daily routines: when we have to be at work, when the bus leaves, when the children have to be fetched from the day nursery. These are things we ourselves do not have very much control over.

One fundamental constraint is connected with our natural needs for sleep and food. It is true that we can postpone these activities a little, and the time we spend on them can vary as well. There are, however, certain limits which cannot be exceeded. A good deal of the day and night, on average between nine and ten hours, is devoted to activities which have to do with these survival projects.

Another kind of control is held by the family. Bengt's family needed to share and co-ordinate the household's activities. Who is going to shop, wash, cook, leave and fetch the children at the day nursery or at school? Mutual consideration within the family is, of course, a positive factor, which is why we do not think much about how this consideration also controls our daily life and limits what each member of the family can do, and when and where. A single person is never faced with the problem of sharing, but also does not have the same social contact with others.

Here we are dealing with various ways of living, whether chosen freely or not, which have different benefits and drawbacks; yet each choice inevitably means booking up future time. If you get a child, your diary is suddenly filled with commitments for several years ahead. When they have their first child many people are surprised by the extent of these commitments. In contrast the empty "diary" of the single person may seem like a future threat.

Thus each way we embark on in our voyage through life implies both opportunities and deadlocks. Our daydreams may fly off in time and space, but when we have to move

How everyday life is controlled. Our everyday life is regulated by a number of constraints – including personal and household constraints, and rules and regulations laid down by authorities and organisations. Every moment of every day we pass through "areas" which are governed by other people's rules.

It is just as difficult to make fair comparisons between yesterday and today. Life on a farm in the last century was so fundamentally different. Sofie, who was born at the beginning of our century, finds it difficult to accept all the innovations. "Some things are good, others bad" is her opinion, based on the sense of values she has about a good life and what sorts of things one really needs. She can't see the point of some of the new things.

In the daytime, the normal working hours, there are plenty of people in offices and factories. Schools, offices, shops and other service institutions are open during the day, or at least in the mornings. At other times of day services are less accessible. In the evenings there are plenty of opportunities for organised leisure activities: cinemas, theatres, restaurants, evening courses and dances. Even at home one can take part in organised leisure activities such as phone-in programmes, television contests and so on.

But all these possibilities also involve deadlocks. The fact that I can go shopping at seven in the evening means that the person in the cash-out is stuck there. My shopping in my free time requires a cashier to be working there then. The fact that I can pick up my children late in the evening from the nursery means that some teacher's working hours are lengthened after I have finished work. But our modern service society does not function without service personnel. Those who work in the service industries also have family and friends to take into consideration, so they, too, have their daily jigsaw puzzle to solve—perhaps an even more difficult one than the more "normal" ones.

physically we have to do it in ways which are firmly bound to time and place.

It is not at all only oneself or one's family that control one's daily life. A very strong external control and regulation of our daily routines lies at higher levels. The Riksdag, the government, private and public companies, both large and small, local authorities, health clinics and hospitals all work according to objectives and values which have been formulated to suit each particular organisation. We are surrounded by laws and regulations which with the best of intentions control our social intercourse and our daily life.

The example of the way milk travelled from udder to stomach showed that many individuals and organisations are involved in its journey through time and space. When many different flows cross in time and space, there will always be conflicts. This is particularly evident when several different organisations are involved.

Our life is spent on territory which is divided up into countless "decision-areas", each with its own decision makers and its own rules. These may be landlords, landowners, shopowners, companies or local or state authorities. One might say that, every day, we pass through other people's decision areas or territories, and we have to take them into account because they control what we may do and how, where and when we may do it.

Milk for breakfast, for example, has to be pasteurised according to fixed regulations. That is why we are not allowed to buy milk regularly at a farm which lies just across the road. On the way to work by car we also meet another totally regulated system; there is a fixed street and road pattern controlled by traffic lights, one-way streets and speed limits. If we go to work by bus, we are faced with the bus company's fixed routes and timetables. Most of us have to get to work at a fixed time and finish work at another equally fixed time. Working hours are determined by agreements between employers and employees. We have to decide on our holidays in good time and within fixed limits. Working hours may clash with banking hours. The children's school times and terms do not usually match their parents' working hours and holidays.

We have shown how Bengt passes through such "decision-areas" controlled by other people. He bumps into many deadlocks in the day, but there are also loopholes in the form of alternatives and possibilities (perhaps in time as well financially). He may, for example, be able to pick up Josefine from the day nursery today earlier than usual. This possibility gives him a bit more time with his children, perhaps under less stressful conditions than usual.

Torsten Hägerstrand once described our control systems in the following way: "In actual fact we are all at one big school, with lesson times and breaks in an unpublished timetable in the background, a timetable which has been drawn up by many headteachers who often do not know all that much about each other's activities and objectives."

Everyday Resources

The characteristic activities of today's way of living are marked by modern technology. Being able to travel quickly and comfortably, keeping food in refrigerators and freezers and being able to cook it quickly, relaxing with television, the radio or newspapers or being able to spend stress-free leisure time playing sports or lying in a hammock in the garden—these are a few examples that show that technology plays a decisive role. A lot of equipment is time-saving, but also requires a not insignificant amount of time to be paid for and maintained. In other words, we have to invest time in order to save time. Perhaps

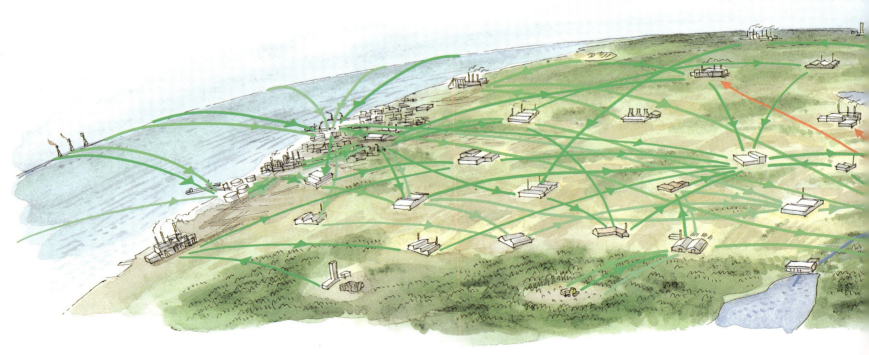

we do not always realise which way the scales of saved time and wasted time tip in the long term, but it is quite evident that our industrial and service society has a great many time and labour-saving devices, both in the home and at work. Does this, however, also give us time to really think about our lives?

When we produce, distribute and consume goods and services, we also deal with many material resources. Raw materials as well as semi-manufactured and manufactured goods are transported on a large scale hither and thither in the world.

Leisure in Sweden also demands large resources, not least because of all the travelling we do. Holiday and weekend trips use up large quantities of fuel for planes, cars and boats. Large areas are taken up by facilities used only for leisure activities, many of them used for only short periods of the year.

We know very little about where parts of our apparatuses come from, and even less about the total demands that each apparatus makes on nature's resources. In addition it is very unusual for producers and consumers to have made preparations for the day when an apparatus is worn out and has to be scrapped. This often means that the apparatus is dumped or is taken to a rubbish tip. It is as yet unusual for resources to be reclaimed from rubbish to protect nature from harmful substances.

That is why our environmental problems are growing. The relationships between all the things in our daily life and our environment are not easily perceived, either for the producer or for the consumer. Moreover, producers of goods and services do not see any profit in taking an interest in environmental problems as long as we go on buying their products. But awareness of environmental problems is growing apace.

The aim of the resources illustration is to provoke thought about the material and substances that surround us. This point is illustrated with a few flows which succeed one another in the manufacturing process from the finished product back to natural resources. We follow other product flows forwards in the process—from the moment when the product is worn out until, in some form or other, it lands up back in nature. Some of the remains can be reabsorbed in natural cycles, others cannot return to nature. These cause long-term damage. Even today, however, a great deal of rubbish is stored or decomposed in special ways.

We showed previously how much forest was needed for a milk carton. How much forest, in fact, has been used up to furnish a modern home? How much iron and steel, aluminium and oil in processed forms do we have round us at home? Every household has a collection of processed products which may be difficult to fit into a natural cycle. These products need not in themselves be harmful to nature, but they may cause damage because we concentrate too much of the same sort in a few spots. And, vice versa, raw materials have been extracted from certain places and spread over vast geographical areas.

In other words there are limitations of a much higher order than those we mentioned earlier. In the long term nature's global limitations will possibly make themselves felt in as concrete a way as when we discover that we have missed the train.

Nature still feels close on a farm. The seasons, rain, sunshine, light and darkness affect everyday life. The town dweller may think he is liberated from nature, but he is fundamentally wrong in that belief. Although many steps in the transformation of nature's resources to household products are concealed, and the connections between our life style and nature's rhythms have become blurred, these connections still exist. If we do not take them into consideration, nature will inevitably revolt— sooner or later.

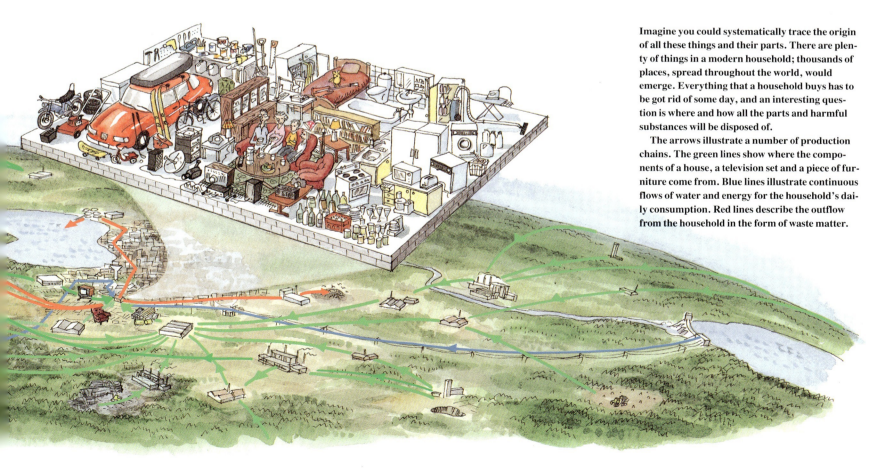

Imagine you could systematically trace the origin of all these things and their parts. There are plenty of things in a modern household; thousands of places, spread throughout the world, would emerge. Everything that a household buys has to be got rid of some day, and an interesting question is where and how all the parts and harmful substances will be disposed of.

The arrows illustrate a number of production chains. The green lines show where the components of a house, a television set and a piece of furniture come from. Blue lines illustrate continuous flows of water and energy for the household's daily consumption. Red lines describe the outflow from the household in the form of waste matter.

Work

The Concept of Work

What does one think of when one hears the word work? A full-time job, perhaps, blood, sweat and tears, part-time work, housework, nightwork, overtime, manual labour, clerical work—there are countless associations, each one different according to the individual's experience of life. Writers and philosophers have for thousands of years expressed a variety of opinions on work.

The word for work *(Sw. arbete)* is found in Old Swedish in the form *arvodhe* (in the Middle Ages), meaning work—toil. In the late Middle Ages this word was replaced by *arbete* from Low German. The word still had a double meaning, including the idea of toil and difficulty.

In the New Testament, Matthew 11.28 in the Swedish translation of 1526, it says: "Kommen till mich j alle som arbeten och ären betungadhe." (Authorized Version of 1611: "Come unto me, all ye that labour and are heavily laden.") In the Swedish version of 1917, it says:"Kommen till mig, i alla som arbeten och äro betungade". The 1981 version reads: "Kom till mig, alla ni som är tyngda av bördor *(Eng. burdens)*". Thus it was not until 1981 that the translation took into account that the word for work had a different meaning from the original sense.

The Swedish word *arvode (Eng. fee)* returns in the 18th century with its present-day meaning. During the Middle Ages pay for work was described as *"arvodets lön"* (The Västgöta Lawbook).

There are also certain moral aspects of work. The Lutheran catechism says: "Work benefits health and prosperity and prevents many opportunities for sin". St Augustine said: "Pray and work".

Work is also one of the classic economic production factors, together with land and capital. And the work factor has been much discussed in both political and economic literature. Our Swedish cultural heritage, as expressed in our proverbs, contains many exhortations to work hard and economize.

For many people work is still associated with hard manual labour, while

Conference hostesses are an example of an occupation that did not exist a few decades ago.

The average length of life has increased and we are physically more active for a longer period of our lives. The traditional picture of life's stages looks different now.

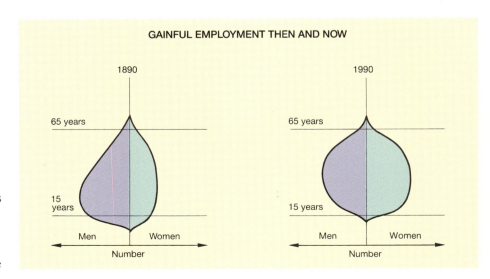

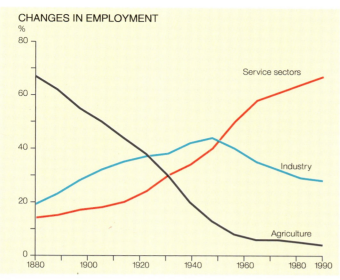

The development of economic life in Sweden closely follows the international pattern: agriculture, industry and services. The next phase lies within the information sector.

for others it is a matter of getting too little physical exercise or being stressed in front of a computer screen.

Thus we can see that both the definition of work and several dimensions of the contents of work itself have varied through the ages. There are also different attitudes towards work. It can be looked upon from an individual or a collective point of view—the church, a trade union, the government, for example. It can also be seen in a time perspective—how long a certain kind of work takes—and in a spatial perspective—it "takes place" somewhere and requires space. These are some of the approaches we shall use in this chapter.

ASPECTS OF WORK

Starting from a simple theoretical diagram, at the bottom of the previous page, we shall discuss various aspects of work in this chapter. The diagram shows the workforce at two different times: the first in the 19th century and the second in the mid–20th century. The first example shows how early people started to work, at the age of 14. Work does not necessarily mean paid work. There was a large amount of unpaid work, especially for women. In the old community everyone had to work, to keep mouths filled and poverty at bay.

The second diagram shows that entry into working life occurred later. Education preceded work and in due course one retired on a pension. Civil servants were the first employees to get a pension. A general pension was introduced by legislation in 1913, when the State took over responsibility. The diagram also shows how the way men and women have participated in working life has evened out. The volume of work per person has diminished, unpaid work is extensive, part-time work, early retirement and unemployment are concepts which were institutionalised by modern legislation.

Work may also be looked upon with regard to its employment and pay functions. Work is the material basis of life; many people would even claim that it also forms a social basis. At the level of the individual it may also be claimed that work is a part of a person's human value. This becomes evident especially in times of high unemployment. Work also facilitates social mobility. Work can be organised and workers can be organised; this is a matter of power.

Work is connected to a place, it has a position, a localisation. How does one get to work? There is a pattern of travel between the workplace and the home: commuting. Work exists at different places, not always where people live, so mobility is necessary to allow people to take up new jobs or to avoid being out of work. The term work also contains an environmental aspect: how are workplaces organised with regard to the physical and social environment? Additionally, work involves questions of health and illness, work satisfaction and disease, as well as feelings of physical, social and mental well-being.

The theme of this chapter, as of others, is that both work and leisure can be described at two levels—that of the individual, which can be called the micro-structure, and that of the framework, which can be called the macro-structure. At the micro-level, with the individual as the starting point, work may be looked upon as part of the life-cycle: time for education, work, retraining, change of employment, perhaps, too, a period of unemployment, early retirement and final retirement on a pension. The macro-level consists of the combined activities of many individuals, companies, employers and employees. There is an interaction between general factors in society—economic cycles, laws and regulations—local factors, and individual factors, as expressed in the form of economic resources, education and the like.

Brick-making at Bockträsk near Sorsele, 1929. The old industries often required a great deal of muscle power and physical effort from the whole workforce, regardless of age.

There are many descriptions of Swedish working life. One novel in which many elderly people have been able to identify their pasts is Eyvind Johnson's *This was 1914*. It is about fourteen-year-old Olof in Norrbotten who has to go out into the world in search of work. One of the passages reads: "He pants, his legs are trembling, his eyes smarting; his arms ache and his hands are blistered from the shafts of the wheelbarrow. When the shift is over, he collapses into his bunk, a broad double one, and sleeps. His eyes close, he falls asleep at once and wakes up feeling tired. Sometimes he thinks that the whole world is standing still, nothing moving and he is getting nowhere. A hell of bricks and mortar."

Occupations and Specialisation

There are about 8.5 million people in Sweden, of whom about 5.4 million are aged between 16 and 64, "the working population". That is the definition today. In earlier days a person was fit for work at a much earlier age and had to work as long as he physically was able to. Those who are counted as part of the workforce today, those who want a job, number some 4.5 million and those who are not in the workforce amount to almost 0.9 million.

There are other ways of describing the workforce: a division into part-time and full-time workers, work for men and work for women, levels of employment in different age groups, the type of education the workforce has or how much people are paid.

"Work" has its own museum housed in a former textile mill in Norrköping.

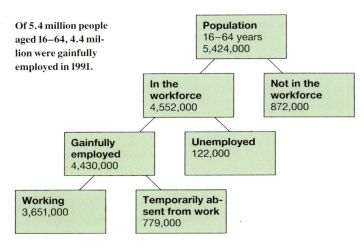

Of 5.4 million people aged 16–64, 4.4 million were gainfully employed in 1991.

CHANGES IN OCCUPATIONS

When the word occupation is mentioned, one thinks perhaps of work in combination with education, specialisation and skills. In earlier days there were few occupations in most villages. Most people worked on the farms, but all the same there was room for specialisation; some people became cobblers, others tailors, carpenters or blacksmiths. The total amount of labour needed in the community was divided between individuals and groups. New occupations arose gradually and work moved outside the farm.

The division of labour also has a geographical dimension. Changes in occupation were in many cases a matter of new locations; people moved from one place to another and changed occupations. When people moved from the countryside into towns, they brought with them skills which could be used in new occupations in the towns. People adapted to new conditions.

It is typical that many of the old occupational names were German in origin and were often craft terms or referred to manual skills. The new occupational terms are often of English origin and are connected with management and service occupations. Some of the old occupations have been given new names. Rat-catchers have become vermin exterminators,

OLD OCCUPATIONS:
- a cooper, made barrels
- a stacker, stacked up planks at a sawmill
- a brass founder, cast bronze and brass
- a last maker, made lasts to be sold to a cobbler

NEW OCCUPATIONS:
- a headhunter, recruits senior executives
- a computer graphics artist, creates layouts with the aid of a computer
- a pooltender, works at a hotel swimming-pool, serving the guests
- a light therapist, makes sure that people have the "right" lighting in the dark months of the year
- a travel manager, plans and co-ordinates business trips for companies and negotiates with travel agencies

Teaching is an example of an occupation that has become more specialised over the past 100 years.

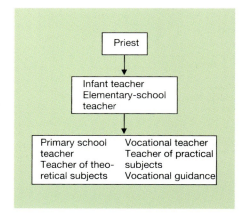

Job advertisements reflect not only the demand for labour but also changes in occupations.

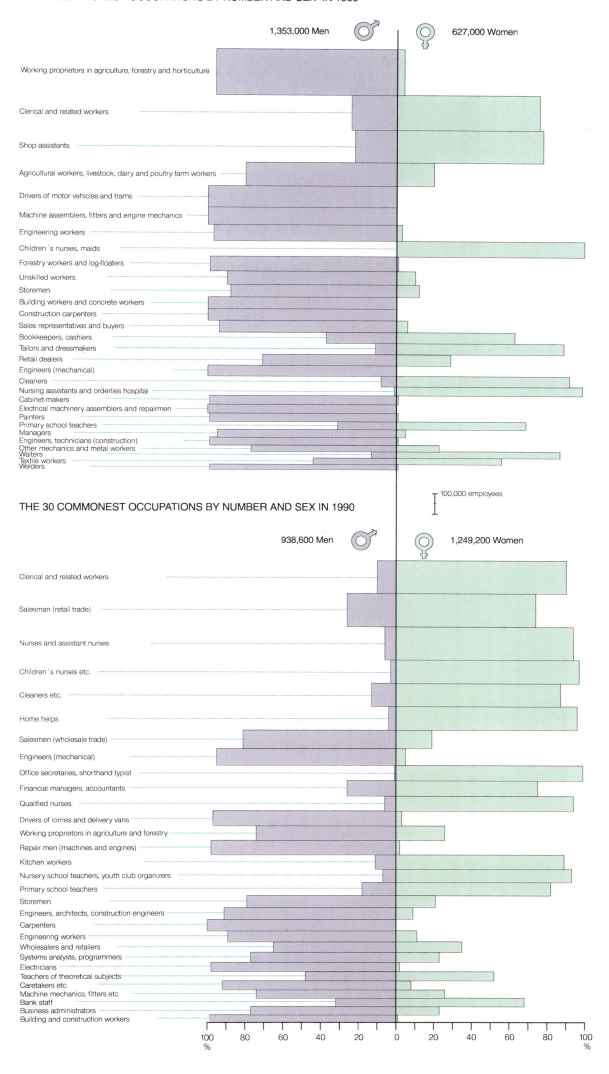

which also reflects a changing sense of values in society. Many occupational names have been depersonified and are often linked to material and technical terms, not least in order to get higher pay.

SPECIALISATION

Changing occupations and jobs usually means that one specialises, that one invests in education or training to get a more skilled job. This is partly an individual consideration, whereby individuals specialise to be able to compete for jobs. But it is also a matter of national competitiveness in relation to other countries. What is happening in the long term on the Swedish labour market? Are more and more people getting highly-skilled jobs, or is the opposite the case?

Most studies of changes in the content of work indicate increased specialisation in work, and many people consider that work has become more skilled. Rapid technological developments and concentration on more knowledge-intensive production methods has led to a need for better trained personnel. The proportion of skilled jobs has increased, while that of unskilled work has decreased.

THE THIRTY LARGEST OCCUPATIONAL GROUPS

We have already pointed out that industry and commerce have changed in the course of time, and this is also true of occupations. In the course of a few decades, between 1960 and 1990, dramatic changes have taken place in the list of the 30 largest occupations. Perhaps the most evident change is that the number of women has increased from just over 600,000 to a little less than 1.2 million, i.e. it has doubled. The number of men, on the other hand, has decreased from 1.4 million to 0.9 million among these 30 occupations. This indicates that there are more male occupations, whereas women are concentrated in certain occupations. It is also evident that occupations based on agriculture and forestry and the industrial sector are diminishing, whereas occupations in the public sector and private services are expanding.

Percentage of men and women among all persons gainfully employed in the 30 commonest occupations. As late as 1960 occupations connected with agriculture and forestry were in the majority. In 1990 the most dominant occupations are service jobs held by women.

43

Education

There are few areas in politics which are so heatedly debated as education. It affects almost everyone. What education have you had? Is it possible to improve one's education? For the country as a whole, education, and the research work that is connected with education, is of vital importance for national competitiveness. These are questions that concern both the individual and society, not least because so much time is invested in education. The local communities where education of various kinds takes place are also affected in a special way.

A BRIEF HISTORICAL SURVEY

The Ecclesiastical Law of 1686 made literacy compulsory. Compulsory schooling in Sweden began in 1842, with the establishment of elementary schools. There was to be an elementary school for all the children in each parish. In fact the Swedish peasantry had been literate for many years, as a result of the Church's catechistical meetings in every household. The six-year elementary school ("folkskola") came in 1882; in 1937 it was extended to seven years. The secondary school regulations of 1905 divided secondary school into two parts: the "gymnasium" and the "realskola". There were separate schools for girls for a long time. From the 1920s onwards girls were admitted to most secondary schools, but there were single-sex secondary schools until the late 1950s. In 1950 the Riksdag passed a law establishing a comprehensive school sys-

Kvarnen School, Lidingö, about 1890.

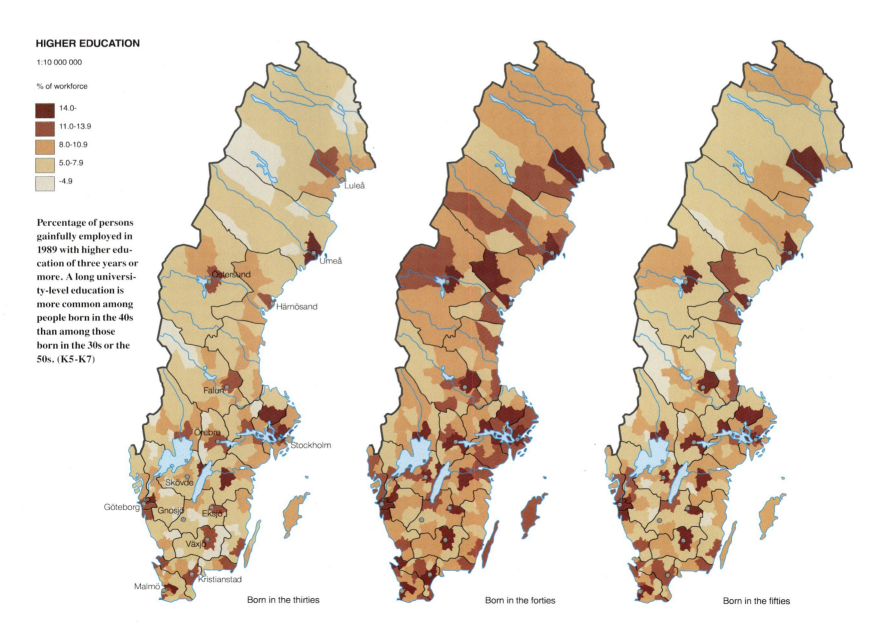

HIGHER EDUCATION

1:10 000 000

% of workforce

- 14.0-
- 11.0-13.9
- 8.0-10.9
- 5.0-7.9
- -4.9

Percentage of persons gainfully employed in 1989 with higher education of three years or more. A long university-level education is more common among people born in the 40s than among those born in the 30s or the 50s. (K5-K7)

Born in the thirties   Born in the forties   Born in the fifties

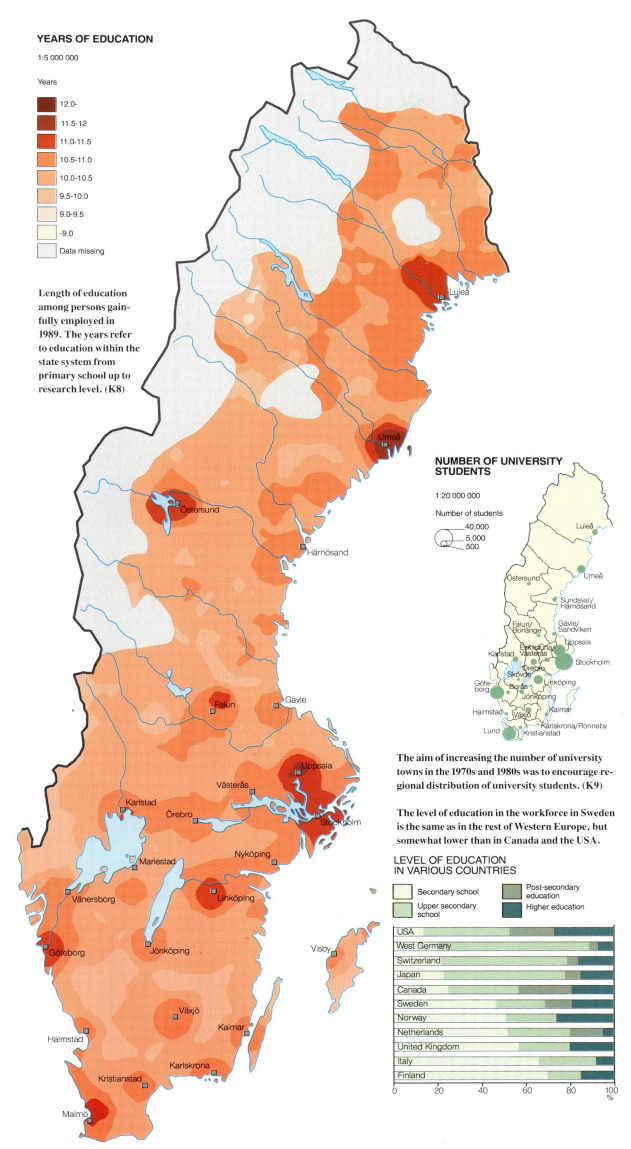

YEARS OF EDUCATION
1:5 000 000

Years
- 12.0–
- 11.5–12
- 11.0–11.5
- 10.5–11.0
- 10.0–10.5
- 9.5–10.0
- 9.0–9.5
- –9.0
- Data missing

Length of education among persons gainfully employed in 1989. The years refer to education within the state system from primary school up to research level. (K8)

NUMBER OF UNIVERSITY STUDENTS
1:20 000 000

Number of students
- 40,000
- 5,000
- 500

The aim of increasing the number of university towns in the 1970s and 1980s was to encourage regional distribution of university students. (K9)

The level of education in the workforce in Sweden is the same as in the rest of Western Europe, but somewhat lower than in Canada and the USA.

LEVEL OF EDUCATION IN VARIOUS COUNTRIES

- Secondary school
- Upper secondary school
- Post-secondary education
- Higher education

tem, and this resulted in the elementary schools and the "realskolor" being amalgamated to create a nine-year compulsory school ("grundskola").

What is characteristic today of Swedish education is its extensive investment in the teenage years, compared with only a few years ago. All children go to the nine-year compulsory school. Today 90 per cent of an age group complete "gymnasium" education (16–19) and about 25 per cent continue to higher education.

The educational career of those gainfully employed in 1989 varied in different parts of the country. In the big cities and most county towns it was long. In contrast educational careers in parts of Norrland, Västergötland and Småland were short. Those with higher education, i.e. tertiary education of three years or more, worked mainly in the county towns.

Many people who would otherwise be unemployed take courses in government training schemes to raise their competence to meet new requirements. It may be said that education today continues throughout one's life, even though the forms of this education vary. The length of education has gradually increased. School is the largest place of work in Sweden.

HIGHER EDUCATION

There was a boom in education in Sweden in the 1960s. The traditional recruitment from the upper and middle classes was complemented by a large intake from young working-class students. The labour market was relatively strong and many people were getting jobs in expanding industries and the public sector.

In order to broaden access to higher education, the State established regional colleges during the 1970s. However, the number of students at the universities of Uppsala, Lund, Stockholm, Göteborg, Umeå and Linköping far exceed the numbers at these colleges. Employees born in the 1940s are more likely to have a long post-school education than employees born in the 1930s and 1950s.

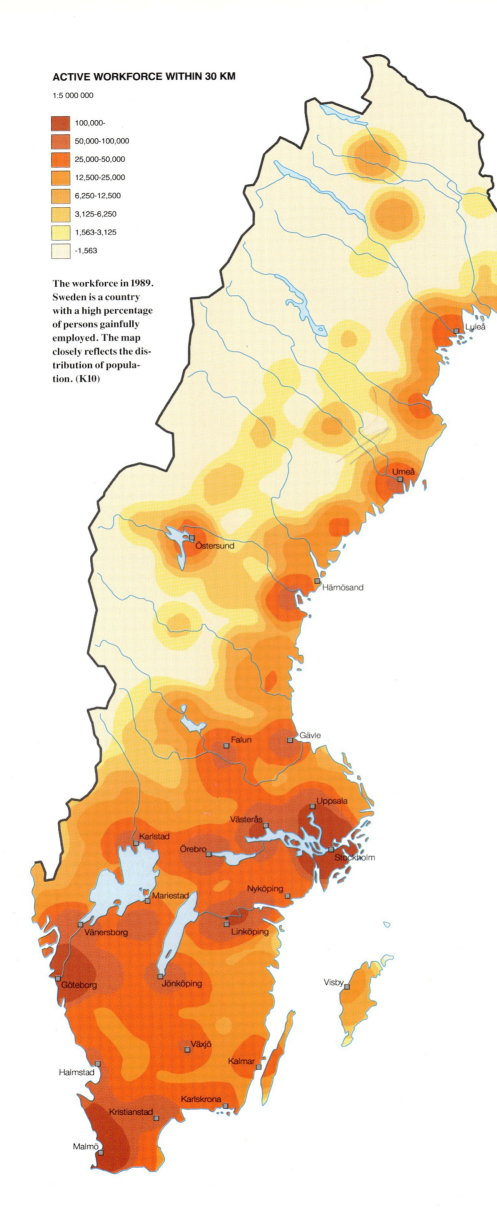

ACTIVE WORKFORCE WITHIN 30 KM

1:5 000 000

- 100,000–
- 50,000–100,000
- 25,000–50,000
- 12,500–25,000
- 6,250–12,500
- 3,125–6,250
- 1,563–3,125
- –1,563

The workforce in 1989. Sweden is a country with a high percentage of persons gainfully employed. The map closely reflects the distribution of population. (K10)

Gainful Employment

"Work refers in the first place to human activity which is defined by the market or the authorities as paid work. In the second place activities that are directly comparable with or exchangeable for paid work are also included. In the third place other planned uses of time which create benefits that meet or may be expected to meet basic human needs are counted as work." That is Statistics Sweden's official definition of work.

For the State it is paid work that receives political attention. There is a broad political consensus about the value of full employment, and the importance of providing citizens with "work, services and a good environment". Paid work provides the material basis for life in industrial and post-industrial society. The many welfare investigations that have been carried out in Sweden in the past few decades support this point of view.

WORK — LIFE FORMS

Work has not only a material aspect; it also has a social dimension, which in turn provides the right conditions for meaningful leisure. In recent years the study of life forms, as they are called, that is, what people do with their lives, has attracted great interest. We give two examples: the life form of the traditional employee and that of the new, increasingly widespread careerist. Changes in values occur slowly and affect all age groups. The pattern of events is not unambiguous.

THE EMPLOYEE

Industrial society developed towards the end of the 19th century in Sweden, bringing with it a new life form in which time was divided into two quite separate areas: work and leisure. Working life and family life became two separate spheres, cut off from each other in both time and

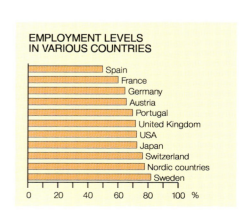

EMPLOYMENT LEVELS IN VARIOUS COUNTRIES

Spain, France, Germany, Austria, Portugal, United Kingdom, USA, Japan, Switzerland, Nordic countries, Sweden

0 20 40 60 80 100 %

space. Work developed into a means for realising various wishes for leisure activities. In order to guarantee enough leisure time working hours had to be regulated. This was done by passing laws which specified the length of time for work, and its distribution over days, weeks and years. These questions were of great importance for the growth of the labour movement in the late 19th century. This life form is dominant in many communities today, particularly in industrial towns.

THE CAREERIST

A majority of the younger generation look upon work differently from the older generation. Work is developing into a means for self-realisation and personality development besides being a source of income. People speak of a new attitude to work, an attitude which also affects everyday life. This way of looking at work is called the careerist life form.

Values and attitudes to work are the result of experiences from the social and economic world one is a part of. Experiences, especially for a specific time, are common to the working population of that time. This generation will continue to carry its values and attitudes throughout life. The generation born in the 1910s, for example, is marked by the war-time years of the 40s. This influenced their material expectations and their concept of the need for consensus solutions for the rest of their lives. Similarly, the generation of the 40s who were at university in the 1960s share common experiences from the student uprisings in 1968. Memories of these events have helped to shape their attitudes towards society, life style and choice of profession.

The careerist life form is maintained by today's well-educated young generation, many of whom have a life style and an attitude to work which replace the old employee life form. Work is more commonly seen as an aim in itself—a means of achieving self-realisation and satisfaction. This may result in work expanding at the cost of leisure. They work overtime, take work home and see no distinction between work and leisure. Whether such changes in values are just ripples on the surface or represent more deep-going changes is difficult to say.

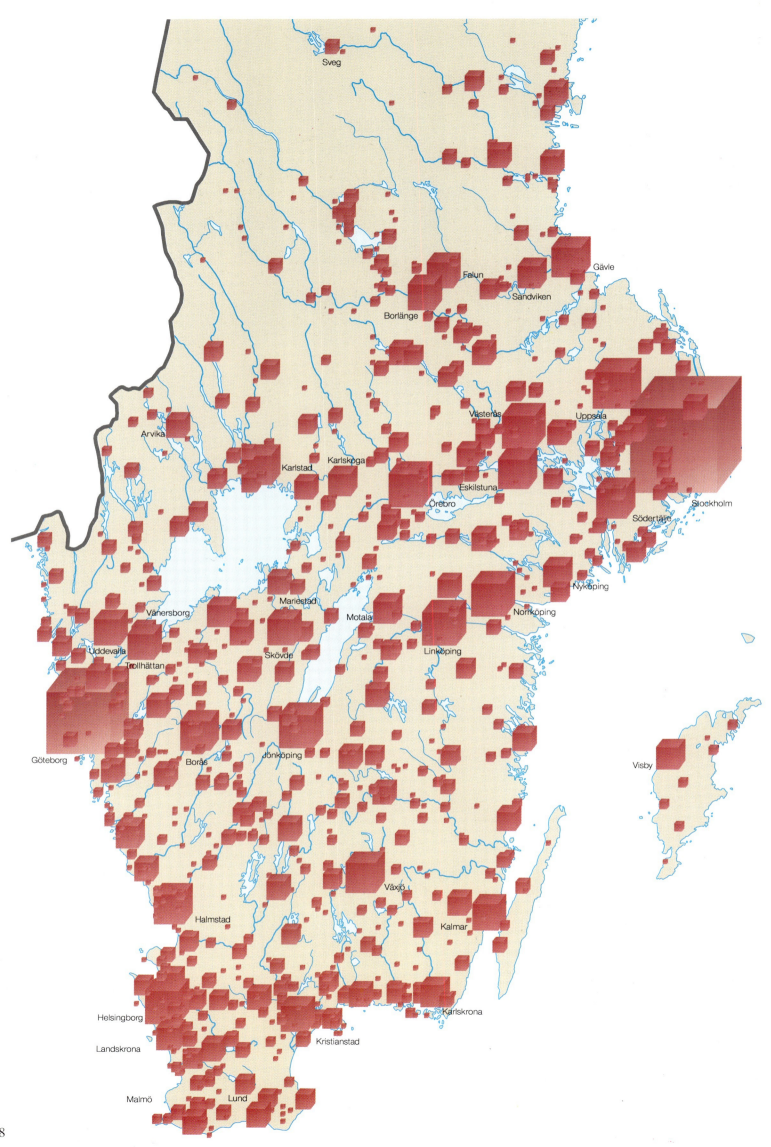

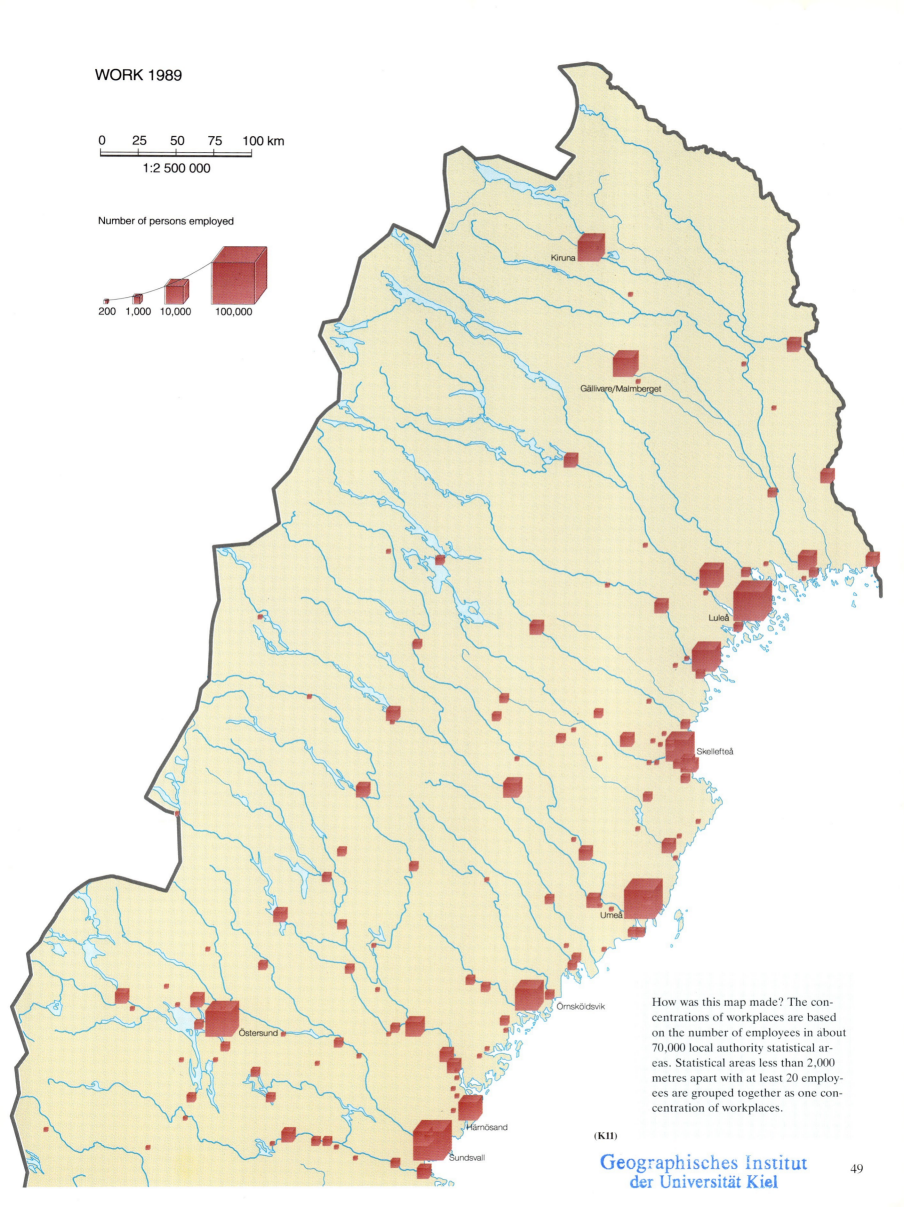

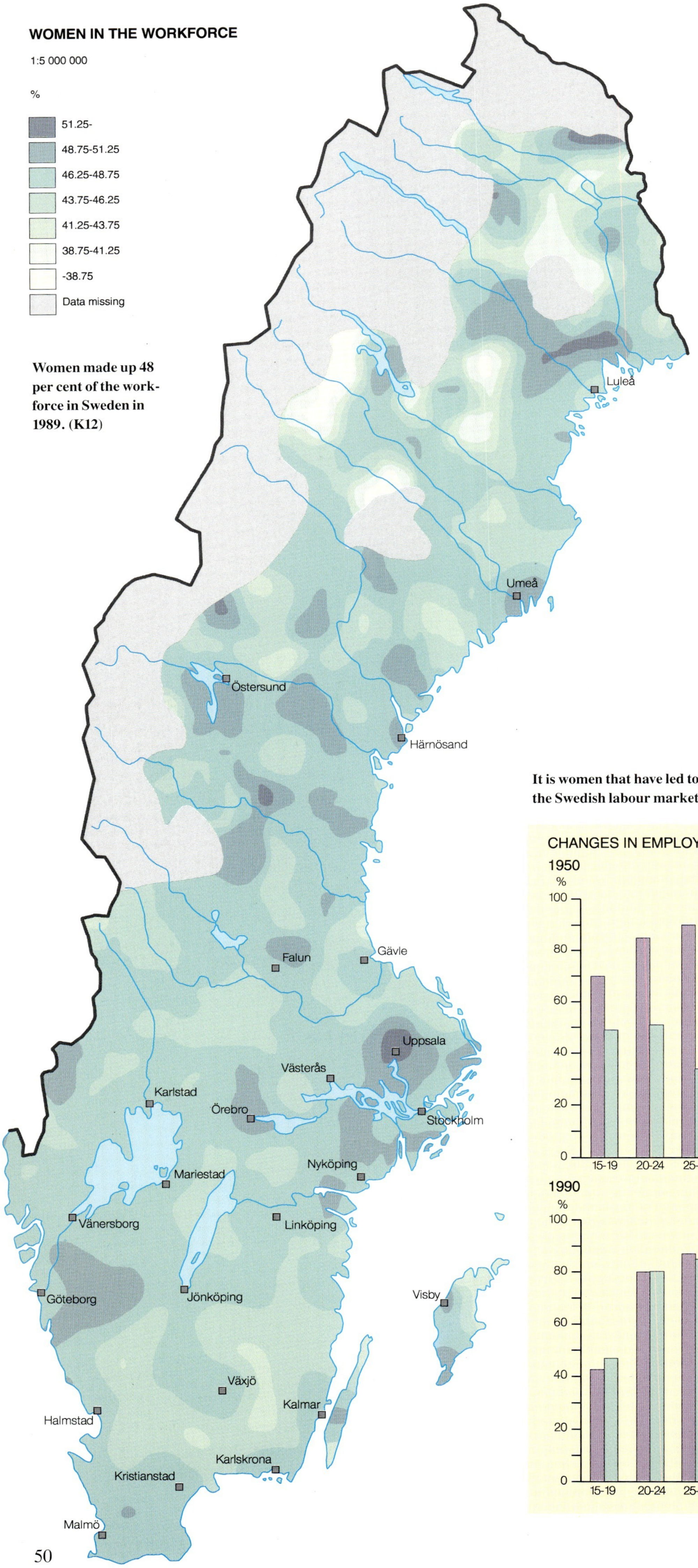

WOMEN IN THE WORKFORCE

1:5 000 000

%
- 51.25-
- 48.75-51.25
- 46.25-48.75
- 43.75-46.25
- 41.25-43.75
- 38.75-41.25
- -38.75
- Data missing

Women made up 48 per cent of the workforce in Sweden in 1989. (K12)

It is women that have led to the great change in the Swedish labour market.

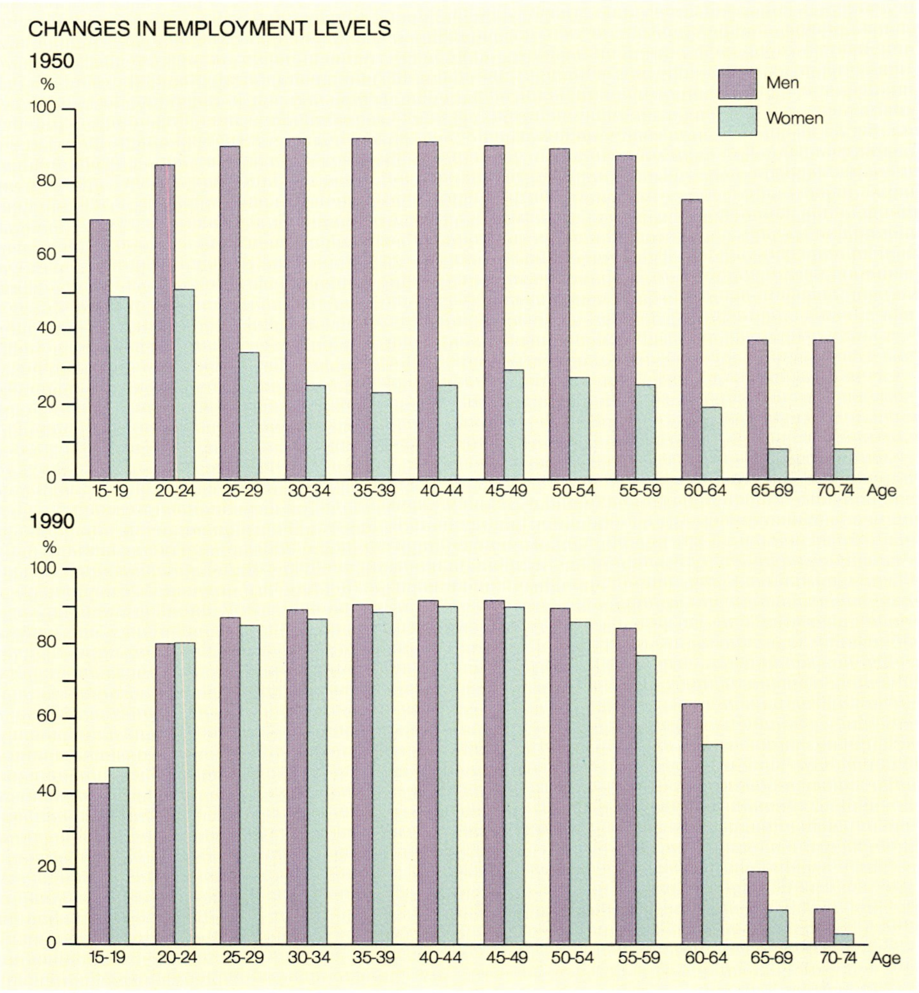

Intensiveness of Economic Activity

One of the major changes in Swedish working life in the post-war years is that more and more people have joined the workforce. This means that the intensiveness of economic activity has increased. Men have by tradition always had a high level of economic activity since they have always been the breadwinners of the family. The greatest change concerns women, not least during the 1970s, as a result of several major developments in society. The growth of the public sector is perhaps the most important change, and there it is the social service sector that has expanded very rapidly and where most of the employees are women. Another explanation of the increased intensiveness of economic activity for women is the expansion of child care; this removed one of the obstacles to doing paid work, which in the first place prevented women from taking a job. Other explanations are the need for two wage earners to manage today's financial obligations. The tax reform of 1973, combined with a higher rate of marginal income tax and separate taxation of husband and wife also made it more profitable for women to go out to work.

CHANGES IN EMPLOYMENT LEVELS

1950

1990

50

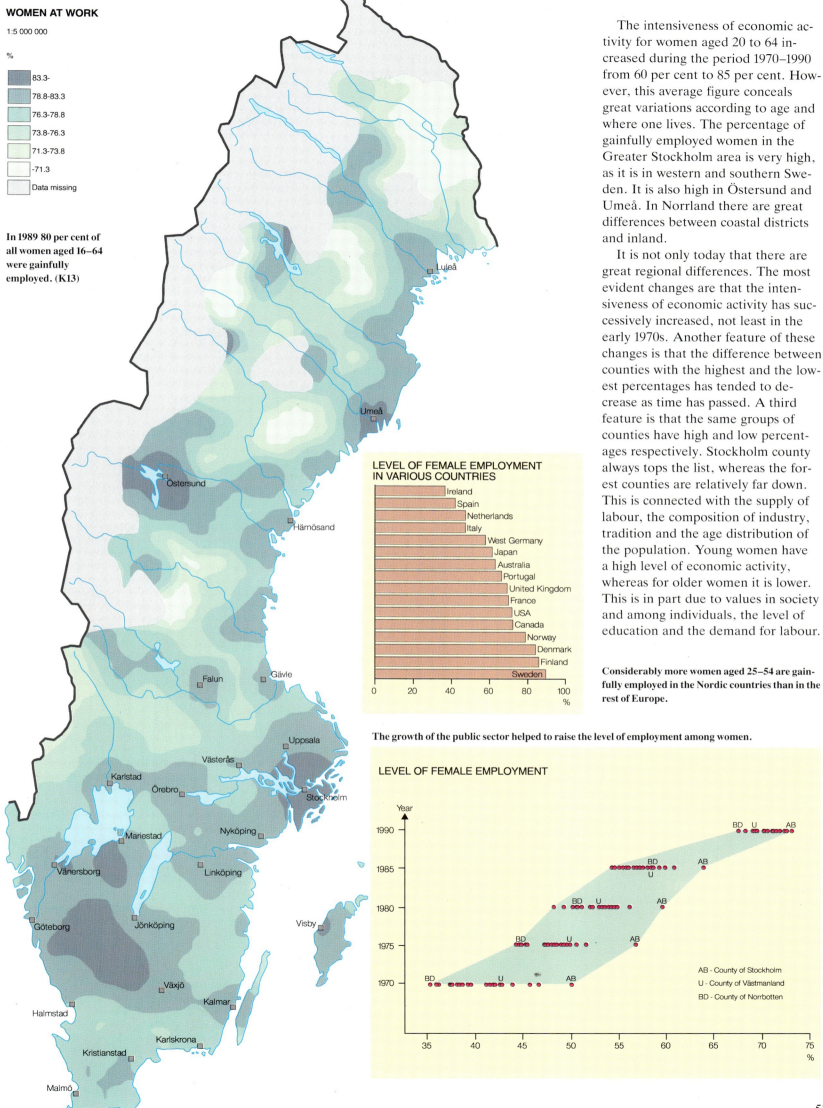

WOMEN AT WORK

1:5 000 000

%
- 83.3-
- 78.8–83.3
- 76.3–78.8
- 73.8–76.3
- 71.3–73.8
- –71.3
- Data missing

In 1989 80 per cent of all women aged 16–64 were gainfully employed. (K13)

LEVEL OF FEMALE EMPLOYMENT IN VARIOUS COUNTRIES

Ireland, Spain, Netherlands, Italy, West Germany, Japan, Australia, Portugal, United Kingdom, France, USA, Canada, Norway, Denmark, Finland, Sweden

LEVEL OF FEMALE EMPLOYMENT

AB – County of Stockholm
U – County of Västmanland
BD – County of Norrbotten

The intensiveness of economic activity for women aged 20 to 64 increased during the period 1970–1990 from 60 per cent to 85 per cent. However, this average figure conceals great variations according to age and where one lives. The percentage of gainfully employed women in the Greater Stockholm area is very high, as it is in western and southern Sweden. It is also high in Östersund and Umeå. In Norrland there are great differences between coastal districts and inland.

It is not only today that there are great regional differences. The most evident changes are that the intensiveness of economic activity has successively increased, not least in the early 1970s. Another feature of these changes is that the difference between counties with the highest and the lowest percentages has tended to decrease as time has passed. A third feature is that the same groups of counties have high and low percentages respectively. Stockholm county always tops the list, whereas the forest counties are relatively far down. This is connected with the supply of labour, the composition of industry, tradition and the age distribution of the population. Young women have a high level of economic activity, whereas for older women it is lower. This is in part due to values in society and among individuals, the level of education and the demand for labour.

Considerably more women aged 25–54 are gainfully employed in the Nordic countries than in the rest of Europe.

The growth of the public sector helped to raise the level of employment among women.

Full-time—Part-time

There are clear sex differences between the percentages of full-time and part-time workers. Traditionally it has been the man who has been the sole family breadwinner. Not until the last few decades has this picture changed. The demand for labour has been so high for some years that women have been needed on the labour market to meet this need. This has been made possible by the State removing many obstacles to doing paid work, which has enabled households to organise the complicated jigsaw of everyday life.

The percentage of men aged 20 to 64 in the workforce has remained very constant, being about 90 per cent in 1990. During the 1970s and 1980s the percentage of full-time-employed men decreased somewhat, but has since then stabilised at about 84 per cent. The percentage of part-time-employed men is low, only 6 per cent, most of whom are elderly.

The intensiveness of economic activity among men aged 55 to 64 varies considerably in Sweden. It is very high in parts of Småland and Västergötland. The figures are considerably higher for the south of Sweden than for the north. In Norrbotten the percentage of working men of this age is remarkably low.

In 1990 85 per cent of women aged 20 to 64 were in the workforce. Half of them had full-time jobs and 35 per cent part-time jobs. The greatest change is that the percentage of full-time workers has increased during the past few decades. It is long part-time work, 30–34 hours, that has increased, while short part-time work, 1–19 hours, has decreased.

It is in the first place women who have part-time jobs. People with short part-time work account for only 5 per cent of all part-time workers.

MEASURING INTENSIVENESS OF ECONOMIC ACTIVITY

There are various ways of measuring intensiveness of economic activity, and there is reason to be sceptical of the traditional method. The starting point for an alternative calculation is the number of men and women of working age, i.e. aged 16 to 64 (1991).

The level of economic activity for

PEOPLE IN GAINFUL EMPLOYMENT, 1991

	Men	Women
Total number	2,753,000	2,671,000
In the workforce	2,369,000 (86.0%)	2,183,000 (81.7%)
Employed	2,299,000 (83.5%)	2,132,000 (79.8%)
Employed, less absentees	1,967,000 (71.4%)	1,684,000 (63%)

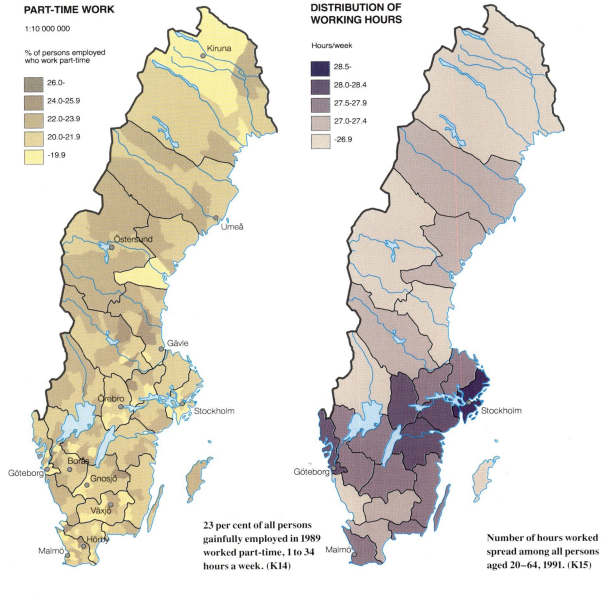

23 per cent of all persons gainfully employed in 1989 worked part-time, 1 to 34 hours a week. (K14)

Number of hours worked spread among all persons aged 20–64, 1991. (K15)

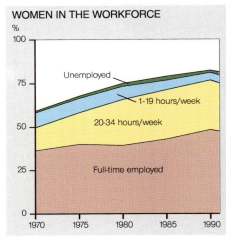

Women aged 20–64 by level of employment, 1970–1991. Short part-time work has decreased and long part-time work increased.

Men aged 20–64 according to level of employment, 1970–1991.

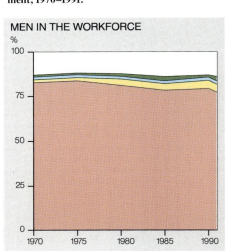

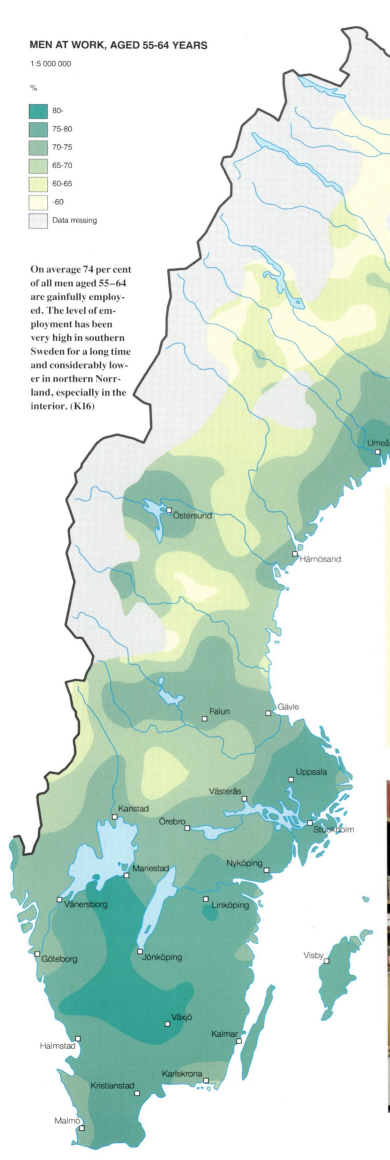

MEN AT WORK, AGED 55-64 YEARS

1:5 000 000

%
- 80-
- 75-80
- 70-75
- 65-70
- 60-65
- -60
- Data missing

On average 74 per cent of all men aged 55–64 are gainfully employed. The level of employment has been very high in southern Sweden for a long time and considerably lower in northern Norrland, especially in the interior. (K16)

GAINFULLY EMPLOYED MEN, AGED 55-64 YEARS, IN VARIOUS COUNTRIES

Italy, Netherlands, Finland, France, West Germany, Australia, Spain, Portugal, Denmark, USA, Canada, United Kingdom, Sweden, Ireland, Norway, Japan

this age group is about 82 per cent for women and 86 per cent for men. Some of this workforce is unemployed, and other groups are away from work for various reasons. Those in work are 63 per cent of the women and just over 71 per cent of the men.

Some employees work less than the normal forty-hour week, while others work more. The average number of hours worked per week is 33.6 for women and 41.2 for men. Taking these figures into consideration, the total volume of work can be recalculated as full-time employment. If the number of full-time jobs is placed in relation to the number of persons of working age, the level of intensiveness is 53 per cent for women and 73 per cent for men.

WORK EXPECTATIONS

Most people are satisfied with their number of working hours; 80 per cent say that they do not wish to change their working hours. Those who work part time, mainly women, compose about one quarter of all gainfully employed persons. Four of 25 part-time employees would like to increase their working time. Fourteen of 75 full-time employees would like to reduce their working time. It is about twice as common for women to want to reduce their working time, compared with men.

Swedish, Japanese, Norwegian and Irish men had the highest level of employment among men aged 55–64 in the OECD countries in 1988.

When the youth centre is closed and the day nursery has its planning conference, children have to go to work with their parents. It is five times more common for women than men to work part time.

PERSONS WORKING IN MANUFACTURING

1:5 000 000

%
- 45.0-
- 37.5-45.0
- 30.0-37.5
- 22.5-30.0
- 15.0-22.5
- 7.5-15.0
- -7.5
- Data missing

Sweden is very dependent on its exports. In 1989 930,000 people, 21 per cent of all persons gainfully employed, worked in manufacturing industries. Districts which are dominated by manufacturing industries are also very sensitive to swings in the international economy. (K17)

Many jobs in the manufacturing industries are heavy and stressful. Smelting plant workers at Swedish Steel in Luleå.

Manufacturing Industry and the Public Sector

Employment in manufacturing industry has been the economic backbone of Sweden for a very long time. These industries are located in the first place in southern and central Sweden. There are many towns, in particular small industrial towns, that are very dependent on manufacturing; some towns are totally dependent on this form of employment. The map shows the large percentage of employees in manufacturing industries in Central Sweden, not least in Bergslagen and Småland. These are areas where the employee life form is most typical.

A question which has often been debated is the recruitment of labour for manufacturing industry. The labour market for young people has undergone great changes. In the early 1980s youth unemployment was a great problem in Sweden, as it was in the early 1990s. Many people believe that there will be a shortage of young people looking for jobs in industry. One reason is that the number of young people aged 16 to 25 will fall dramatically in the next 10 to 20 years, because of the small number of babies born in the 1970s and early 1980s. The attitudes of young people to industrial work have become more negative, which is evident not least in the fact that not so many of them

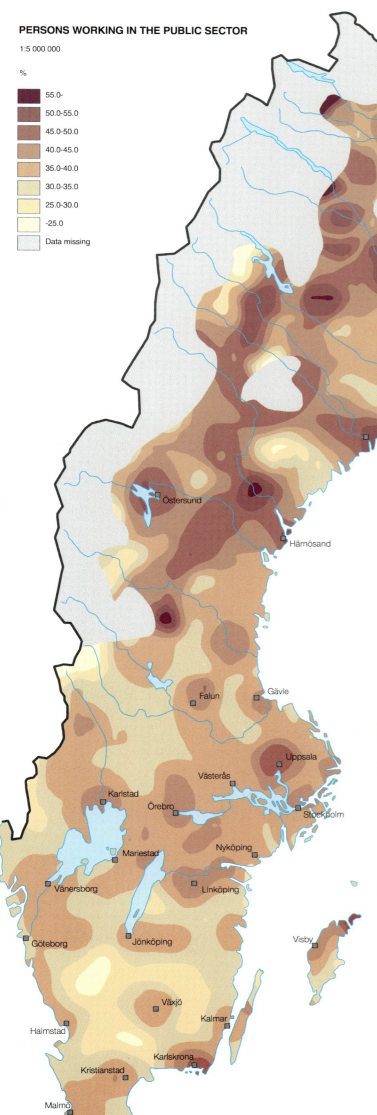

PERSONS WORKING IN THE PUBLIC SECTOR

1:5 000 000

%
- 55.0-
- 50.0-55.0
- 45.0-50.0
- 40.0-45.0
- 35.0-40.0
- 30.0-35.0
- 25.0-30.0
- -25.0
- Data missing

Almost all education is organised within the public sector.

GAINFULLY EMPLOYED IN 1989, AGED 16 AND UPWARDS

	Number	Men	Women
Agriculture and forestry	174,423	5.4%	2.3%
Mining	11,861	0.4%	0.1%
Manufacturing	933,861	28.7%	12.3%
Electricity, gas and water utilities	34,460	1.2%	0.3%
Construction	290,679	11.3%	1.2%
Retail trade, hotel and catering	632,738	13.4%	15.0%
Transport, post and telecommunications	315,092	9.2%	4.6%
Bank, insurance and consultancy	375,351	8.7%	8.0%
Public administration, other services	645,980	20.0%	54.9%

Total gainfully employed, 1989 (including unspecified)   4,480,665

The public sector grew very rapidly during the 1970s and comprised 37 per cent of the employees in 1989. A large number of services are organised via the public sector. In an international comparison Sweden has a large percentage of public employees. (K18)

want to work in industry. Surveys of the attitudes of 18-year-olds show that the most popular occupations are the intellectually free and socially and geographically mobile ones. Young people tend more and more to reject industrial work, mainly because of the lack of intellectual stimulation and poor working environments. Young people want interesting jobs and a good working environment rather than more leisure time and more flexible working hours. This was their opinion in the 1980s. It is not clear whether, and if so to what extent, a change in the availability of jobs will affect attitudes towards industrial work in particular.

The public sector grew rapidly in the 1970s and 1980s. The largest absolute number of jobs is to be found in towns in southern and central Sweden. On the other hand it is apparent that the percentage of employees in the public sector is very high in the interior of Norrland. The local authority is often the most important employer, and employment in health care and social welfare is large. Growth in the public sector slowed down in the 1980s, and in the 1990s the tendency is rather towards a decrease in the number of public employees. In view of the overwhelming dominance of women in this sector and considering regional distribution patterns, it may be assumed that many of these jobs are endangered, not least in Norrland. The difference in the distribution of the sexes is most noticeable between manufacturing industry and public administration.

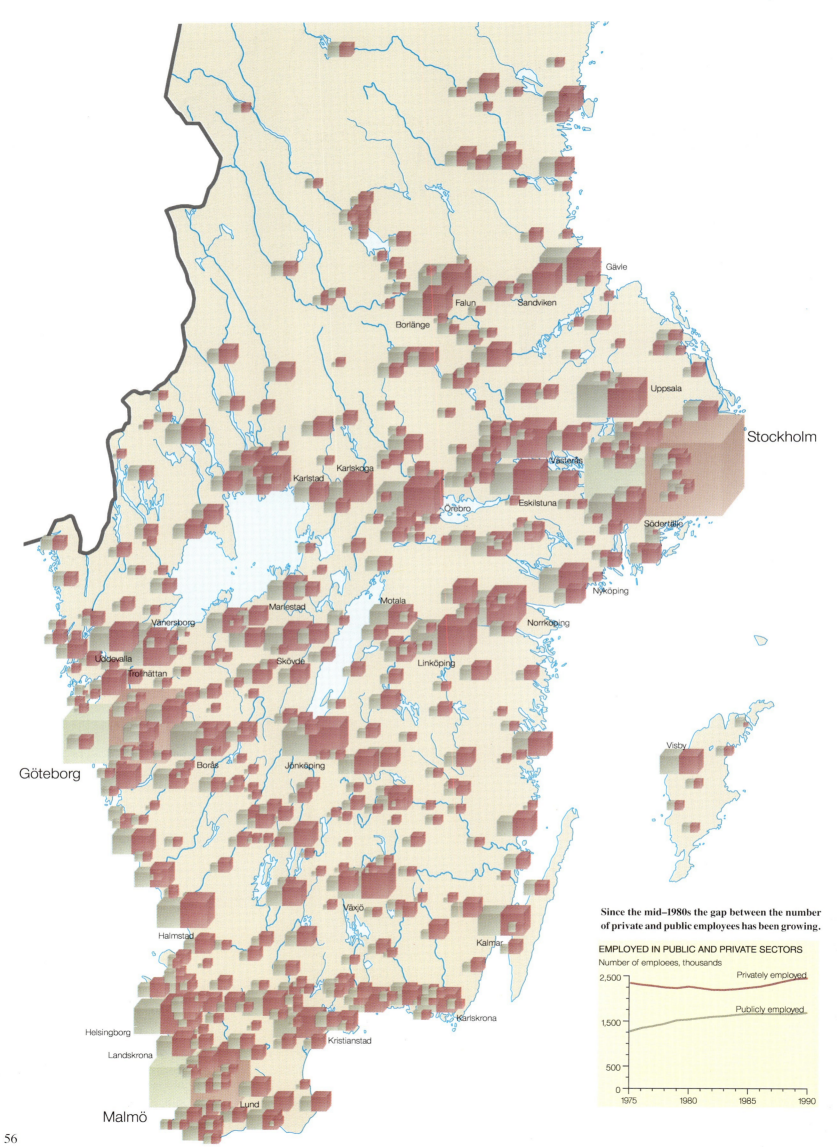

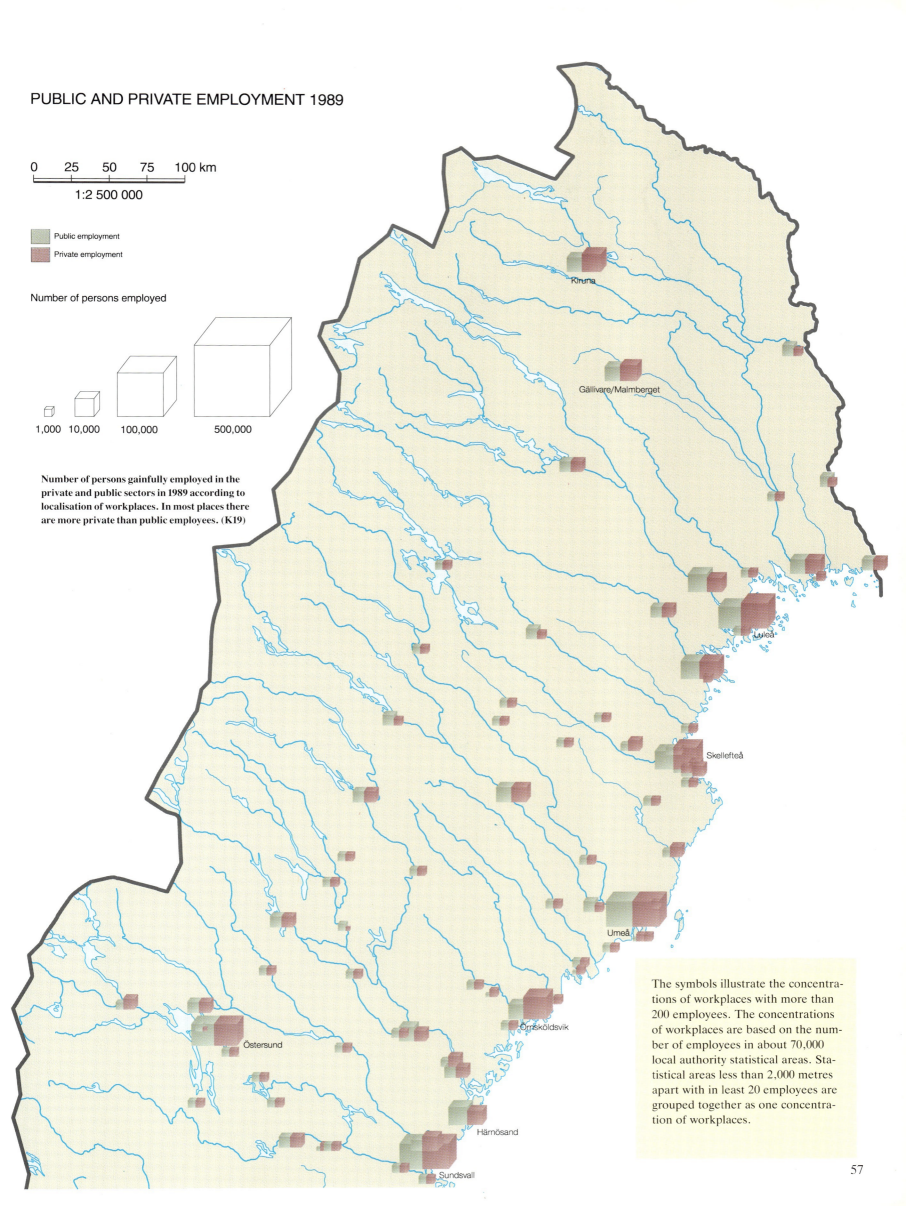

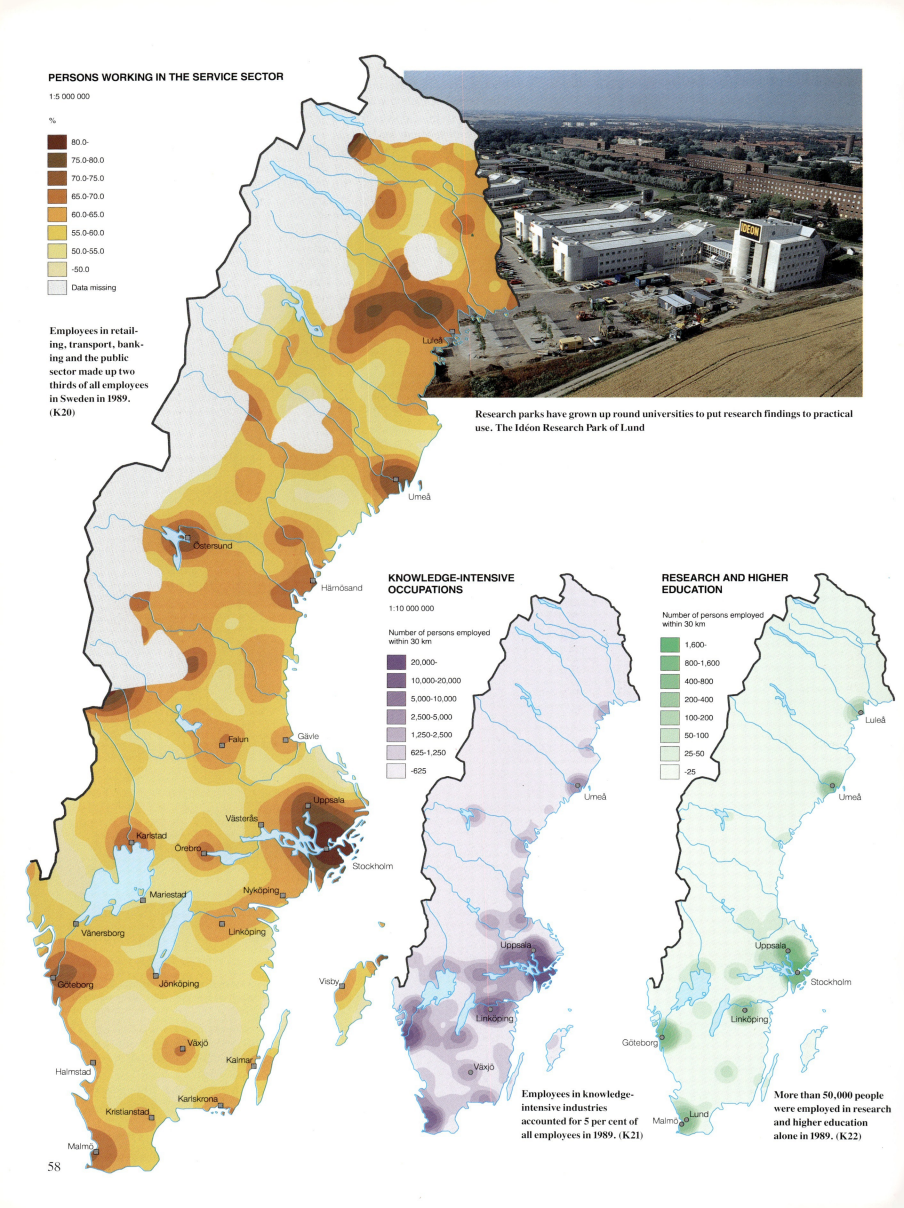

PERSONS WORKING IN THE SERVICE SECTOR

1:5 000 000

%
- 80.0-
- 75.0-80.0
- 70.0-75.0
- 65.0-70.0
- 60.0-65.0
- 55.0-60.0
- 50.0-55.0
- -50.0
- Data missing

Employees in retailing, transport, banking and the public sector made up two thirds of all employees in Sweden in 1989. (K20)

Research parks have grown up round universities to put research findings to practical use. The Idéon Research Park of Lund

KNOWLEDGE-INTENSIVE OCCUPATIONS

1:10 000 000

Number of persons employed within 30 km
- 20,000-
- 10,000-20,000
- 5,000-10,000
- 2,500-5,000
- 1,250-2,500
- 625-1,250
- -625

Employees in knowledge-intensive industries accounted for 5 per cent of all employees in 1989. (K21)

RESEARCH AND HIGHER EDUCATION

Number of persons employed within 30 km
- 1,600-
- 800-1,600
- 400-800
- 200-400
- 100-200
- 50-100
- 25-50
- -25

More than 50,000 people were employed in research and higher education alone in 1989. (K22)

Employment in the Service Sector

A distinction is usually made between employment in the production of goods and in the production of services.

The former sector has declined in terms of employment in Sweden, as in the whole of the Western world. It is instead the production of services that has grown very rapidly. In Stockholm no less than 80 per cent of workers are employed in this part of the economy. As the service sector has grown, there has been an increased differentiation of jobs. The percentage of employees in the service sector is very high in northern Sweden. Western Småland is an example of an area with relatively few employees in this sector.

The Information Society

Our modern society, which has evolved from industrial society as technology has progressed, has often been called "the information society". This means a society with a completely new system of production. The basis for employment and the economy is no longer the production of goods. Instead it tends to be activities connected with information in the widest sense of the word that attract labour. Broadly speaking we have moved from being farmworkers or industrial workers to being processors of information. This shift to the information society is made via the service society. The service sector has included much of what was dependent on the industrial era, such as commercial and distributive trades, salesmen and drivers. But the new era has brought new services that are dependent on new information technology—including everything that has to do with computers.

The building stones of the information society are the microchip, the computer and electronic communication. If the car may be said to be an expression of the industrial era, the personal computer is an expression of the new information era. To begin with the car was looked upon as a strange creation that later became a necessity. The personal computer will be a necessary tool for every citizen in the information society for the collection, processing and creation of information.

> The percentage of persons employed in 1989 in company services such as legal and accounting work, computer services, and advertising, PR and market research activities is 2 per cent of all those gainfully employed, or a total of almost 80,000 people. Outside the major cities the percentage of persons employed in company services is high in Skellefteå, partly because of extensive computer services.

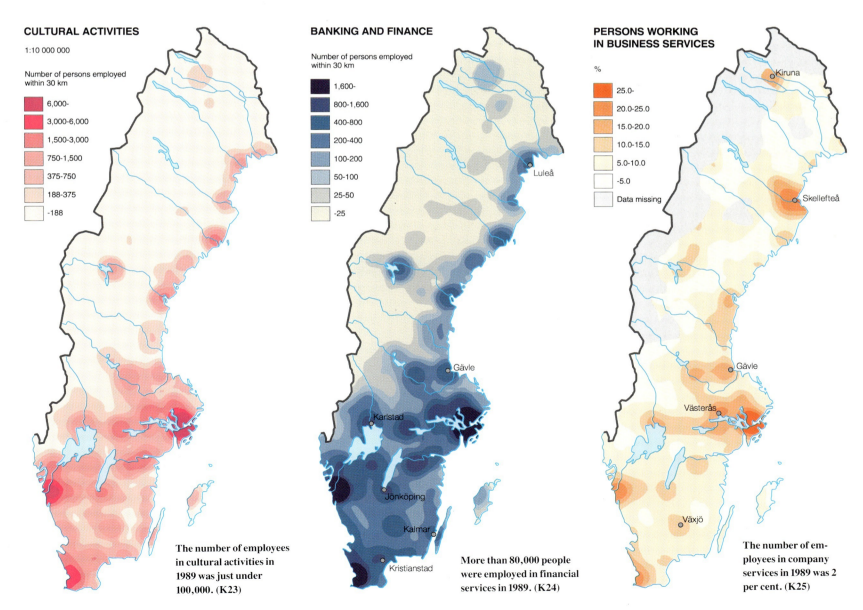

The number of employees in cultural activities in 1989 was just under 100,000. (K23)

More than 80,000 people were employed in financial services in 1989. (K24)

The number of employees in company services in 1989 was 2 per cent. (K25)

Local Labour Markets

The local community has become a central concept—central in the sense that much effort is being put into improving the local environment in various ways. Questions concerning "work, services and a good environment" have long been national goals, and they imply a well-functioning local community, or a community with work within commuting distance. In recent years discussions about the local community have also embraced questions concerning local identity, or where people belong and what they like to call their territory. This has also touched upon questions of culture. All in all it may be said that the local community has more and more come to include both material and immaterial dimensions, not only the standard of living but also the quality of life. The home is for most people a kind of focal point in life. It is the starting point for various kinds of activities. The local community is the arena, the platform, where people live, work, love and die. The following section will discuss the ways in which the individual acts, behaves, in order to get access to work, and how these local labour markets function. How far is one prepared to commute to get a job, or does one have to move out of the local market? But let us start with a look at history.

WORK MIGRATION IN THE PEASANT SOCIETY

In the old peasant society most people were tied down to their farm and their village. This was the field of their daily activities. There were, of course, exceptions: trips to market, to church, to a wedding in the next parish. And there were groups of people

People carry their skills around with them. A lumberjack from Mora. Painting by Pehr Hilleström, the Zorn Collections at Mora.

who were more mobile than others, for example maids and farmhands. To earn their daily bread, when there was not enough work obtainable locally, many people worked outside what we today call the local labour market.

Historically, work migration was no unusual phenomenon. It was particularly common in 19th-century agrarian society. Regional variations in agriculture formed the basis of seasonal work migration. In the 18th and 19th centuries it was necessary in many districts to take jobs periodically somewhere else to provide for the family. The best-known examples are the migrations from Dalarna to Stockholm, where the girls often worked as boat rowers and "mortar boards" on building sites, while the men were building workers.

The plains of Skåne also received seasonal workers for threshing from Halland, Småland and Blekinge. Another example is provided by the women's "winter walk" from Jämtland and Härjedalen to work in Hälsingland and Ångermanland.

Changes in industrial life, from agriculture to increased industrialisation, created conditions which allowed employment all the year round instead of seasonal employment. A contributory factor was emigration to America in the latter half of the 19th century. A large proportion of the seasonal workers came from districts with a high level of emigration. Forest work and log floating in Norrland and the sugar-beet season in Skåne are examples of seasonal work that survived into our own times.

COMMUTING AND URBANISATION

A characteristic feature of the pre-industrial town was the proximity of workplace to home. To begin with, industrialisation in Sweden grew up round companies that exploited raw materials from agriculture, forestry and mining for export. Important parts of the new industries grew up where the raw materials or water power were to be found, outside the towns. For this reason urbanisation developed less hectically in Sweden than in other countries. Another influential factor was that the industrial workforce commuted weekly or seasonally to work. Thus there was a time delay in Sweden between industrialisation and urbanisation.

New forms of energy and new technology with the benefits of mass-production led to a concentration of the workforce at fewer places. Industrial work took place in factories.

Land which was not used for industrial or commercial purposes was used for housing. In the late 19th century

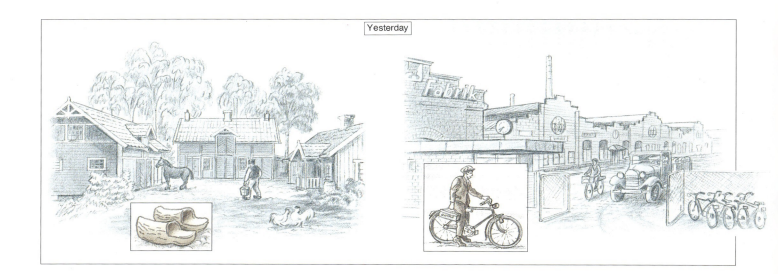

The expansion of the railway network at the end of the 19th century encouraged the growth of suburbs.

Factories were often located at cycling distance from the workers' homes. Bicycles parked outside the Rex shoe factory in Örebro, 1946.

The development of transport systems, for example the growth of private motoring, was a prerequisite for the expansion of towns.

the outer areas of towns were used to build working-class estates. Improvements in public transport, with suburban trains and trams, made it possible to live farther away from one's place of work. Later the upper social classes moved out to newly-built mansions in attractive locations on the city's outskirts. Housing areas had become segregated. A typical feature was the mixture of dwellings and workplaces in the inner cities, which continued right into the 1950s and 1960s. The distance between home and workplace was not great in most towns. The bicycle was a common means of transport.

The 1960s brought dramatic changes. In order to improve housing conditions for those living in the town centres, and in order to attract labour to the expanding industrial sector, new homes were needed, in large numbers. During a ten-year period starting in the mid–1960s one million new housing units were built in Sweden. Geographically there was an expansion to areas outside the towns, at the same time as workplaces and services moved out from the centre. The planning theory was to divide towns up into different functional areas.

When the location of both housing and workplaces had been changed, the number of journeys to and from work and their length also increased. It was also during the fifties and sixties that private car-ownership increased dramatically, which was necessary if one was to live outside town.

The number of journeys to work across municipal boundaries increased by 118 per cent between 1970 and 1989, while the number of employees increased by only 30 per cent in the same period. Every fourth employee in 1989 had his place of work in another municipality than his home municipality. More than half of all commuting across municipal boundaries is to the 20 largest commuter municipalities.

THE 20 LARGEST COMMUTER MUNICIPALITIES

Workplace	No of commuters, 1989
Stockholm	243,145
Göteborg	87,398
Malmö	46,424
Solna	45,736
Lund	20,511
Huddinge	19,001
Mölndal	17,317
Helsingborg	15,033
Karlstad	13,349
Sundbyberg	12,846
Sigtuna	12,598
Sollentuna	11,506
Danderyd	11,257
Uppsala	10,368
Trollhättan	10,174
Järfälla	9,951
Örebro	9,896
Linköping	9,811
Södertälje	9,646

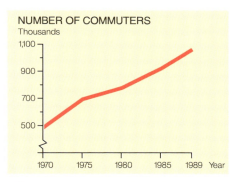

The number of commuters has doubled since 1970, at the same time as travelling distances have increased (commuting across municipal boundaries).

1:1 250 000

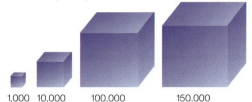
Number of journeys to work in each 100 km square
1,000   10,000   100,000   150,000

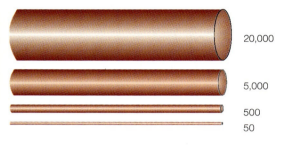
Number of journeys to work between 100 km square
20,000
5,000
500
50

HOW WAS THIS MAP MADE?

Sweden is divided up into 10 x 10 km squares. Journeys to work between these squares are illustrated by commuter links. These links show flows of more than 50 commuters; the size of the links is proportional to the number of commuters. Two links between the same square mean commuter flows in both directions. The cubes symbolise journeys to work in each square with more than 100 journeys; the size of the cubes is proportional to the number of journeys.

It should be noted that the map is based on information as to where the employees have their homes and places of work. They do not necessarily commute daily. People may live where they work without being registered as residing there. Thus the map slightly exaggerates the extent and distance of daily commuting to work.

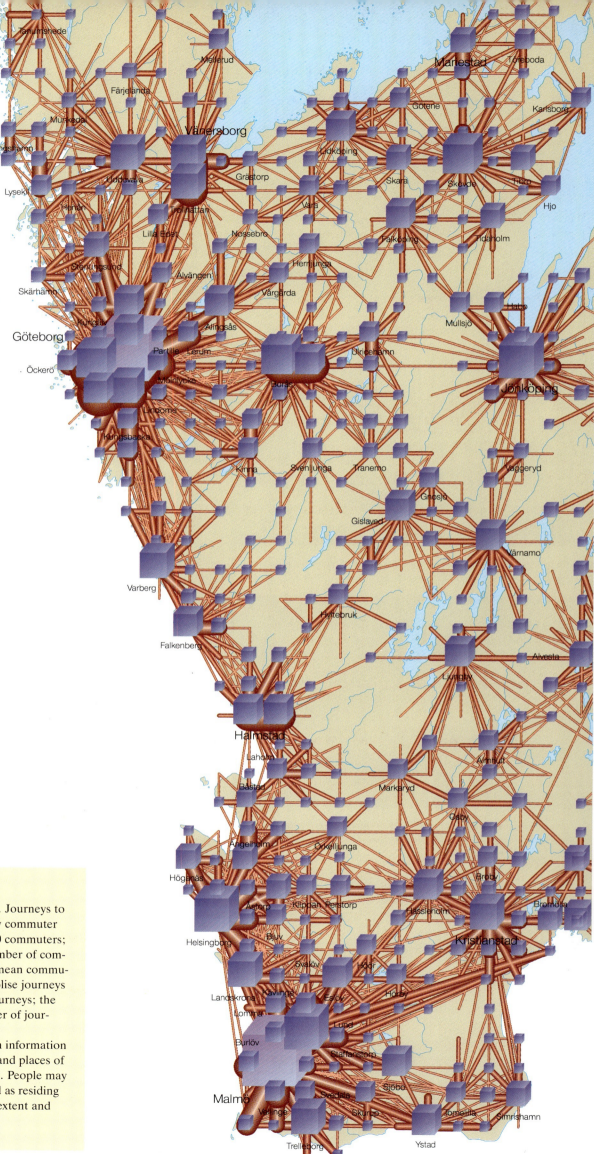

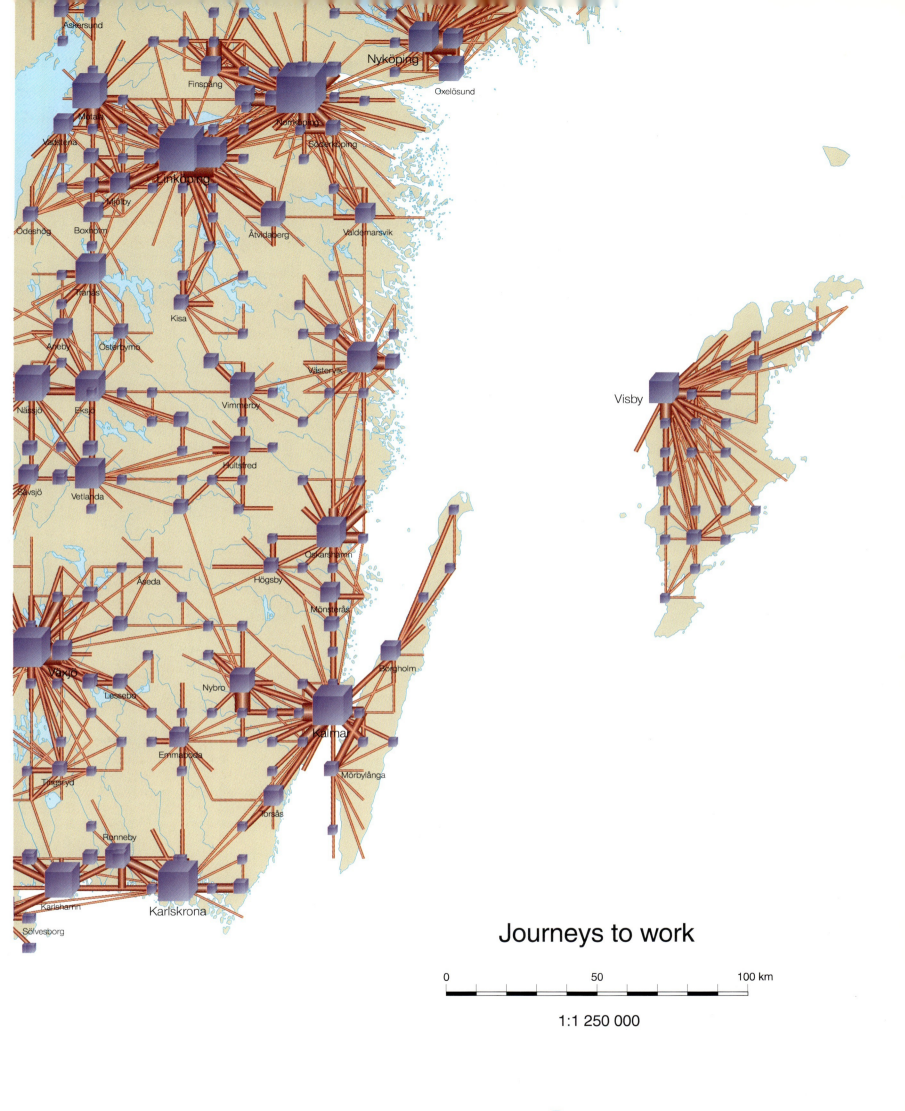

Journeys to work

1:1 250 000

JOURNEYS TO WORK

1:1 250 000

Number of journeys to work in each 100 km square

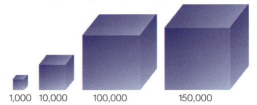

1,000　10,000　100,000　150,000

Number of journeys to work between 100 km square

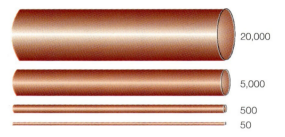

20,000
5,000
500
50

A car is often the only realistic way of getting to work for those who live out in the country.

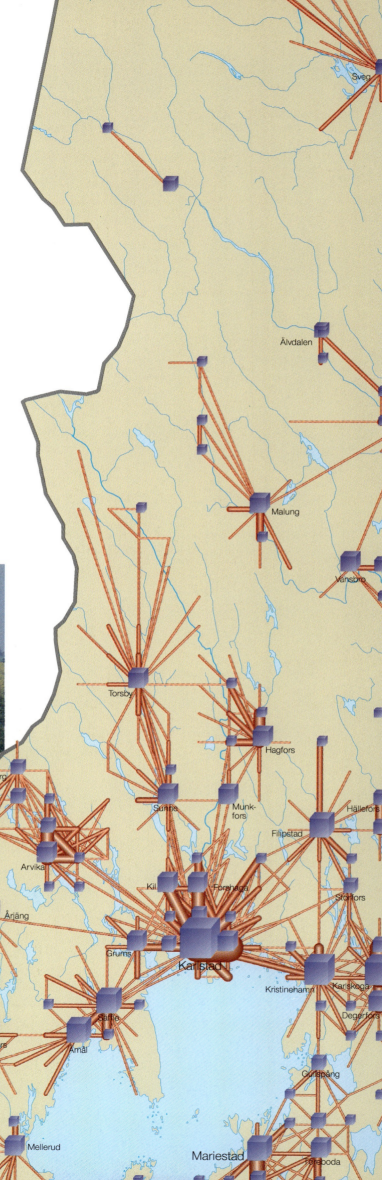

64

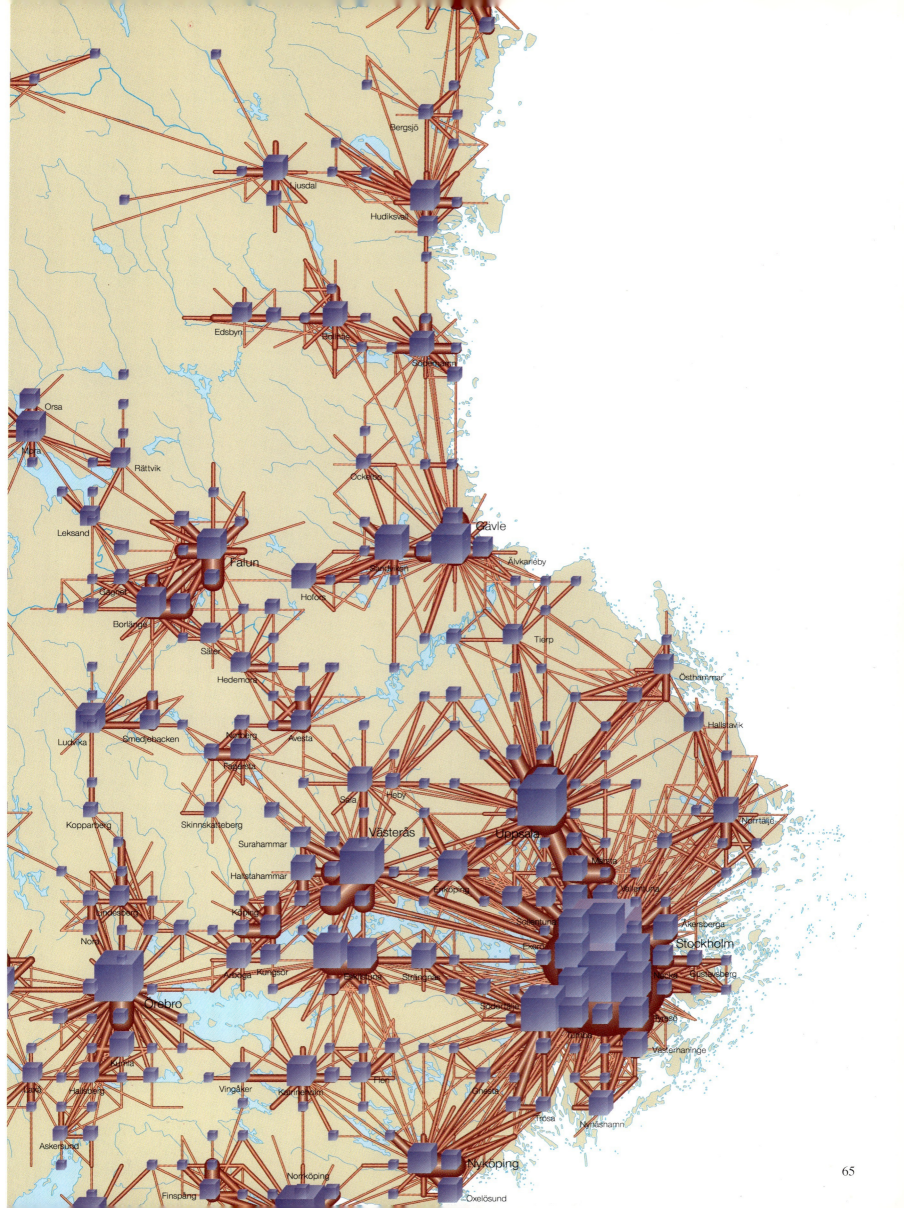

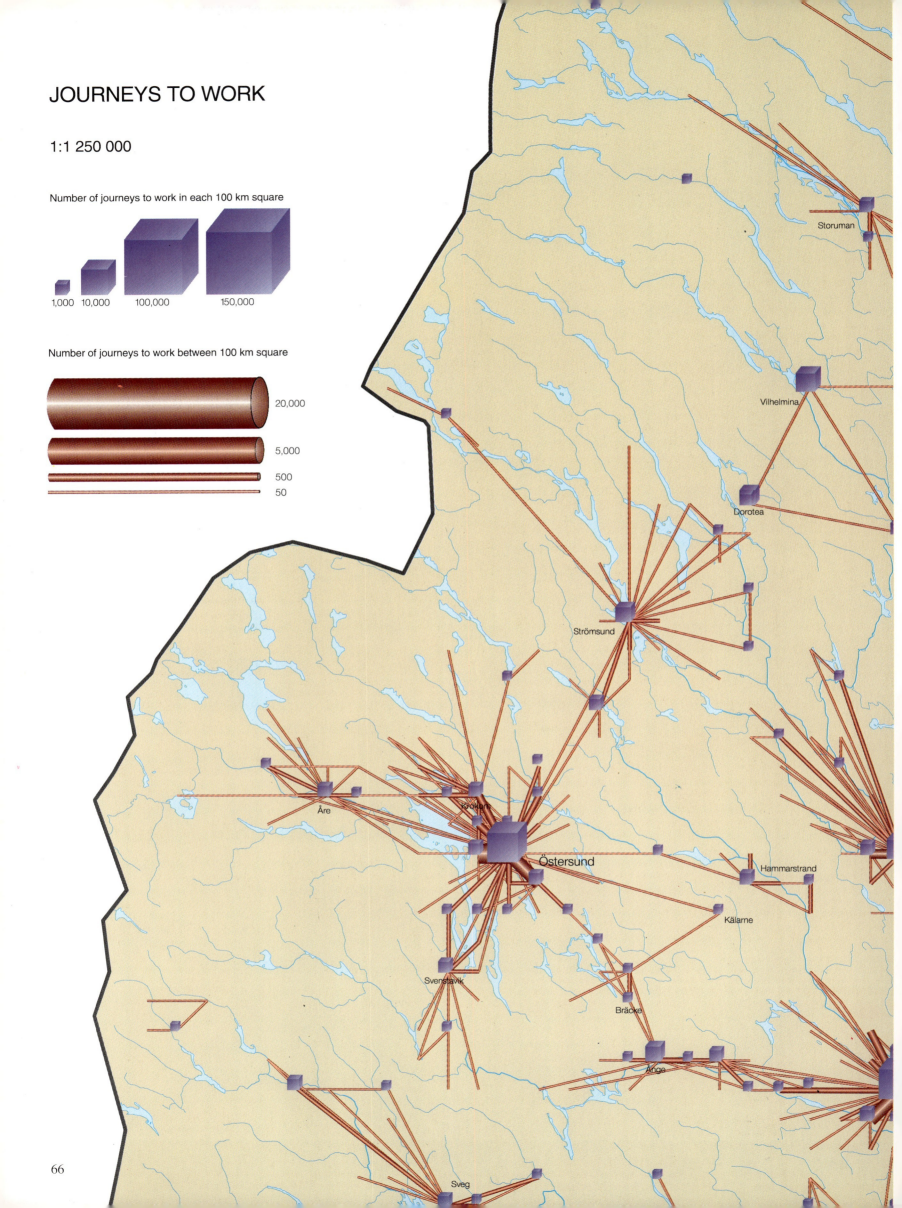

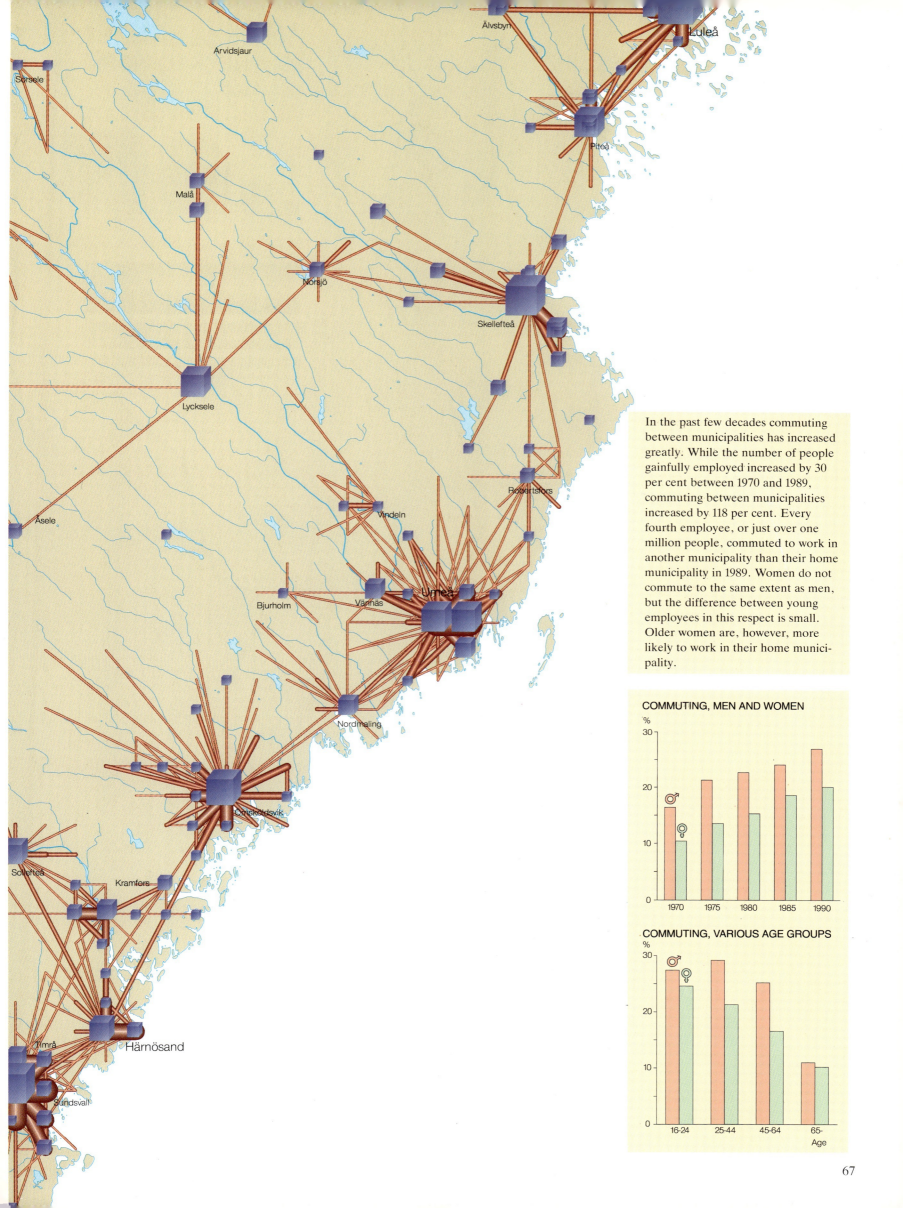

In the past few decades commuting between municipalities has increased greatly. While the number of people gainfully employed increased by 30 per cent between 1970 and 1989, commuting between municipalities increased by 118 per cent. Every fourth employee, or just over one million people, commuted to work in another municipality than their home municipality in 1989. Women do not commute to the same extent as men, but the difference between young employees in this respect is small. Older women are, however, more likely to work in their home municipality.

COMMUTING, MEN AND WOMEN

COMMUTING, VARIOUS AGE GROUPS

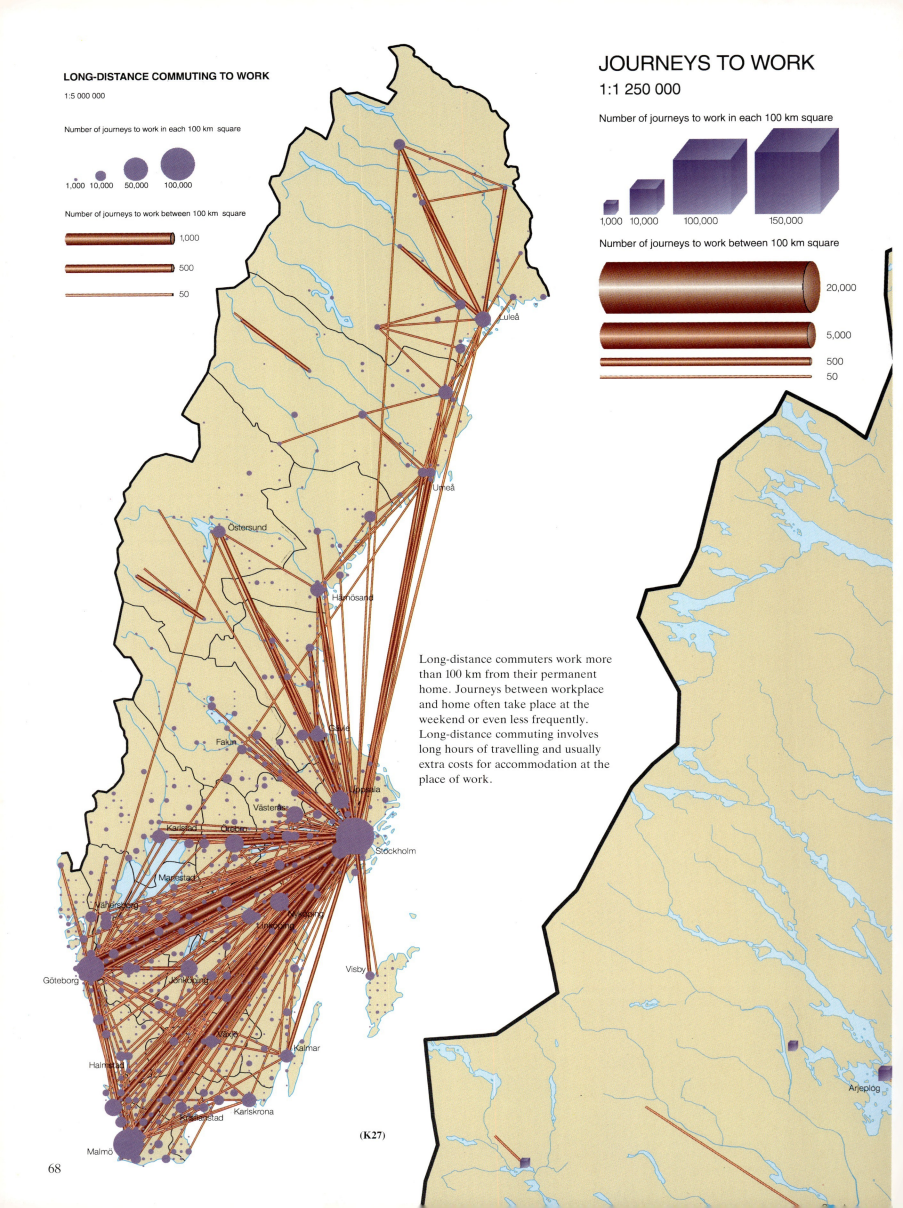

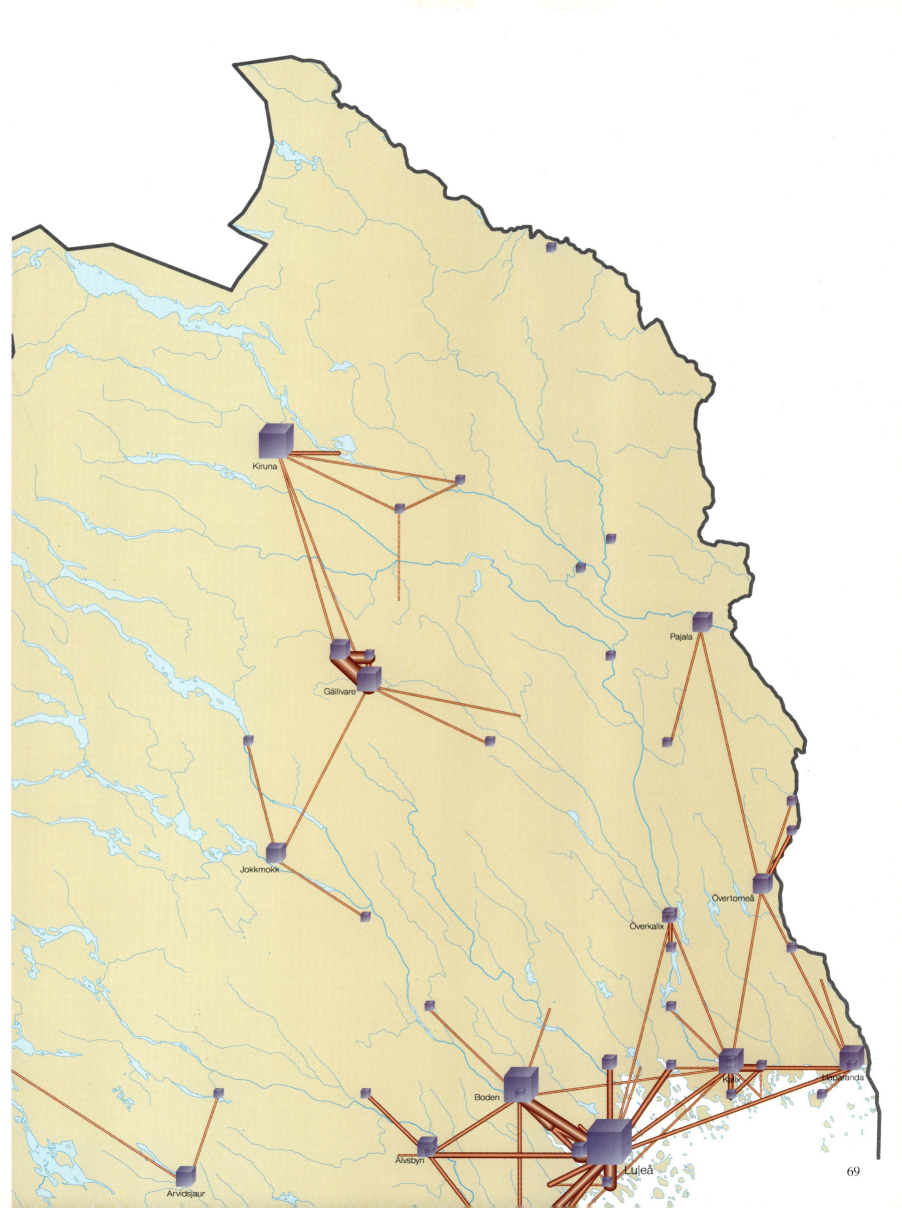

LOCAL LABOUR MARKETS, 1970

■ High commuting intensity
■ Low commuting intensity

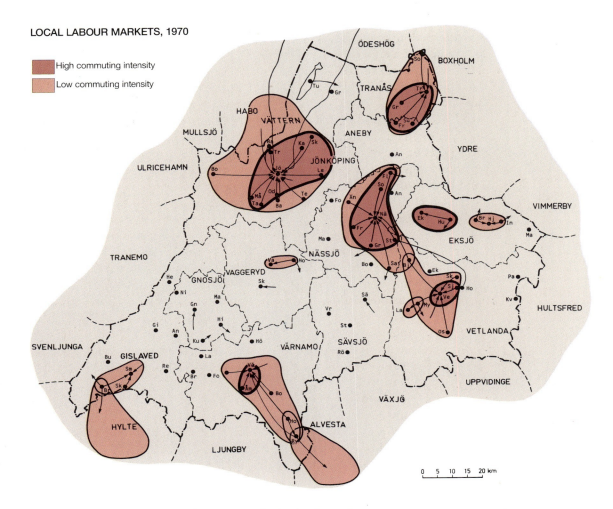

Local labour markets are marked off on these maps by showing the number of business journeys. The level of commuting is higher in the dark areas than in the light areas. (K28, K29)

LOCAL LABOUR MARKETS, 1980

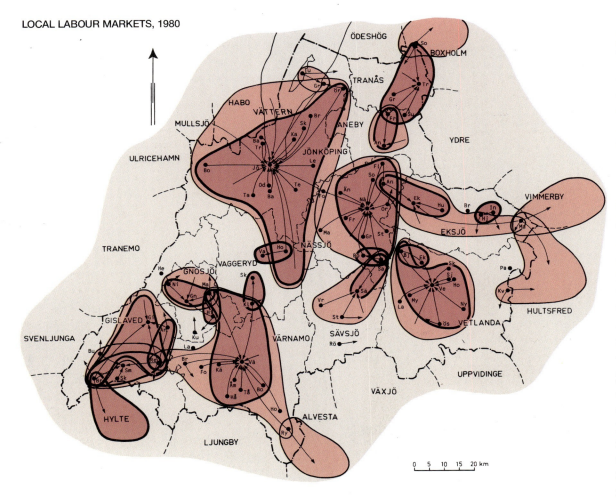

From Local to Regional Labour Markets

In the past, work and leisure were two separate worlds. The worker put his packed lunch in a box in the morning, walked or cycled to work, worked his shift, came home, put his lunch box away and read the newspaper. Short journeys between home and workplace took hardly any or very little time at all. That's how it was right into the 1950s in industrial towns. But the structure of society has changed, its physical location, too, and people's behaviour has adapted to these changed conditions. We can see, for example, that commuter distances have gradually increased. A Labour Market Board survey in 1964 showed that the distance between home and workplace was only 2 km or less for half of the workers. As many as 87 per cent lived less than 10 km from their place of work. The number of people who commuted more than 10 km increased from 26 to 29 per cent between 1978 and 1983. This increase was greatest outside the metropolitan regions. Several surveys show that an increasing number of the working population are faced with longer journeys to work.

If then we are able to establish that travel distances have increased, which is indisputable, one may wonder about the time taken by commuter journeys. Many experts claim that there is a critical figure of 45 minutes, perhaps an hour, which people are willing to spend on commuting. If that figure is exceeded, people take action by changing jobs or homes. One can speculate about this time and how it is used. Is it working time or leisure time?

LOCAL LABOUR MARKETS— JÖNKÖPING COUNTY

Commuting can be seen as a series of circles on a map. The centre is usually in a main town to which many people travel to work. Right up to the 1950s these circles were small and did not overlap. Every main town had its hinterland, whose size varied according to the size of the town, the number of jobs in the surrounding area and the competition from other towns. Increased car-ownership, better transport services, the transformation of industry, increased professional specialisation and the entry of more and more women onto the labour market made the previously simple commut-

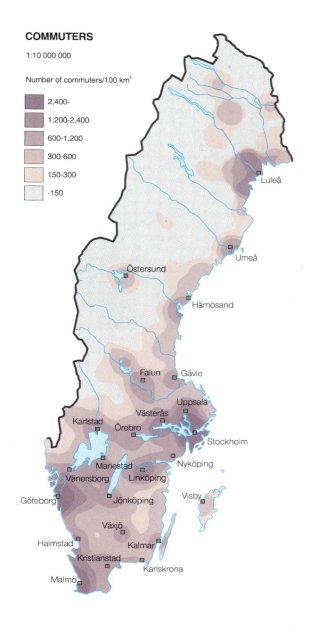

COMMUTERS
1:10 000 000

Number of commuters/100 km²
- 2,400-
- 1,200-2,400
- 600-1,200
- 300-600
- 150-300
- -150

There are a great many commuter journeys in and round our large cities, but also in the district comprising Boden, Älvsbyn, Piteå and Luleå. Here Sweden is divided into squares measuring 10km by 10km. The map shows the number of commuters travelling between them in 1989. (K30)

ing pattern more and more complex. An example of a regional commuting pattern is shown in two diagrams of Jönköping County, one dated 1970, the other 1980.

In 1970 the commuting areas are clearly centred on the main towns and correspond on the whole with municipal boundaries. We can refer at this point to the reorganisation of the municipalities at that time, which was partly based on commuting patterns. Administrative and functional regions corresponded with each other. The picture in 1980 is somewhat different. It is quite evident how much larger the commuter belts round the main towns are. These belts also cross the municipal boundaries more often and to a certain extent overlap. In the south-west corner of the county the commuter belts overlap to a very great extent. The pattern is very complex, without any natural central place.

What does the situation look like ten years later? The pattern is even more complex. Commuting by both men and women has to be integrated with the household's time budget and daily field of activities. This is a very complicated business, requiring many households to make difficult decisions. One such problem is described below: to commute or to move.

TO COMMUTE OR NOT TO COMMUTE, THAT IS THE QUESTION

We saw in the introductory chapters that each household is enclosed in a time-space prism, in which both time and space are limitations on what can be done in a day, a week or a year. There are many opinions and wishes to be accommodated and these accommodations are expressed in various spatial ways. All activities "take place" somewhere: the children's schooling, the wife's work, the husband's work, trips to see friends and relations, holidays and so on. One has to be located somewhere, live in the "right" place for all the pieces to fall into place. In the old society with the breadwinning husband, the housewife at home and the children going to the local school, the choice was fairly straightforward. The field of activities was restricted and there were few options. In modern society both options and restrictions as to where one should live and work are more numerous.

In many cases commuting is one way of adapting spatially, of stretching the household's time and pushing the time budget to breaking point. There is a limit somewhere, and that is where the choice between commuting or moving lies. A household's decision to commute or to move is a lengthy business, requiring answers to a number of important questions: Will the new job, or jobs, work out all right? Can we sell the house? Will we be able to get hold of an equally good home in the new district? Will we lose contact with our friends and relations if we move? Will we be able to create a new social life for the family?

The form of dwelling is an important factor when characterising which households choose to commute or move. There is a greater probability that a family will move if they have a rented apartment than if they own a house. The difficulty of finding a buyer and the fact that one has invested work in one's own house creates restrictions. If the members of the household are young, the chances of choosing to move are also greater. Single persons are also more inclined to move to work in a new town than married or cohabiting couples, and this is particularly true of women. In many families it is the woman's career that takes second place to the man's. Studies show that priority is given to the man's career, because the man usually has a higher salary.

The young bachelor girl moves to the municipality where she has found a new job while the married middle-aged man chooses to commute to his new job outside his home municipality.

Working Locally

Most people change their working situation during their lifetime. They start work, are perhaps unemployed for a while, get a new job, move and change jobs, or commute, and then retire and leave the workforce. People also start new careers. Individuals make a great many changes and choices, which together create the local labour market and make it work.

These changes may be seen as a system in which the main difference is between those who are gainfully employed and those who are not. If the municipality is seen as the local labour market, commuting in and out may also be seen as a flow to and from the municipality, as well as moving in or away. By using links between the National Census data for 1985 and 1990 these flows may be studied in a few municipalities. Those we have chosen are Gnosjö and Eksjö

MOBILITY WITHIN A LOCAL LABOUR MARKET

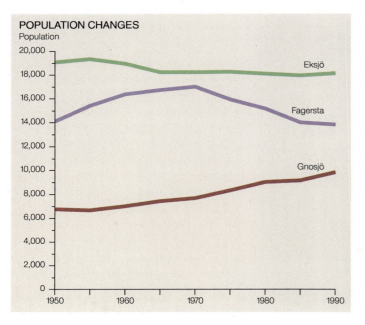

These diagrams illustrate the number of people moving into and away from a municipality, and the residents in a municipality who start working and who retire. The size of the arrows is proportionate to the number of people.

POPULATION CHANGES

Fagersta has long been dominated by the iron and steel industry. Its history goes back to iron production in the 17th century.

Eksjö is a market, craft and garrison town which was granted a charter at an early date.

Gnosjö is famous for its many industrial firms. The level of employment here is one of the highest in Sweden.

LABOUR MARKET MOBILITY, FAGERSTA

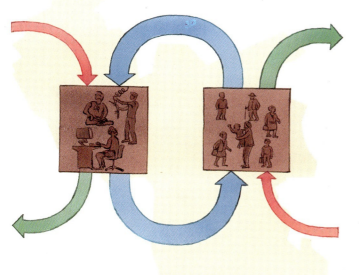

LABOUR MARKET MOBILITY, EKSJÖ

LABOUR MARKET MOBILITY, GNOSJÖ

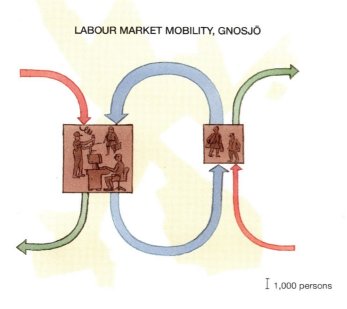

I 1,000 persons

FAGERSTA
Number of persons employed

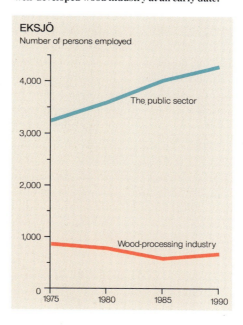

The number of employees in manufacturing industries has decreased in Fagersta. The decrease is particularly large in metal production.

The richly-forested areas round Eksjö created a well-developed wood industry at an early date.

EKSJÖ
Number of persons employed

A very large proportion of the working population of Gnosjö are employed in small engineering firms.

GNOSJÖ
Number of persons employed

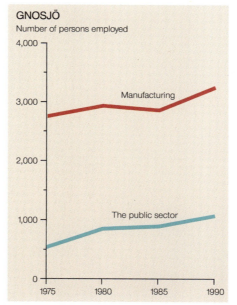

in Jönköping County and Fagersta in Västmanland County.

Changes in the population have varied for Fagersta, Eksjö and Gnosjö. The population of Fagersta has been decreasing continuously since the 1970s. In 1990 it was about 14,000, of whom 6,800 were gainfully employed. The number of inhabitants of Eksjö has changed only marginally since 1950. About 18,000 people lived there in 1990, of whom 9,100 were gainfully employed. The population of Gnosjö has been slowly increasing since the 1950s. In 1990 it was 10,000, of whom 5,700 were gainfully employed.

Labour market movements in these three municipalities are illustrated here by flow arrows proportionate in size to the number of persons. In spite of differences in their industrial structure, these municipalities are similar in many ways. It is the marginal changes that are of interest.

In Gnosjö 85 per cent are still gainfully employed in 1985; in other words, 20 per cent of those who were gainfully employed in 1980 have left the workforce. Both Eksjö and Fagersta show greater mobility. In these two municipalities 23 per cent and 27 per cent respectively left the workforce during the same period.

The new workers are mainly the municipality's own inhabitants. Just over 16 per cent are Fagersta's own inhabitants; the percentage is higher for Eksjö and Gnosjö, 18 and 22 per cent respectively. Gnosjö gets more workers from its own inhabitants and fewer workers leave than in the other municipalities. Hardly 12 per cent of those gainfully employed in 1985 leave their jobs and remain in the municipality. The corresponding figures for Eksjö and Fagersta are 14 and 16 per cent respectively. The internal turnover between those gainfully employed and those not gainfully employed among the municipalities' own inhabitants is largest in Fagersta and smallest in Gnosjö.

The attractiveness of each municipality is reflected in the fact that the number of those moving to take up employment is proportionally largest in Gnosjö and smallest in Fagersta. Moreover the number of those moving away from Fagersta is proportionally larger than from the other municipalities. This applies both to those gainfully employed (16%) and to those not gainfully employed (13%), for example young people and people out of work.

Localisation of Workplaces

In the old society home and workplace lay close together, but industrialisation separated them. The milltown worker, however, did not have far to go to get to work. Being within walking distance was almost a condition for getting workers.

Some cottage work continued right into the 1950s, for example the women sewers who worked for the shoe industry in Örebro or the women textile workers in Västergötland. Each region had its own industries and this type of cottage work has a long tradition. It was advantageous for the employer, who did not have to provide premises for all his workers. It was advantageous for those who worked at home, especially at a time when there were hardly any public day nurseries. But the system had its drawbacks, too. It was difficult for the employer to control production and the workers lacked social stimulation.

There has been a growing tendency to separate home and workplace, not only in the division of functions but also in the greater distances they lie apart.

In Sweden's well-organised society there was, as early as the 1940s and 1950s, a clear tendency to divide up different functions physically. The in-

Right up to the 1950s working at home was common in certain industries such as shoemaking. A leather seamstress.

creasingly tight planning laws of the 1960s led to a conscious segregation of functional areas for housing, work, commerce, outdoor recreation and travel.

There were rational grounds for these divisions; it facilitated planning for industry with its need for transportation, and commerce also needed its own supply system. This development was common to the whole western world. The watchwords were function and separation, so that differing interests did not clash. Different interest groups were weighed up against each other.

One consequence of this system, of dividing up an area geographically, was that people could spend different times of the day in different places in the town. An example of the way people would be grouped together during different hours of the day is shown in the diagram here. People are in the housing estates in the evening, at night and until early in the morning; after that there are considerably fewer people there. One might say that the separation between where people live and where they work leads to a wave of movement in the urban landscape. In the morning people are washed into the town centre and out to the workplace areas, often on the edge of town, and in the evening this wave of people washes back again. This topography of human activity in a town may be illustrated by two maps of Gävle, one showing where people live and the other where they work.

The 1970s brought a reaction to this increasing division between dwelling-work-leisure. Many people proposed integration instead of segregation. The whole of society was, in fact, marked by this ideology. On the housing estates different social classes, age groups, ethnic groups and so on were to live together; segregation was to be actively avoided. Workplaces were to be brought into the housing estates, or at least placed close to the housing estates. It was not only all

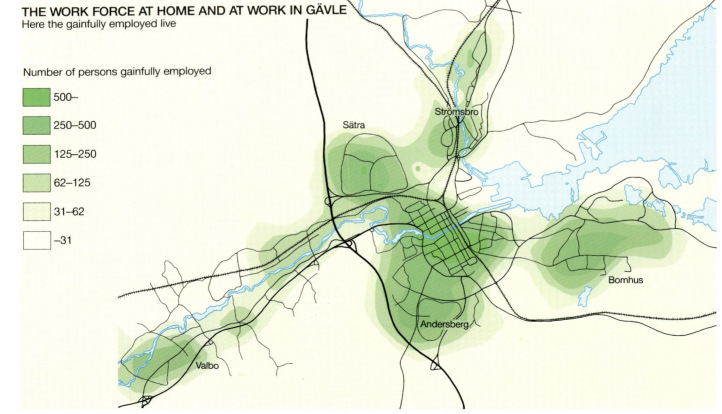

Home and workplace at some distance from one another means daily travelling. The maps show where employees in Gävle in 1989 lived and worked. (K31, K32)

THE WORK FORCE AT HOME AND AT WORK IN GÄVLE
Here the gainfully employed live

Number of persons gainfully employed
- 500–
- 250–500
- 125–250
- 62–125
- 31–62
- –31

Gävle is a medium-sized Swedish town with an old export harbour and an old industrial tradition. This view from the south shows how the E4 highway runs past the Andersberg and Sätra housing estates to the south and the north respectively.

The town centre is the most important place for work, living and visits. Number of people in the town centre during a three-day period.

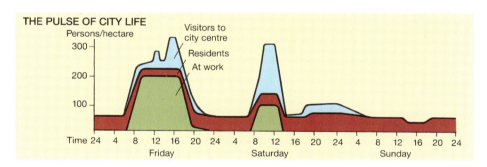

the travelling backwards and forwards in town that led to traffic problems, but also the social problems; "emptying" the housing districts in the daytime and filling them up again in the evening gave society an artificial life style. The term "dormitory suburb" was coined.

But these plans did not get very far, perhaps because urban society was not planned like this and because it is difficult to change established patterns of behaviour. In addition, people do not like to change their workplaces much in Sweden.

In recent years, however, new efforts have been made, some of them inspired by the House and Home Exhibitions which have been held in Sweden since 1985. Herrgårdshagen in Gävle, for example, which won an award, is an example of craft centres placed close to dwellings.

An extensive experiment in Nykvarn in the 1970s attempted to decentralise workplaces, using computer technology to bridge the distances. One aspect criticised by the trade unions was that it was not socially acceptable to be alone at home with work. The unions also saw problems in organising the workforce.

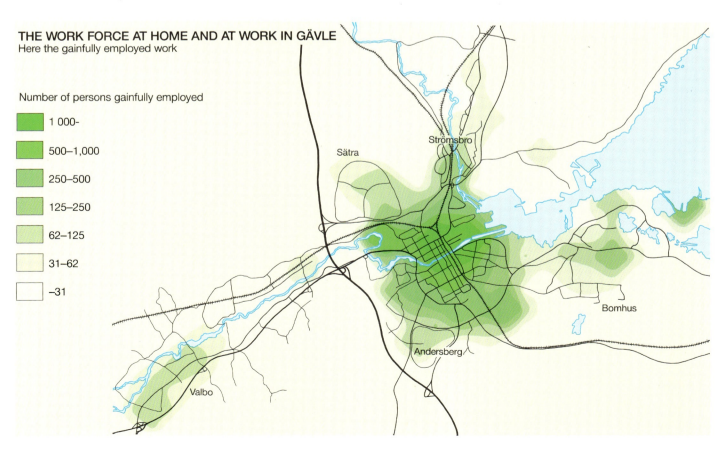

Mobility on the Labour Market

There are several types of mobility on the labour market. The first is to enter and leave the market. People get educated or find a job or become unemployed or retire or choose to stop working. Then there is geographical, spatial mobility; people move to another job or to find work or because there is no work any longer. This is where commuting also comes into the picture. There is also occupational mobility; people change occupations, which includes internal mobility within firms. There may be a career ladder in the firm, promotion.

Furthermore there is the mobility that is connected with changes in industries. Certain industries grow, others shrink. In the simplest case any one of these types of mobility will mean that the individual makes a change. In more complex cases mobility on the labour market may mean a series of simultaneous changes: industry and occupation, home and region. This is illustrated by the ten largest inflows to Umeå, Västerås and Borås in 1991, shown on the map on the following page. Immigration is mainly from neighbouring municipalities and from the densely-populated cities of Stockholm and Göteborg.

What basically creates mobility on the labour market is the availability of jobs, which may also be expressed as a lack of jobs. There is a balance between labour and its competence on the one hand and work requirements on the other. These requirements may be expressed in terms of qualifications.

MIGRATION AND EMPLOYMENT

Young people move more often than old people, for a variety of reasons. When people are young, they look for education, work, someone to marry or live with, and somewhere to live. This search for life is also reflected in the statistics. Those who do not have a job move more frequently than those who do have a job. The total migration frequency in a typical year is just over 20 per thousand for those who have a job and about 30 per thousand for those who do not have a job.

VACANCIES

One of the measures of mobility on the labour market is the number of job vacancies. Availability of jobs leads to migration to take up the jobs that exist in various parts of the country in various occupations. There is a clear relationship between the level of vacancies and migration across municipal boundaries—the curves run parallel. However, it is apparent that vacancies in the early 1980s did not lead to high migration. The same is true of the boom years in the late 1980s. Although the number of vacancies increased, this was not matched by increased migration across municipal boundaries. The obstacles to migration seem to have grown in importance.

NUMBER OF YEARS SPENT IN VARIOUS OCCUPATIONS IN THE SAME MUNICIPALITY	
Manual labourer	3.6
Timber-yard worker	4.8
Carpenter	5.2
Metal worker	5.7
Vocational teacher	6.5
Secretary	6.9
Military personnel	7.2
Nursing orderly	8.8
Nurse	9.3
Farmer	11.0
Primary school teacher	12.9

OCCUPATIONAL MOBILITY

On average men change jobs six times during their lifetime and work on average a little less than seven years between each change. Women change jobs five times in their lifetime and work on average seven years between each change. Changing jobs also has other effects. Those who leave an occupation, either to change occupations, to move or to stop working, create vacancies. These vacancies result in more than 90 per cent of the turnover on the labour market. This means that fewer than 10 per cent of vacancies are caused by structural changes in the demand for labour. About 20 per cent of vacancies are the result of old-age retirement.

How long do people stay in the same job in the same municipality? If the labour market is divided up into occupations, one gets a rough idea of the number of years people stay in various occupations. The diagram above shows some occupational groups and their average "staying power".

Municipal boundaries are most frequently crossed by young people who are not gainfully employed.

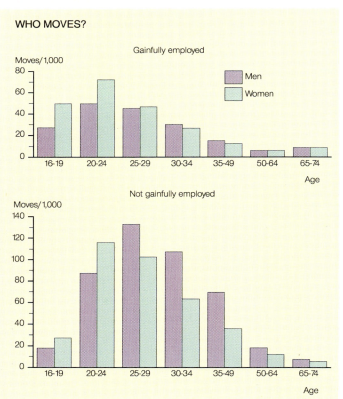

Availability of job vacancies leads to migration.

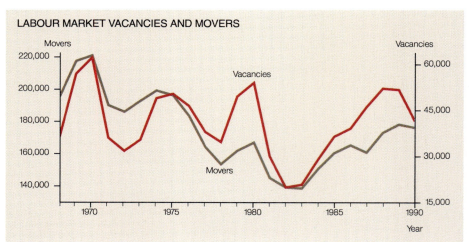

MIGRATION INTO THREE MUNICIPALITIES
1:5 000 000

Number of migrants
→ 40
→ 80
→ 160
→ 240
→ 320

Movements of people are relatively constant in both size and direction. The largest in-migrations to Umeå, Västerås and Borås in 1991. (K33)

EDUCATION

Migration and level of education are related; this connection can be noticed even in very limited data. The movements of a class of school leavers over a period of 25 years is an example of a small study. The group that left upper secondary school in Uppsala in 1948 spread across the whole country. What is remarkable is that the majority ended up in large towns, above all the county towns. This may be explained by educational careers and the availability of jobs. The more specialised the work, the more probable it is that the jobs are in the large towns.

INTERNAL MOBILITY

For many years mobility on the labour market was regarded as a mainly external phenomenon; workers moved from company to company or from industry to industry. Today, however, the importance of internal mobility is receiving close attention. The growing size of companies and workplaces means that much of the previous external mobility between workplaces now occurs internally.

Various factors explain the importance of external stability and internal mobility. Stability in employment may well be in the interest of both the employee and the employer. The employee may be the family breadwinner and has perhaps made a long-term investment in a home close to his or her place of work. It will certainly be of very great importance for this employee to have a secure, long-term job at one and the same workplace. Nor should the value of a well-developed circle of friends among the other employees be underestimated. From the employer's point of view there are other positive factors. Studies have shown how productivity in an industrial firm increases with the length of employment of the employees. The explanation is presumed to be that the employees learn their jobs better and their team spirit improves. The importance of skill transfer between employees and willingness to accept new technology are also seen as significant factors in high productivity.

All this presupposes that employers do not look upon their employees as expendable or exchangeable parts.

Immigration and the Labour Market

The labour market is the decisive factor for mobility, even across national frontiers. Seen in a historical perspective, immigration to Sweden was encouraged as early as the Middle Ages, when Germans came and dominated political and economic life in many towns. In the 17th century skilled workers were recruited from present-day Belgium; the Walloons are a well-known feature of the mining districts round Finspång. Finns immigrated in the 17th century from Finland to the forest districts, where new land was opened up; and in the 19th century, too, labour was recruited from abroad to work in the sawmills along the coast of Norrland. While industry was expanding in the north, there were problems in the south. People moved away, partly because of over-population and lack of land. From the mid–19th century up to 1930 Sweden was a land of emigrants. All in all some 1.5 million people left the country and 0.4 million immigrated. The balance since 1930 has been different. About 1.7 million people have immigrated to Sweden, while 0.8 million have emigrated.

In the late 1940s there was a wave of labour immigration that continued into the 1970s. These were the years of strong growth both in industry and in the fast-growing public sector. Swedish companies went abroad in search of labour.

Immigration to Sweden was very dependent on trade cycles until the mid–1970s, but since 1975 its character has changed, mainly due to a large increase in the number of refugees. Consequently, there here has also been a change in the immigrants' country of origin. Labour immigrants during the fifties and sixties came mainly from Europe, whereas immigrants in the seventies and eighties to a large extent came from countries outside Europe.

The intensiveness of employment among immigrants during the 1950s and 1960s was at times greater than among Swedes, but today immigrants have a lower intensiveness of employment and a higher rate of unemployment.

A recession affects foreigners worse than Swedes. In spite of the upward trend of the 1980s and the lack of labour in the last few years of the decade, the intensiveness of employment among immigrants continued to decline throughout the 1980s.

The recession of the early 1990s hit immigrants very hard, and particularly workers from outside Scandinavia. The later their immigration, the higher their rate of unemployment. This was particularly true of women from Iran and Iraq. Immigrant women often face a double handicap when they want to enter the labour market. Unemployment is generally speaking twice as high among foreigners as among the population as a whole. For those who have become Swedish citizens the rate of unemployment is the same as for the population as a whole.

Immigrants meet a good many obstacles on the Swedish labour market. In general immigrants end up in more poorly-qualified occupations than Swedes. The immigrants' qualifications and previous work experience from their home countries are often not recognised. But it is not a question of a straightforward barrier between Swedes and immigrants. A complex hierarchy of ethnical groups and social spheres has grown

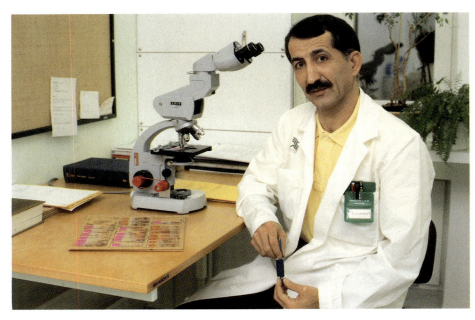

Many immigrants are well educated, but a large number of them are obliged to work in jobs below their level of competence.

Immigrants often get jobs in badly-paid service occupations like catering.

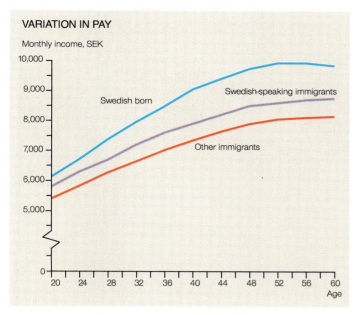

Generally speaking immigrants have lower wages than Swedes. One reason is poor language competence.

The percentage of people born abroad is unevenly distributed in Sweden. Most of them live in the metropolitan areas, the old industrial regions in Bergslagen, Västergötland and Småland and close to the Norwegian and Finnish borders. (K34)

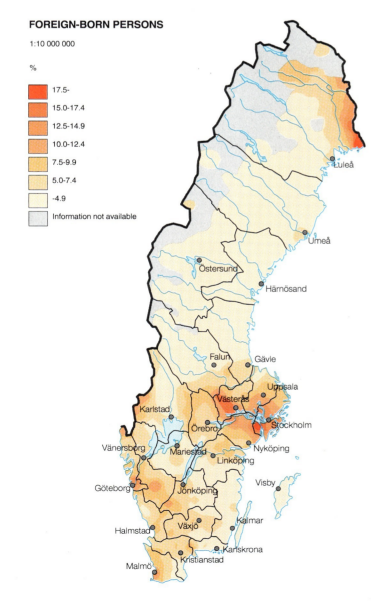

up within industry. Certain ethnical groups have a relatively strong position in more attractive occupations, while others tend to remain in monotonous jobs year after year.

COMPETENCE AND CAREER

As new forms of work have evolved, attitudes towards immigrant workers have also changed. The introduction of new organisational forms involving autonomous work groups, industrial democracy, new technologies and so on has focused attention on individual differences. This also means that the ethnical differences that exist within the labour collective have come into the limelight. Cliché attitudes towards immigrants as a group tend to become more widely accepted. The competition that exists between different decentralised units seems to be affecting relations between Swedes and immigrants to a very high degree, and often to the immigrants' disadvantage.

Immigrants often end up in jobs well below their level of competence in their own country. Immigrant graduates are to be found in manual occupations far more than their Swedish counterparts. The percentage of graduates in manual occupations is particularly high among those from countries outside Europe. In the latter case the percentage among men is as high as 25 to 30 per cent.

There are, however, great differences between different groups of foreigners. Examples of groups with relatively slow socio-economic mobility upwards are men born in Greece, Yugoslavia and to some extent Finland. In contrast immigrants from Czechoslovakia and Western Europe, for example, move more rapidly up the socio-economic ladder than their Swedish counterparts.

INCOME

Studies carried out in the 1970s showed that immigrants' pay was at a medium level. Low and high pay levels were less common than among the rest of the population. The fact that so few were in the lowest income brackets is explained by foreign women working part time to a lesser extent than Swedish women. The small percentage in the upper income brackets is explained by the high concentration of manual work. Studies carried out in the 1980s reveal a similar pattern, except that more have fallen into the lowest income bracket.

The average annual income of foreign citizens was very high in the late 1960s. In 1967 the relative income per person was 22 per cent higher than in the population as a whole. In the 1970s it fell and was in the 1980s below the level of the population as a whole. In 1987 the income per person was more than 20 per cent lower than for the population as a whole.

The difference in language competence is perhaps the most significant factor underlying the difference in pay between Swedes and immigrants. Studies reveal clearly higher pay for Swedes within those occupations that require a good command of Swedish. Differences in pay between Swedes and immigrants show that the differences tend to increase with age. The situation is somewhat better for immigrants with a good command of Swedish, but their pay is still clearly lower than that of their Swedish counterparts.

HEALTH

First-generation immigrants have rather more health problems than the rest of the population, which may be partly explained by a larger proportion of workers in immigrant groups and the previous stresses that refugees have been subjected to and which may result in mental health problems.

In an investigation foreign-born people were asked whether they had had any problems such as sleeplessness, stomach trouble, coughs and other illnesses during a particular month. A larger percentage of immigrants than Swedes reported that they had had trouble one or more times a month.

POLITICAL ASYLUM AND WORK

One of the problems of the increase in immigration was that it took a long time to process the refugees' applications. Another problem was that a person who sought political asylum in Sweden did not have the right to work. This state of affairs has been strongly criticised, primarily because enforced idleness leads to passivity among those seeking asylum. Active, competent, energetic persons may lose their power of initiative and drive if they are not allowed to make a living by working. In order to remove this problem the government has put forward proposals allowing certain kinds of work for those seeking asylum.

Unemployment

The level of unemployment was relatively low during the last few years of the 1980s but increased rapidly in the early 1990s. Unemployment is usually measured in relative figures, that is to say, the percentage of unemployed persons of the total number in the workforce.

The diagram below shows the average annual figures for the period 1970–92. The method for measuring unemployment was changed between 1986 and 1987, so the figures before 1987 are not wholly comparable with those from 1987 onwards. In 1986 the rate of unemployment for the whole country was 2.7 per cent. According to the new method applied since 1987 this corresponds to 2.2 per cent. This type of conversion cannot be made for the forest county and metropolitan sub-groups.

In general the graph shows that Sweden had a low rate of unemployment in the 1970s and 1980s, by international standards as well. Despite variations and sporadic peaks the trend was fairly constant. Developments in 1991 and 1992 show a clear rise to levels which have not been experienced in modern times.

Apart from unemployment at the national level figures are also given for the metropolitan counties (Stockholm, Göteborgs and Bohus, and Malmöhus) and the forest counties (Värmland, Kopparberg and the Norrland counties). Developments in the rest of Sweden correspond closely with national trends and are therefore

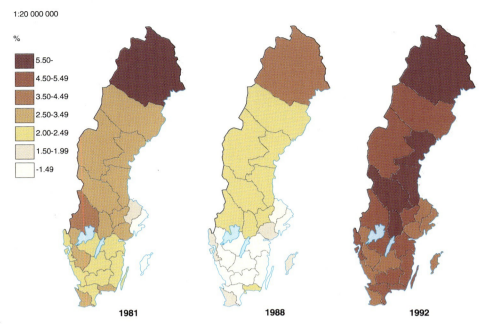

In the early 1990s Sweden began to come up to Western European levels of unemployment. By 1992 unemployment had risen in every county and was higher than in 1981 and 1988. (K35–37)

Unemployment levels differ greatly both between counties and within counties. Examples from the counties of Jönköping and Norrbotten. (K38, K39)

Since 1990 unemployment figures have reached levels which up to now have been uncommon in Sweden.

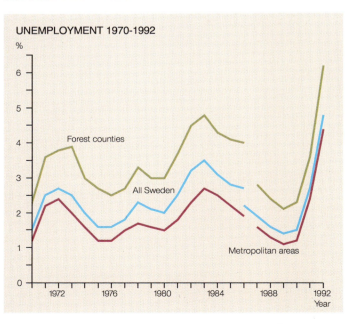

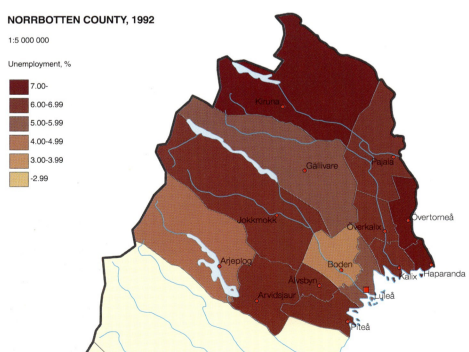

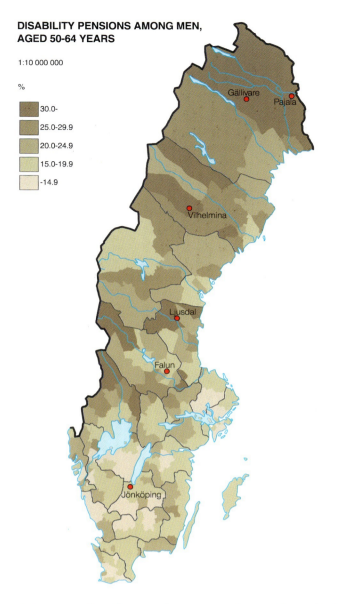

DISABILITY PENSIONS AMONG MEN, AGED 50–64 YEARS

1:10 000 000

%
- 30.0–
- 25.0–29.9
- 20.0–24.9
- 15.0–19.9
- –14.9

In large parts of Norrland more than one man in four aged 50 to 64 has been granted an early retirement pension, while the figure for southern Sweden is usually below 20 per cent. (K40)

not reported separately. Deviations between the national figures and the special regions (the metropolitan counties and the forest counties) seem to be of a structural nature. Unemployment in the forest counties, regardless of the general labour market situation, is always higher than the national figure, and the reverse is true of the metropolitan counties.

Unemployment at the county level is reported with average annual rates for 1981, 1988 and 1992. In most counties unemployment was lower in 1988 than in 1981. The counties of Stockholm and Uppsala were still among the lowest while Gotland was the only county with a higher rate in 1988. Changes up to 1992 meant that all counties had a higher rate than previously, that the lowest county rate in 1992 corresponds to the highest county rate in 1988 and that the differences between the counties have decreased. Unemployment also varies within counties, as the maps of Norrbotten and Jönköping county show.

Unemployment is unequal. People have different opportunities of getting a job. It is above all young people, immigrants and those with a poor education that are more often unemployed than the average.

EARLY RETIREMENT

The number of people retiring early on disability pensions has increased greatly in the past few decades, from just over 300,000 in 1981 to more than 360,000 in 1990. Early retirement may

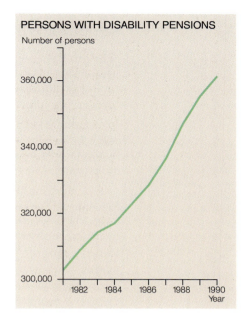

PERSONS WITH DISABILITY PENSIONS

The increase in the number of early retirement pensions is large and constant. A long period of unemployment often results in early retirement.

be granted to those in the national insurance scheme who are over 16 but not yet 65 and who, on account of poor health, can only work half time or less. Early retirement may also be granted to insured persons who are 60 and who have been out of work for a long period and are judged to have little chance of getting a job before their retirement at 65. There are great regional variations. In the group of men aged 50 to 64 the relative share of early retirement pensions is high in the forest counties, not least in inner Norrland.

In 1991 unemployment was greatest among young people. It was also higher among immigrants than among Swedes.

Jobcentres in Sweden are a part of the public sector.

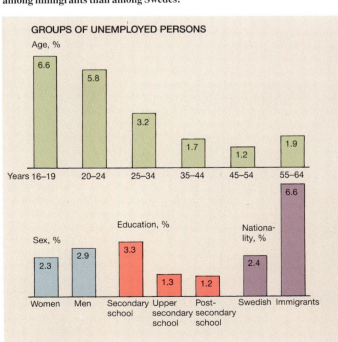

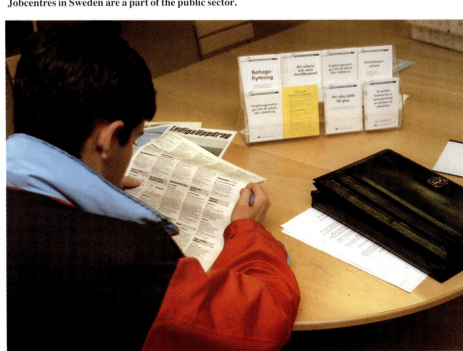

Absence Due to Illness

It is often said that absence due to illness is very high in Sweden compared to other countries. It is strange that Sweden can afford to have such a high rate. It is also often hinted that the work ethic is weak. That is what one hears. Is it true that Sweden has a high rate of absence due to illness?

It is not the malingerers that keep the figures high, but rather those with long-term illnesses. The regulations in Sweden are that sick workers are not forced out of the sickness benefit scheme as they are in other countries, where they would have to claim social welfare instead. The high intensiveness of employment in Sweden has also led to "marginal" labour coming onto the market, some of whom appear in the absence statistics. International statistics in this field are less specific than the Swedish data, so it is difficult to make direct comparisons.

Absence through illness is very unevenly distributed. Long-term illness lasting at least seven days accounts for four fifths of all days of illness and more than 40 per cent consists of days in especially long cases of at least three months. Two per cent of all employees account for more than 50 per cent of all days of illness, while 30 per cent have not been absent for illness once during a year.

We can see today that a number of employees have long-term illnesses; this is one consequence of having a larger percentage of people in work. Even a marginal increase in employment means that more sick and vulnerable people are drawn into the workforce, thereby affecting the average rate of absence through illness.

The increase in absence through illness occurs in precisely those groups and sectors which show the major increases in intensiveness of employment: women, not least in the provinces and within the public sector. Studies of the established part of the workforce, those who have worked for at least one year at one and the same place, reveal a higher rate of absence among women. Between 1975/76 and 1968/69 women's absence through illness increased by 5.2 days to a total of 24 days. Absence through sickness among men, on the other hand, decreased by almost one day to 16.2 days. This is due to a certain decrease in employment in the form of early retirement and to the fact that the number of physically demanding jobs in the traditionally male occupations has decreased. The mental and ergonomic demands placed on women in work seem, however, to have increased. The illness rate varied considerably from region to region in 1990. The highest number of days absent per insured person, 30 days, occurred in Göteborg and Malmö, followed by the counties of Västerbotten and Gävleborg with 29 and 28 days respectively. Halland had the lowest absence rate in 1990 with 20 days, closely followed by Skaraborg and Kronoberg.

Following the introduction of new sickness benefit regulations on March 1st, 1991, the number of those reporting sick fell by about 20 per cent. This lower level continued throughout 1991 compared with the previous five years. This sudden decrease can hardly be interpreted otherwise than as the result of the reform. However, it is unlikely that the whole of the decrease was solely due to the change in regulations. Weaker business conditions and rising unemployment are factors that lead to fewer people reporting sick. The consequences for absence through illness as a whole was a decrease of 10–11 per cent compared with the previous year.

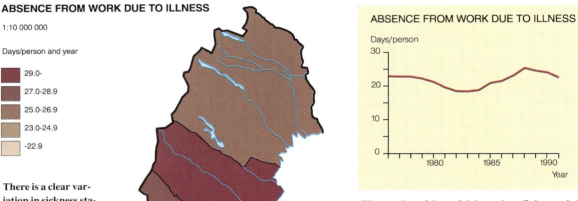

ABSENCE FROM WORK DUE TO ILLNESS
1:10 000 000

Days/person and year
- 29.0-
- 27.0-28.9
- 25.0-26.9
- 23.0-24.9
- -22.9

There is a clear variation in sickness statistics from county to county. Halland has an average of 20 days of absence due to illness, the lowest figure in the country. (K41)

The number of days of sickness benefit has varied since the 1970s between 18 and 25 days per person per year.

Greater attention has been paid in recent years to the working environment. Many people have monotonous jobs.

Different occupations demand different amounts of effort. Some lead to stomachache, other to backache. Approximately 90 per cent of those interviewed in male occupations consider their work physically arduous.

WORKING ENVIRONMENTS

Working environments are an important factor for the occurrence of illnesses and disease. Certain occupations are physically demanding, for example work involving lifting, heavy vibration, awkward body positions or repetitive movements. The jobs considered most demanding physically are to be found in male occupations such as construction work and forestry work. Corresponding jobs in female occupations are, for example, nursing assistants and home helps.

Looking at the occupations which involve lifting weights of at least 20 kg several times a day, we find somewhat surprisingly that the largest group of employees concerned today are not men but women in health care. Almost 45,000 women in this field report that they have to lift heavy weights several times a day. This may be compared with 33,000 men in the construction industry and 29,000 in engineering and metal construction work.

The Swedish labour market is very sex segregated. Men are more highly represented in heavy and dirty industrial and trade work. Women mainly work in offices and in health care. Consequently men are more exposed to noise, cold, draughts and vibration, while women are more exposed to cleaning agents and dry air, but also to lifting heavy weights.

Other occupations are more mentally demanding. Teachers form a category who consider that their work is to a high degree mentally exhausting. So do people working in health care, such as nursing assistants, and policemen. As for psycho-social working conditions, there are great occupational variations as well as variations between men and women. Women seem more often to have less influence on their working conditions than men, even in those cases where they have equivalent occupations and educational backgrounds.

Occupational accidents also contribute to absence through illness. In 1989 more than 97,000 accidents were reported among employees. Most of them occur in manufacturing industries. Slaughterhouses report the highest relative frequency of accidents.

UNEMPLOYMENT AND ILLNESS

The increased rate of unemployment has been seen as a national health problem. There is a connection between unemployment and a decreased sense of well-being, increased illness, increased consumption of medicine and increased use of health care. Unemployment leads to an increased risk of alcoholism, in the first place among young men. The risk of death is 1.5 to two times greater among unemployed people, and mental problems also increase to the same extent. Thus unemployment has a series of negative effects.

> A passage from Eyvind Johnson's novel *This was 1914* describes how hard work in the old days ruined the body. "His son was fourteen years old, red-eyed like his father and his back stooped, reeking of soot and smoke. He looked like a spoon and if you'd picked him up by the legs you could certainly have bailed a boat with him. His face was already that of an old man, he had deep furrows in his brow and faltering, wrinkled hands..."

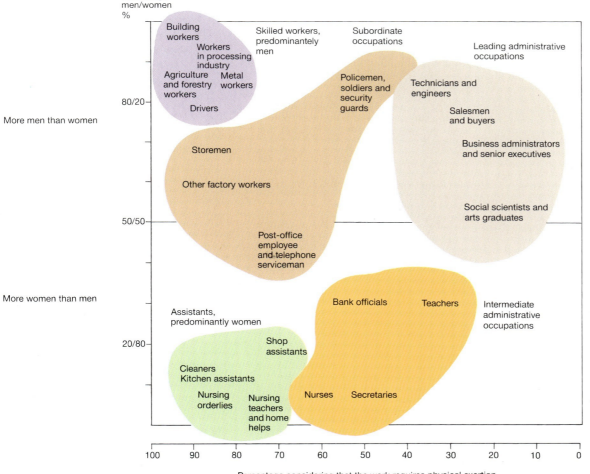

OCCUPATIONS AND RELATED PHYSICAL EFFORT

PAY IN THE COMMONEST OCCUPATIONS IN 1990

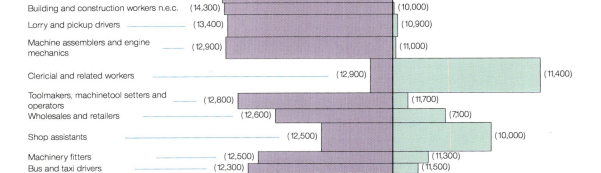

The mean income in 1990 for gainfully employed men and women above the age of 15 who work more than 35 hours a week.

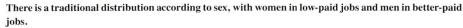

There is a traditional distribution according to sex, with women in low-paid jobs and men in better-paid jobs.

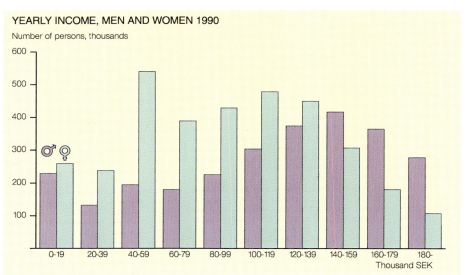

Pay

"Getting paid for one's trouble" is a common expression. Officially pay is defined as payment for a certain piece of work, either in the form of wages or a salary. Income is a broader term. Total income is the sum of six forms of income: income from gainful employment, capital, other property, temporary economic activity, agricultural property and business. This is the fiscal picture of income. It does not include home production.

Sweden has the most even distribution of income among individuals of all the countries in the world. There are, however, variations between different groups of people, according to sex, occupation and education and where one lives in Sweden.

MALE AND FEMALE

During the past few decades Swedish women have entered the labour market on a large scale. Almost as many women as men are gainfully employed today. The fact that women have entered the labour market does not mean, however, that they share men's labour market conditions in every respect. Almost half of all women work part time. Women and men usually do completely different kinds of work and women's pay is consistently lower. Total incomes for men and women are distributed as follows.

Men have a 50 per cent higher income than women. This can be explained in various ways. Women work part time to a larger extent than men, women do less skilled jobs than men, women work in occupations where the pay is lower than in typically male-dominated jobs. If persons with exactly the same education, age and occupation are compared, it is nevertheless evident that there is a 10 to 15 per cent pay difference between men and women. Many studies have proved that women have consistently lower pay than men. The only reason seems to be that women's work is valued lower than men's. The whole-year, full-time employed women in labour union jobs had an average annual income that was about 80 per cent of men in labour union jobs in 1991. The differences in the salaried workers (TCO) and graduate (SACO) union jobs were even larger, 76 and 77 per cent respectively.

If the male employee is the norm throughout, it will also be male values that dominate economic structures

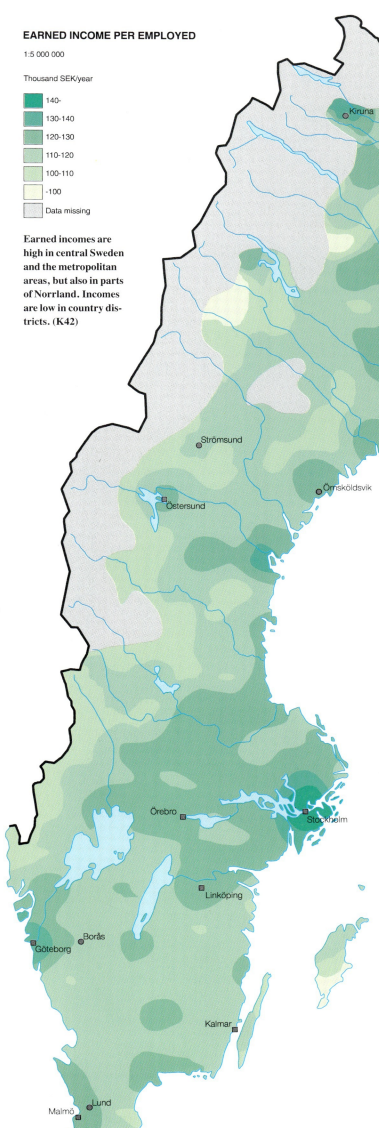

EARNED INCOME PER EMPLOYED

1:5 000 000

Thousand SEK/year
- 140-
- 130-140
- 120-130
- 110-120
- 100-110
- -100
- Data missing

Earned incomes are high in central Sweden and the metropolitan areas, but also in parts of Norrland. Incomes are low in country districts. (K42)

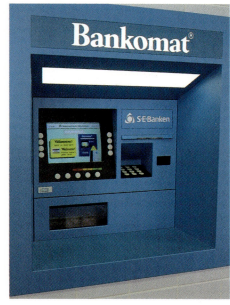

From pay packet to automatic bank account payment.

and what is taken to be rational behaviour. In working life, whether one is an employee or an employer, one is expected to maximise one's pay, fight for a higher post and increase one's influence. In other words one is expected to seek power and recognition. This is economically rational behaviour.

When a woman enters working life, she is expected to behave in an economically rational way. But she has other aspects to take into consideration. Women are often, as a result of tradition and social pressure, responsible for the home and the family, which means that they also have to behave in a socially rational way. People's time is divided up into work or leisure. For most women, especially those who are married and have children, there are three kinds of time — working time, leisure time and household time. From an economic point of view it is rational to devote as much time as possible to paid work. But the work done at home may also prove to be very economical, as well as directly necessary. Admittedly work done at home brings in less income, but it also often reduces the household's expenditure.

Women's responsibility for their families, and above all for their children, can also be seen in time-geographical terms. If a working mother has to accompany her child or children to the day nursery, her choice of workplace may be affected. There may be only one day nursery available for her children, and its location may force her to take a less skilled job because of the time available to her for travelling. This may be economically irrational, but without a shadow of doubt socially rational.

INCOME AND EDUCATION

Historically speaking, income and education are closely connected: the higher one's education, the higher one's pay. In the opinion of some people, including some employers' representatives, this connection has been rather too weak in Sweden. They claim that education has not affected pay levels sufficiently strongly.

REGIONAL PAY DIFFERENCES

In the mid–1970s a group of experts investigating regional development (ERU) showed that pay levels varied considerably from region to region. Average incomes were highest in the big cities. The most striking fact was that inner Norrland had relatively low income levels. This was explained by unemployment, early retirement and informal, unpaid work. It might also be maintained that costs are lower, so that such regional differences hardly reflect differences in material standards of living. Despite decreasing regional pay differences this pattern is recognisable in the regional distribution of average incomes for 1989.

Measuring and Evaluating Time and Work

Some years ago Lars Ingelstam wrote a book about the value of work and the use of time, in which he distinguishes between various economic systems and ways of organising work. These different economic systems are given colours: yellow, blue, black and white.

The yellow economy, the colour of gold and wheat, is what we usually call business life or the market economy. The blue economy, the main colour of Sweden's flag and coat of arms, consists of tax-financed production of services for private consumption. The blue and yellow systems together make up the formal economy. This is the money economy measured in terms included in the national budget.

The black economy comprises illegal economic activity, everything from pure theft to sophisticated tax evasion.

Finally, the white economy consists of the completely legal production which takes place outside the formal economy. This includes household work, unpaid work in various kinds of organisations run on a non-profit making basis, and the legal exchange of goods and services that takes place outside the market. Money is not a measure of value in the white economy.

In all these economic systems or sectors there are people at work. All working people invest both time and money in the informal, white economy as well as in the formal, blue-yellow economy. Estimates indicate that people of working age devote four hours a day to work at home, which includes household work, mending, child care and so on. In other words work at home accounts for 45 per cent of productive activity in the Swedish economy.

But work at home in the white economy is in principle no different from work on the market. How and where the work is carried out is an organisational question, in which choice of organisation may vary with time and among the various economic systems. In the relationship between market production and household production the latter may well be seen as the primary form—production that converts resources into welfare for the individual. From this point of

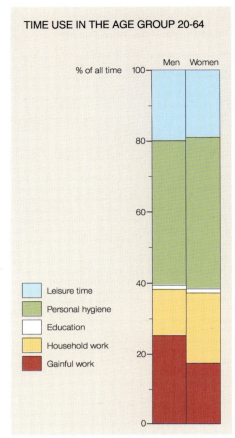

There is a considerable difference between men and women in the amount of time they devote to household work and paid work.

Households devote about three and a half hours a day to looking after the home.

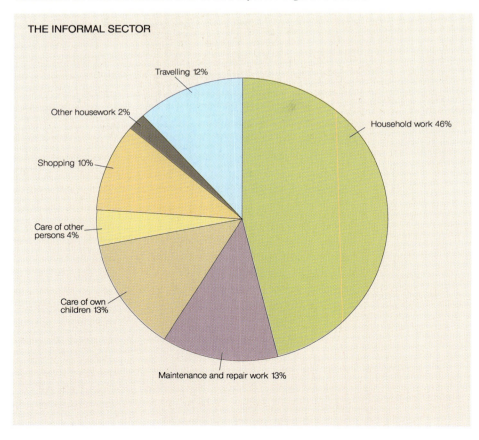

"HOUSEWIFE"

I do the housework
on the way to the bathroom

Walking through the livingroom
I water the flowers
dust the fireplace
tidy the papers

In the kitchen I feed the dog
put the cups away
and make the coffee

In the hall
I shake the carpet
and put the gloves away

The bathroom:
I fold up the washing
change the towels
and put the washing machine on

Now I'm on the loo
And while I sit there
I mop the floor

Berit Østberg

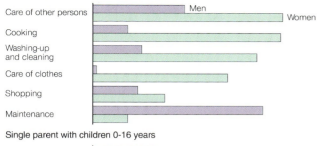
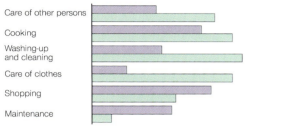
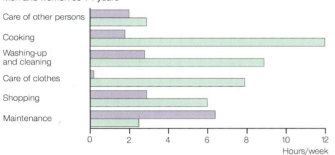

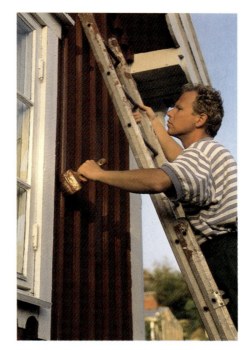

House maintenance is a common leisure-time activity.

The traditional sex roles are evident in the three groups of households. Women look after cleaning, cooking and clothes care and men look after house maintenance.

A good deal of the household's leisure time goes to unpaid work.

view work on the market is merely a means of getting resources for this kind of production.

One of the greatest changes in the use of resources in the economy in the past few decades has been the transfer of women's production resources from the home to the market. A complementary factor here has been a reallocation of men's time between the home and paid work. Between 1960 and 1970 men transferred on average eight hours per week from paid work to other activities, including work in the home. During the 1980s, however, the time men devoted to paid work increased again. Women, on the other hand, transferred during the same period six hours per week from work in the home to paid work. Half of this increase occurred in the 1980s.

The time men and women devote to work in the home is, however, very different. On average women devote more than 33 hours per week to work in the home, while the figure for men is just over 20 hours. The difference between the sexes is less at the weekends but greater on weekdays. Within the home there is also a division between male and female activities, whereby women carry out work in the home which is difficult to combine with paid work because of its time requirements. Men are responsible for maintenance work and repairs at home while women are responsible for cooking, cleaning and child care. The time devoted to housework varies greatly between men and women and at different stages of life. The workload is heaviest in families with small children, but is also considerable in periods when there are children up to the age of 12. The difference between the sexes is also greatest in families with children, when women devote more time not only to child care but also to household work.

Unpaid work, work in the home, often affects paid work with regard to working hours, place of work and type of work. Work in the home is often less flexible than many paid jobs and affects women's paid work in particular. To a great extent women choose work and working hours that take the family and the household workload into consideration. Women have always made this choice, but instead of leaving the labour market today to give birth to children and look after them, they now take temporary leave of absence and part-time work.

Organisation of Work

Sweden is a country with a long tradition of trade union activity. People have joined trade unions to protect their rights and to improve working conditions. This has taken place in a mixture of conflict and consensus between the workers and their organisations and the employers and their organisations. The percentage of the workforce organised in unions is in an international perspective very high.

HISTORY

Following the abolition of the guild system in 1864 and the industrial revolution in Sweden the first trade unions were formed in the 1870s. During the 1880s these unions strengthened their positions by forming confederations and in 1898 these confederations formed a common central organisation, *Landsorganisationen (LO)*, the Swedish Confederation of Trade Unions.

The employers replied four years later by forming the Swedish Employers' Confederation (SAF). The first agreement of importance between LO and SAF was made in 1906. In this "December compromise" employees' rights to form trade unions and employers' rights to direct and assign work and to employ and dismiss employees were recognised.

The organisation of office workers came considerably later, partly because there were relatively few office workers at the beginning of the century and partly because staff in executive positions felt a certain loyalty towards their employers. Office staff did not become a significant factor in union negotiations until the 1930s, and the first central organisation for office workers was formed in 1931. At a later stage (1944) private and public office employees were organised in the Central Organisation of Salaried Employees (TCO). A few years later yet another central organisation was established, the Central Organisation of Swedish Graduates (SACO).

During the 1930s legislation on the right to strike was discussed, in part to protect third-party rights and to prevent industrial action that might interfere with vital government functions. SAF and LO agreed to try to solve these problems by negotiation, and in 1938 a main agreement was reached including regulations for negotiation procedures, dismissal procedures, a ban on industrial action in certain cases and the treatment of conflicts "dangerous to society".

This agreement, the "Saltsjöbaden agreement", demonstrated the ability of the employees' and employers' unions to regulate conditions on the labour market without government intervention. The era that ensued was infused with the "Saltsjöbaden spirit", a spirit of co-operation and consensus whereby the parties managed their affairs without the government intervening.

This is one part of the "Swedish model", signifying peaceful and trusting relations between the labour market parties. This model also includes the "Rehn-Meidner model" for a wage policy of solidarity with low-paid workers, structural rationalisation and active labour market policies. This has contributed greatly to the rapid restructuralisation of Swedish industry and the consequent urbanisation of Swedish society.

In the 1970s a number of changes were made to Swedish labour laws. One of the most radical of these Åman laws (named after the chairman of the commission that preceded the new legislation) was the law on security of employment (LAS). LAS abolished the employer's right to employ and dismiss employees without cause; today employees may only be dismissed on grounds of fact.

The most important of the labour laws is the 1976 law on co-determination (MBL). This law regulates the relationship between trade unions and employers on the whole labour market. The obligation for the employer to provide information and conduct negotiations laid down in the MBL has resulted in limitations of the employer's traditional rights to direct and assign work.

WORKING HOURS

The number of hours worked has successively decreased during the 20th century. Since 1890 the annual number of hours worked has been almost halved, from about 2,800 hours to about 1,500 hours per year today. More and more people are in work, but the number per individual and even totally has decreased throughout most of the century. Shorter working hours are a consequence of fewer hours worked per day and week, longer holidays and a decrease in the number of years people work. The resources created by improvements in productivity have largely been used to

A worker. Painting by Albin Amelin.

The labour organisations today are LO (The Confederation of Trade Unions) with 2.2 million members, TCO (The Central Organisation of Salaried Employees) with 1.3 million members, SACO (The Central Organisation of Swedish Graduates) with 330,000 members and SAC (The Central Organisation of Swedish Workers) with 13,000 members.

The employers are represented by SAF (The Swedish Employers' Confederation), SAV (The National Agency for Government Employers), The Association of Local Authorities, The Federation of County Councils, The Negotiating Committee of the State Companies and the Negotiating Committee of the Cooperative Society.

TIME OF WORK

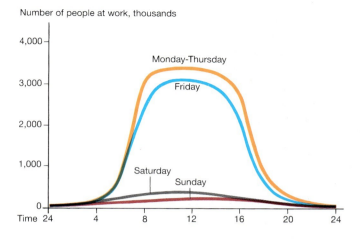

Most people work at some time between 7 in the morning and 5 in the afternoon on weekdays.

> **LEGISLATION ON WORKING HOURS**
>
> 1920 The 48-hour week
> 1938 Twelve days' paid holiday
> 1946 Three weeks' paid holiday for young people under 18 years of age
> 1951 Three weeks' paid holiday
> 1957 The 45-hour week
> 1963 Four weeks' paid holiday
> 1966 The 42 1/2-hour week
> 1970 The 40-hour week
> 1977 Five weeks' paid holiday

The Social Democrats' proposal that Employee Funds should be set up caused Sweden's employers to protest and form the 4th of October Committee.

The Labour Movement's great parade on May 1st in Stockholm.

shorten working hours.

The normal working week has been reduced since the turn of the century from about 63 hours a week to today's considerably lower level. The average number of hours worked in 1990 amounted to 37.9 per week. Men work on average 41.5 and women 33.7.

Thus the main tendency during the 20th century has been a continuous reduction in working hours. This trend was broken, however, in the early 1980s. The number of hours worked began to increase, both for the individual and totally. The average number increased from 36 hours in 1981 to 37.9 in 1990. There are several possible reasons for this break in the trend. Real pay had been decreasing for several years, there were changes in the age structure of the workforce and there was a greatly increased demand for labour.

WHEN DO PEOPLE WORK?

Working hours regulate everyday life to a great extent. Most workers, about three million of a total of some 4.3 million, work daily from Monday to Friday. On Saturdays about 200,000 to 380,000 people are at work between 8 a.m. and 7 p.m. and on Sundays the number of people at work varies between 180,000 and 250,000 between 8 a.m. and 7 p.m.

The number of people working irregular or unsocial hours is increasing. In 1974 20 per cent worked these kinds of hours, and by 1988 the figure had risen to 27 per cent, corresponding to somewhat less than 1.2 million people. Of these 170,000, most of them young men, work shifts. About 30 per cent of all employees work on some occasion on a Saturday and/or a Sunday.

Regional Policies

Many government white papers state that regional development started in 1964, when the report on active regional location policy was submitted. But there is nothing new under the sun, including regional development, at least if one defines it as political measures which have a direct effect on the economic and social development of a region.

The State has, for example, pursued a policy of colonialisation ever since the time of Gustav Vasa with the purpose of creating more tax-paying homesteads, from which most of the State's income was derived in the past. Some examples are the Lappland Bills of 1673 and 1695 and the Lappland regulations of 1749, legislation that was intended to assist people in cultivating land in Lappland territory by granting them tax exemption.

In the latter half of the 18th century it was feared that the forests in central Sweden would disappear because of the large quantities of wood, mainly in the form of charcoal, that was taken from the forests round the ironworks. For this reason the State encouraged the establishment of ironworks in northern Sweden, where there were forests in abundance. Thus when new settlements were established, it was to secure labour for work in the forests, at the ironworks and for all the necessary transportation.

What today is often called the infrastructure was one of the State's methods for attracting people to Norrland—the expansion of the railways in the late 19th century, for example, and as late as the 1930s the route of the Inland railway line. As far as dwellings were concerned, Crown crofts and "colonies" were built in the late 19th century and right up to the 1930s. This was also mainly to meet the demand for forestry labour. The State was trying to exploit the resources of land, forest, iron ore and water power that were to be found in Norrland, which was for many years the land of the future.

DEPOPULATION

During the crisis years of the 1930s the State made investments in order to reduce unemployment. Roads and bridges were built. After World War II Swedish society was radically transformed; the key words were economic growth, urbanisation and rural area problems. Agriculture and forestry were radically rationalised with consequent redundancies in the workforce. Unemployment was particularly bad in the five Norrland counties and in Kopparberg and Värmland. These counties were very dependent on agriculture and forestry.

At the same time as there were redundancies in the forest counties, industry, above all in the south of Sweden, was crying out for labour. The result was the "flight from the countryside" and the rapid growth of towns and new urban areas. New homes and premises had to be built on a scale that had never before been experienced in the towns to which people moved. As a result the construction industry expanded enormously. Both labour and materials were needed, while in Europe the demand for industrial goods was almost unlimited during the gigantic post-war reconstruction programmes of the 1950s and 1960s. The export market was, to say the least, attractive.

MODERNISATION

In the early 1960s politicians and planners realised that developments were getting out of hand and leading to serious consequences, not only for individuals, those who moved house, but also for those who stayed put and for the whole social structure of Sweden. It was being undermined. Work and services go together. "Population basis, scope, level of services" were terms often used in the debates on regional development. Something had to be done. The first regional development report was submitted, involving the not insignificant sum of 800 million kronor for development work. This grant was the first phase in modern regional development—the modernisation phase, as it was called. The central concept was to support the establishment of industry. People were leaving agriculture and forestry to work in industry in southern and central Sweden, so it was in the north that industrial investment was needed. The aim of this policy was to move jobs to people instead of people to jobs. By means of various kinds of grants and subsidies attempts were made to move companies, especially subsidiaries with good prospects, from the more industrialised parts of the country to designated development areas, whose boundaries have changed but which have always been in the north and the west. What was forgotten at this stage was that industrial employment as a result of rationalisation had not merely stagnated throughout the country but had even started to decrease, as it had already done in agriculture.

REGIONAL DEVELOPMENT

A new phase in regional policy was to try to provide equal access to work, services and a good environment. This was done by attempting to set up a place system with strong regional centres. The term "strong centre" became something of a slogan. One means of achieving a strong labour market was to invest in the public sector, which grew rapidly in the 1970s. Another method was to decentralise higher education by creating regional colleges.

Trees used to be felled in the winter to make it possible to transport the timber away.

When road construction was given high priority, simple road bridges were built in some places, called Rosén's Corsets. Vojmån in Vilhelmina.

The whole forestry process, from felling to finished product, is a highly technical business nowadays.

Concerning the relocation of the public sector, two underlying factors may be discerned. One was the rapid growth of Greater Stockholm and the consequent overcrowding there. The other was the realisation that growth was strongest in the public sector and that there was a great need for "support bases", regional centres in the country.

It was mainly the county towns that received the relocated government departments, with about 11,000 jobs. The local effects were large, because only a few of the staff with the highest educational backgrounds moved from Stockholm. This meant that the authorities had to recruit new staff. The most qualified personnel were recruited from the whole country while the less qualified were usually employed locally.

HOW WELL HAS THE STATE'S RELOCATION POLICY SUCCEEDED?

Sweden is by no means unique in its relocation policy. More or less the same process has been going on all over the western world, which is quite natural since the patterns of migration and population growth are rather similar in Western Europe.

The goal of reducing growth in the Stockholm region has not been reached. Nor have the hopes that private companies would move away from Stockholm and relocate in the regional centres been realised. The effects in the new towns have, however, been more positive. Both populations and tax revenue have increased and the labour market has been broadened. The Agency for Administrative Development, which carried out evaluations, points out that the relocated government departments have become an important resource in regional development work. This is primarily true in northern Sweden. It has also been shown that the greatest benefits have been achieved where departments work in the same field, for example in Gävle where three departments are concerned with social planning. These departments co-operate with university colleges, county

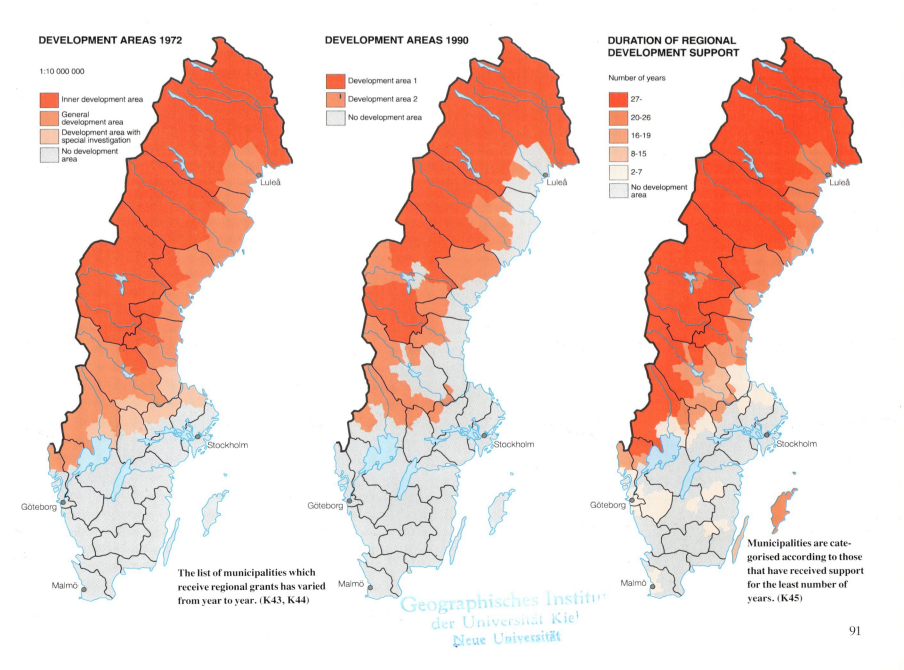

The list of municipalities which receive regional grants has varied from year to year. (K43, K44)

Municipalities are categorised according to those that have received support for the least number of years. (K45)

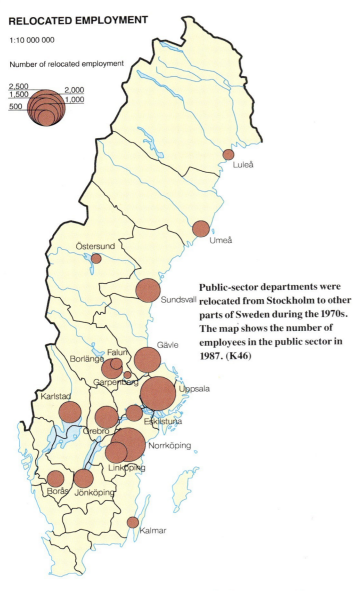

RELOCATED EMPLOYMENT

Public-sector departments were relocated from Stockholm to other parts of Sweden during the 1970s. The map shows the number of employees in the public sector in 1987. (K46)

ling costs have increased.

More relocation took place in the 1980s, though not on the same scale as during the 1970s. The goals were the same, to slow down growth in the Stockholm region and to increase employment and broaden the labour market in the regional centres.

New Structural Problems — Mobilisation

There were major changes in industry in the late 1970s. Those most affected were companies in the iron and steel, paper and pulp and textile industries. Towns and regions offered development packages providing various combinations of financial support. These measures were aimed at Norrbotten, the interior of northern Sweden, Västernorrland, Bergslagen and Blekinge. To compensate for the closing down of the shipbuilding industry towns like Malmö, Uddevalla and Karlskrona received large "crisis packages". Local and regional mobilisation comprised companies, municipalities, county authorities and development companies. In general emphasis was placed on mobilising people locally. Many municipalities took the opportunity to initiate their own industrial development policy.

CULTURE, ATTRACTIVENESS AND COMPETENCE

In the late 1980s some regional policies began to provide more general financial support, not only for the development areas. There was competition for labour of various kinds. One

REGIONAL DEVELOPMENT GRANTS, 1965–93

One of the basic principles of regional policies is to give development grants to certain geographical areas or regions.
- grants to manufacturing companies
- grants to rural areas
- reduced employment taxes
- grants for freight transport
- grants for passenger transport
- grants for computerisation
- special infrastructure investments
- "package incentives" in regions undergoing major structural change
- creating regional investment and development companies
- local planning
- relocation of government offices
- grants to service companies in selected areas

Although the list is long, it shows that over a long period of time there has been agreement as to which geographical areas should receive grants.

aim was to attract people with good qualifications to the central places. Methods in these campaigns included attractive housing estates, good public transport, access to higher education and cultural development.

STATE TRANSFER PAYMENTS

Apart from what are called regional development policies, the State greatly influences employment in various parts of the country, and thereby regional development, in many other ways. This is done by means of tax equalisation grants and at an earlier stage by direct State grants to economically weak municipalities, so that they are able to offer work and services to their inhabitants and prevent the standard of living from deviating too much from the national average.

If we look at the way money is allocated from the national budget to the inner regions of the north and the west, we see that one third may be termed transfer payments to individuals there as consumers. Approximately 20 per cent goes to industry for production and improved productivity. About the same amount consists of direct State grants, for example for construction work and for various types of services the State offers its citizens. The remainder consists mainly of tax equalisation payments and State grants. All of these grants create work opportunities, either directly

authorities and the municipality as well as with each other. Of course relocation has not been painless, either for the individual and the household or for the department as such. On the other hand government costs have fallen. It is mainly cuts in office rents that have led to savings, while travel-

As a part of the relocalisation programme a number of government authorities were moved from Stockholm to regional centres. The Swedish Meteorological and Hydrological Institute (SMHI) moved to Norrköping.

REGIONAL DISTRIBUTION OF STATE SUBSIDIES

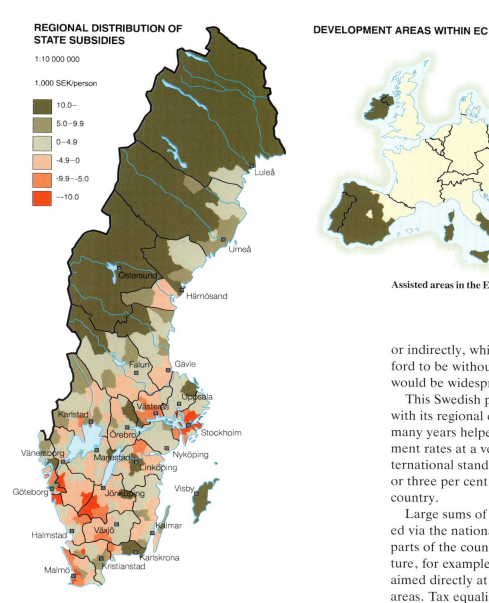

The state transfers funds to the municipalities. Distribution, 1985/1986. (K47)

Assisted areas in the EC. (K48)

Allocation of funds among municipalities by state income and expenditure, 1985/1986.

REGIONAL DISTRIBUTIONS OF STATE SUBSIDIES

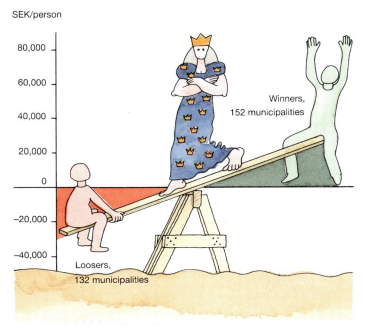

or indirectly, which society cannot afford to be without. The alternative would be widespread unemployment.

This Swedish policy of equalisation with its regional consequences has for many years helped to keep unemployment rates at a very low level by international standards, in general two or three per cent, throughout the country.

Large sums of money are reallocated via the national budget to various parts of the country. Certain expenditure, for example regional grants, is aimed directly at supporting exposed areas. Tax equalisation payments also have a direct regional equalisation function. The labour market incentives also tend to have a similar profile, since unemployment is highest in the high-priority development areas. Other support, such as company assistance, services provided by the State itself and transfer payments to households do not have a clearly defined regional development purpose. Nevertheless these, too, reallocate large sums of money regionally, to some extent in the same way as the regional development grants, but the total sums involved are very much larger. Thus the State is, for many municipalities, the most important "basic industry". When the national budget is cut, different sectors are affected to a greater or lesser extent.

A sum corresponding to almost one tenth of national expenditure and income is redistributed among the municipalities. This means that almost 10,000 kronor per person is transferred from the "losing" to the "winning" municipalities. Some of this, however, can be ascribed to the fact that expenditure on universities, county administration, military activities and the like neither can nor should be shared equally by each municipality.

Europe — a Threat and a Promise

During the 1990s European integration has entered the field as a new factor in regional policy. If Sweden becomes a member of the new European Community, decisions made outside Sweden will greatly affect Swedish policy. European integration is described in the political debate both as a threat and as a promise. One of the questions is how regional development areas in Europe are classified and what grants different areas may be given. Sweden emphasises low population density, a harsh climate and long distances as development criteria, while continental Europe concentrates on areas with low levels of income and high rates of unemployment. Another question concerns what support of a general nature and what incentives to companies and activities may be made by each country without unfair competition occurring, for example for exports.

A BROADER PERSPECTIVE

There is a formal aspect of policy-making which is called regional development policy. There is also a policy that is regional in its effects, even though its name does not indicate anything to do with regions or the redistribution of funds to different regions. The "little", official regional policy corresponds to SEK 3bn a year. The "big", concealed regional policy reallocates about ten times as much among the municipalities. Both policies, however, are affected by a shrinking national budget and European integration. During the 1990s it is probable that more attention will be given to the "big" rather than to the "little" regional policy. Redistribution policies may also be lifted out of today's system. A typical example is the Swedish State Railways' "collective ticket". Instead of subsidising uneconomic lines internally within the company by means of an operating subsidy, the State will commission and pay openly for certain traffic on certain lines which is not a paying proposition. The advantage of dividing all sectors in this way into two parts is that it is easier to see how well they achieve their own goals.

Leisure

Aspects of Leisure Time

Those parts of the day, week, year and life that are devoted to paid work have successively, at times at a fast pace, at times more slowly, decreased for everybody. At the beginning of the 20th century more and more salaried workers gained the right to a holiday, which could vary in length from 20 to 45 days.

In the Occupational Safety and Health Act of 1931 everybody was granted the right to at least four working days' holiday. The first Compulsory Holidays Act of 1938 gave each employee the right to two weeks' holiday. It was seen to be in the national interest to provide for the employees' need for rest and recreation. Some people were worried about the leisure time problems that might arise. Would people use their newly-won leisure time sensibly? A few people were in fact unwilling to take their holidays. In order to meet this threat information films were made and handbooks were published entitled "Planning a Happy Holiday". The war broke out, however, and in the post-war decades part of the improved standard of living was taken in the form of leisure time. Laws adding to the holiday entitlement were passed in 1951, 1963 and 1968. Many groups had already made agreements to this effect. The sixth holiday week has still to be granted to about 60 per cent of employees. Every change in holidays has been preceded by debates about the choice between more leisure and more pay, and the fact that leisure time is both a product of and a prerequisite for work.

Discussions about work and holidays are relatively recent. Previous generations were in a totally different position, where the choice lay between quite different alternatives than leisure time or higher pay. Previous generations of young people provided their own entertainment and leisure activities. It was not until the 20th century that a commercial entertainment and leisure industry developed, creating an almost endless variety of ways of spending one's leisure time.

What did people do on their holi-

There seems to be an endless range of leisure activities available to us.

days? Most people stayed at home, or went on day excursions to bathe or to visit friends and relations. The thirties and the forties were also a time for cycling holidays, when you camped or stayed at a youth hostel. This was also the heyday of the boarding houses. The economic boom of the post-war period brought the motor car into the picture, assisted by the 1953 law on hire-purchase. The road network and road standards were improved, more and better camping grounds were established, tents and other such equipment became more practical. The caravan came in the 1950s. Having a car brought freedom and made travelling an individual matter. The whole family could go off on holiday. The only restriction was the length of the holiday. Collective travelling, previously by boat or train, was replaced by coach trips to the continent and package tours to Mallorca and Italy.

Leisure Time?

The rise in productivity and the decrease in the number of hours worked have kept pace with each other and have meant that time is used more now for consumption than for production. We surround ourselves with more and more things and our home living space is increasing. A large part of our consumption is devoted to leisure articles and investment in capital goods intended for leisure. Looking after and making use of all these things takes time. The media boom has multiplied the choice of entertainments. It is getting more and more difficult to find time for all the things that have to be done. Rush and stress are increasing in the recreational ratrace. Anyone who stops to think realises that prosperity is not necessarily synonymous with well-being. The time that is left after paid work and household work have been done, leisure time, may well have increased and it is well needed. But leisure time has also become more and more busy and we sell it, voluntarily, for a multitude of organised and institutionalised activities. These comprise an extensive industry continuously providing us with new needs, fashions and investment goals.

DO CLOTHES MAKE THE MAN?

Thoughts on this theme are just as topical as ever, even though we may now talk of life styles. The ways in which we can express ourselves in this respect are endless, not least in our choice of leisure activities. Take the jogger, for example, plodding along in his cushioned shoes of the right make, wearing the right super tracksuit and sweatband in the right matching colours, with a programmed time, pace and pulse counter on his wrist, equipped with the latest energy drink and a walkman giving him his course in French or Zen Buddhism as he jogs. He, or she, is transmitting a message about a life style: fit for life.

The popular movements expressed a community of interests. The banner and the flag were rallying signs, showing what one was fighting for, or against. There was no doubt as to the values one wanted to communicate.

A sense of community or affiliation may be expressed by gathering round an activity, as participants, spectators or officials. Taking part in events like the Vasa Race, the Stockholm Marathon, the O-ring, Round Gotland, the Spring Art Show or a dawn picnic in Haga Park may tell us something about the participant, about his or her capacity or qualities.

Fetish-like objects such as banners, badges or buttons have the same function, to confirm the perhaps well-known fact that one belongs to an exclusive brotherhood. What the supporters on the football stands carry on with is basically the same thing.

The Royal Swedish Yacht Club

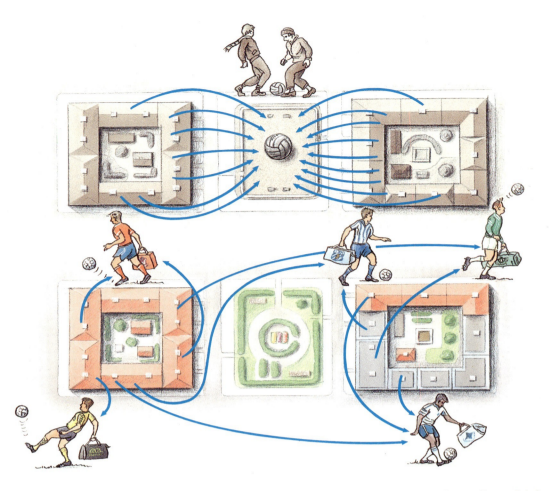

When sports are organised in clubs, the pattern of leisure-time movement changes. Parental choice, or absence of choice, regulates the ways in which children spend their leisure time.

The costs of leisure-time activities vary greatly.

WE PLAYED FOOTIE IN THE PARK...

A couple of good bounces with the football was the signal for enthusiasts of any age living in the block. Time for football for an hour or so on the gravel pitch, on the grass in the park or in the street. Those were the days before clubs and the municipality took over. Not many players were any good, but everyone had fun. Nowadays youngsters go to their training sessions at different times according to their age. They are given technique training and are reminded about the importance of eating and drinking the right things, paying their registration fee and wearing their club jersey. There is a break in training in July unless there is a special competition. Trainers wrinkle their brows and talk about unorganised youth...

Spontaneous forms of "sport and play" have been replaced by organised activities. What has happened?

SPORT FOR EVERYBODY?

When spontaneous sport began to disappear, the range of players decreased. An investigation showed that more than half (53%) of 15-year-old boys kicked a football or played some other game now and then in 1968; by 1984 the figure had fallen to seven per cent. Nowadays practically all sporting activities for young people are organised by clubs. Not so long ago most new talent was discovered in schools. The School Games, the annual sports events, got a lot of publicity.

The more dominant role played by the clubs is the result of the form of official financial support. Municipalities give a grant per activity and member which is the same for all clubs, but these grants represent only half of the subsidies which municipalities pay to clubs. The major costs are for municipally-owned facilities like sports, swimming and ice stadiums, football pitches and the like. They are rented out free in principle, which means a large subsidy for those clubs that use them. The sports that benefit most are, for example, football, ice-hockey and basketball, as well as swimming and athletics.

One effect of this system is that money is distributed unevenly. Thus girls usually have to pay a considerably larger share of the costs of their leisure activity if it happens to be riding, while the boys in the ice-hockey team are heavily subsidised.

The extent to which children and young people actively take part in sports or athletics, and their choice of activity, depends to a high degree on their social background. As sports have become more and more like school subjects, well-planned, theoretical and evaluated, we find that the children that take part in sports and thus use the sports facilities most frequently are those that do well in school. The proportions between the social classes have shifted with the increase in organised sport. L-M Engström, a social researcher, reports: "You need to have the right parents if you are going to take part in sports, parents who take the trouble to place their six to eight-year-olds in a club. And they should have time to give encouragement and a car to drive the kids to the club. Such parents are to be found mainly in the upper social classes."

In junior school three times as many children from the upper social classes choose to play sports than children from lower social classes. The higher their social status, the greater the likelihood that the children will choose an individual rather than a team sport. A general conclusion is that the percentage of passive children has increased markedly since the disappearance of spontaneous sport.

It is easy to get the impression that many leisure activities have become over-organised and institutionalised. This may reflect the well-known tendency for Swedes to form a club with a formal structure of rules and regulations whenever the occasion arises, so that a certain activity may be pursued in a secure, organised form. All this takes time. Another factor is that many leisure activities have become more and more specialised, requiring special equipment, membership of a club, and plenty of free time and physical, financial and social resources. The variations among different kinds of activities are striking. Thus choice of leisure time interest controls to a greater or lesser extent the individual's life style.

THE BROADCASTING MEDIA

Radio broadcasting became a widespread and significant feature of social life from the 1930s onwards. However, none of the mass media has had a greater power to influence people's use of time than television.

The diagrams show some of the technical developments in radio and television sets. Parallel with these developments there has been an enormous increase in the number and range of programmes broadcast to the public.

Concerning the development of the broadcasting media in the 1980s, it is evident that most attention has been given to television. The growth of cable television in the latter part of the decade led to a great increase in broadcasting time.

But it was in fact radio that accounted for the major change in this respect in the 1980s. This increase in broadcasting time came mainly from community radio stations. National radio cannot increase very much more since the channels already broadcast more or less round the clock.

What have increased above all in Sweden are popular music programmes. During the 1980s the number of hours of music played on the radio increased ten times over. This trend, reinforced by the expansion of commercial broadcasting, is expected to continue during the next few years.

Despite this increase in broadcasting time it does not seem likely that radio listening will increase. It has remained constant at about two hours a day throughout the 1980s. Instead audiences will be more clearly specialised. The same is true of TV-viewing, which takes up on average two hours of the day in Sweden. Nor has this time increased during the 1980s, in spite of the increase in broadcasting time. Each new television channel has to compete for a limited amount of viewer interest.

The influence of television on reading habits is not disputed but is not unambiguous either.

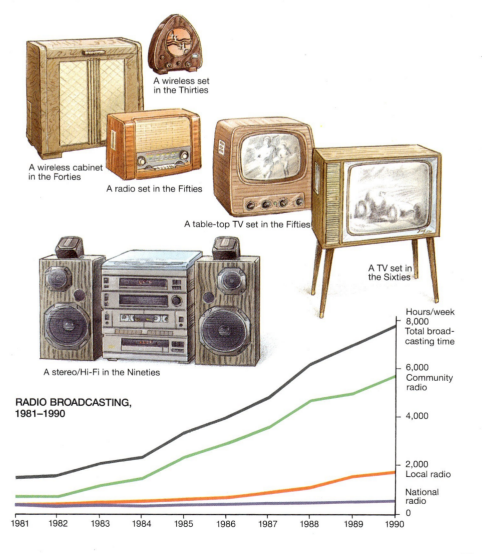

Leisure Time Activities

DAILY LEISURE

Once when working hours were at the centre of political debate, the following slogan was coined: "Eight hours' work, eight hours' sleep, eight hours' play". This referred to normal working days. But not all time outside work and sleep is available for free activities.

A large part of the free eight hours, as well as the weekends and holidays, is in fact committed in various ways. Everyone has to use part of his or her time to keep the home running. Time is put aside for shopping, cooking, cleaning, mending and so on. Families with children have part of their time committed by their children's activities: going to the day nursery or the baby minder, for example. Most people also use up part of their time in travelling to work, which has grown in both time and distance in the 1990s.

Thus according to each person's situation there is a varying amount of free time available. These variations depend on each person's stage in the life cycle: age, sex, size of family, home district, distance from work and so on. Information about how different groups of people use their leisure time is often unreliable. The difference between free time and committed time is to some extent vague and shifting, depending on the individual's situation. The following discussion is therefore partly based on rather rough estimates. On average free time is about 20 per cent of all the time one is awake. Of course it is unevenly distributed on the different days of the week. There are also natural variations over the year, but in the reports on everyday activities holidays are not included.

Women often work shorter hours outside the home than men, but in the family women tend to have less free time than men. These differences between the sexes are also to be found in their choice of activities in their free time.

Everyday free time is mainly used within or close to one's home. Only exceptionally do people go on long journeys during the week in connection with leisure activities. Saturdays and Sundays provide better opportunities for travelling.

LONG WEEKENDS AND HOLIDAYS

Long public holidays like Christmas/New Year and Easter, like normal holidays, provide much better opportunities for spreading one's activities geographically. This explains the large seasonal migrations and peak-traffic periods. One can live in one's second home, visit friends and relations who live a long way away, visit various types of tourist attractions or travel abroad. Long weekends also provide opportunities for activities away from home such as hunting, fishing, hiking in the mountains and so on.

This chapter will deal with a number of leisure time activities. Since people enjoy such a wide range of activities, the sample will not be complete.

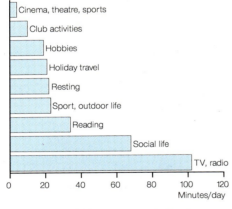

Television, social intercourse and other home activities fill most of our leisure time. The leisure time which we have at our disposal freely and without constraint is a little less than 20 per cent of our everyday life.

Everyday leisure time is concentrated to the hours between 6 p.m. and 11 p.m. Shift work, part-time work and work in the home may lead to some distribution of leisure time through the day.

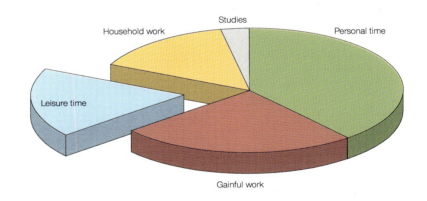

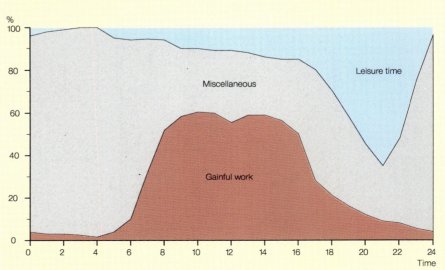

BOOK LOANS FROM PUBLIC LIBRARIES, 1989, EXCLUDING CHILDREN'S BOOKS

1:10 000 000

Book loans/person
- 4.50-
- 3.80-4.49
- 3.42-3.79
- 2.90-3.41
- -2.89

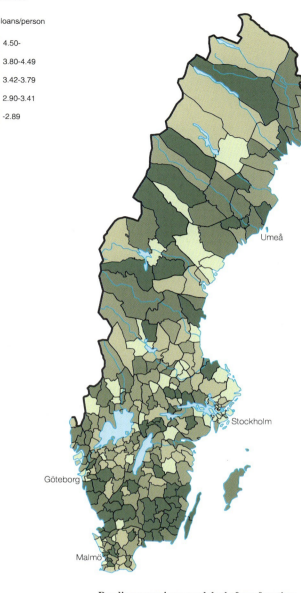

Reading occupies a good deal of our free time. In Småland, Jämtland and Västerbotten many books are borrowed from libraries, while fewer books are borrowed per person in the big cities. (K49)

Chatting over a cup of tea.

Men and women choose different kinds of leisure-time activities. Needlework is a typical women's hobby, while men have more technical interests.

Sedentary Leisure

Most leisure time is taken up by activities tied to the home. During a normal week about 70 per cent of this time is devoted to such activities. Apart from television Swedes spend time on a variety of social activities, reading and what might collectively be called hobbies.

SOCIAL INTERCOURSE

About 15 per cent of time is spent on conversations, both face to face and on the phone, visits by friends and relations and parties. The differences between men and women are mainly that women spend more time on the phone, which can probably be seen as an indication that they often manage the contacts with friends and relations.

READING

Besides reading newspapers (19 minutes) an average of 10 minutes per day is spent reading books. There are differences between families in this respect, but are there any differences between different parts of the country? A clue is given by book loans from public libraries, which are in general very well stocked in spite of local variations. The distribution of loans of literature to adults shows that parts of Småland, Västerbotten and Jämtland have more active borrowers, while the big cities show lower figures. Here we are disregarding the fact that certain towns with higher educational institutions have a very high level of book loans, which hardly has anything to do with the population as a whole.

HOBBIES

We devote about as much time to hobbies as to reading, but here there is a clear difference between men and women. Women spend twice as much time on hobbies as men. Instead men give more time to sport, outdoor life and club activities outside the home. In so far as men devote time to hobby-like activities at home, they are likely to be within the field of technology.

Television's Dominance

Television was introduced to Sweden in the 1950s and regular broadcasts began in 1956. After a very rapid expansion of the transmitter network, television was soon everyman's property. To begin with there was only one channel, but in 1969 a second terrestrial channel was established. It has long been possible to see television programmes from our neighbouring countries in certain parts of Sweden, but it was not until the 1980s that the number of television channels was increased. Viewers were offered more channels thanks to the introduction of commercial satellite and cable broadcasts. In 1992 yet another terrestrial Swedish channel was established, financed by commercials.

From 1956 onwards the development of TV has had a considerable influence on the way people use their time. More and more leisure time has been used for watching television. This "activity" is now by far the largest single activity during people's available free time. Almost one third of the time between 6 and 10 p.m. any weekday evening is often spent watching television.

On average in the late 1980s Swedes spent just over 100 minutes a day watching various television programmes. There are some regional differences in viewing time, but they are fairly small. The variations are not more than +/–9 minutes from the average. Regular investigations of audience figures are made by the Swedish Broadcasting Company's Audience and Programme Research Unit, which has found that Blekinge has the longest viewing time, while the counties of Stockholm, Malmöhus and Älvsborg have the lowest figures.

The number of people that watch television on a normal day shows hardly any regional differences. Variations in viewing are not more than +/–3% of the county average.

The present large number of channels, provided above all by cable television, has increased the amount of viewing. The difference between those people who can only see terrestrial broadcasts of Channel 1, TV2 and TV4 and those who have access to the greater range of channels is between 10 and 15 minutes a day.

Young people, but above all those above the age of 65, watch a lot of television. The lowest frequency of television viewing is found in the

When television first came into Swedish homes in the 1950s, many people from several families would gather round one of the few sets available. Looking at television in this way was something of a social event.

15–24 age group. Less well-educated people watch television more than other groups, which also agrees with the distribution of ages. There are also seasonal variations in viewing.

It should also be noted that women watch television more than men.

Women, however, seem to have a more "extensive" style of viewing. This means that it is more common for other activities to be dominant, but that the TV set is on and that they watch when something of interest comes up.

Television takes up such a large part of our leisure time that, together with work, school, and personal time for sleep etc., it has become in terms of time the most important part of many people's lives. Almost 40 per cent of the population watch TV around 7 o'clock every day.

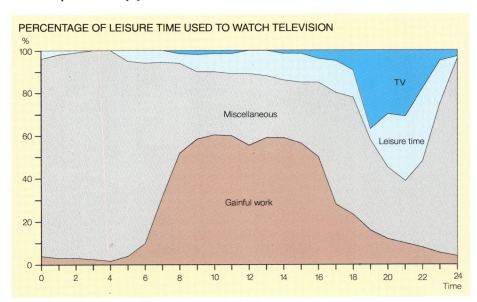

VIDEO

Video is closely connected with television. An interesting phenomenon may be observed here. Ownership of VCRs increased greatly throughout the 1980s, but the percentage of video viewers per day peaked in 1986 and since then has declined somewhat. This may be due to several factors. One is perhaps that total television transmission time and the number of channels available increased during this period, providing several more attractive programmes. The amount of time available for viewing has, of course, not increased.

RADIO

The radio set at home or at work is often on, but there are not many people who listen intensively to radio programmes more than a few minutes a day. Radio does not tie the listener to the set in the same way that television does. Other activities are dominant and listening becomes passive.

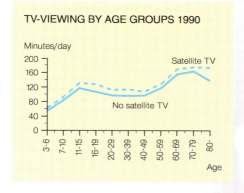

TV-VIEWING BY AGE GROUPS 1990

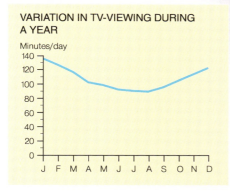

VARIATION IN TV-VIEWING DURING A YEAR

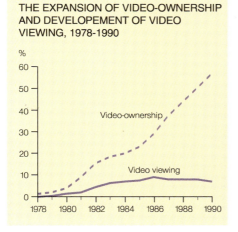

THE EXPANSION OF VIDEO-OWNERSHIP AND DEVELOPEMENT OF VIDEO VIEWING, 1978-1990

TV programmes on Monday, 6 September 1992, between 7.00 and 7.30 p.m., published in a national newspaper

Channel 1
7.00 Educational radio: Stenography

TV 2
7.00 Regional news
7.15 Sports report

TV 3
7.00 Jackpot, general knowledge contest

TV 4
7.00 News
7.25 Weather

NORDIC
7.00 Glamour, American series

BBC
7.00 News and weather

CHILDREN'S CHANNEL
5.30–8.00 T.C.C with C.D.Q., Fifteen Part 1, Swedish subtitles Saved by the Bell Part 1 and Fame Part 1

CNN
7.00 World News

DANISH TV 1
6.55 History Quiz

DANISH TV 2
7.00 News

DISCOVERY
7.00 Beyond 2000. New inventions (Swedish)

3-SAT
7.00 Heute
7.20 3sat Studio

EUROSPORT
7.00 Volleyball World League

FILMMAX
6.00 Gimme an F

FILMNET:
7.00 A Dry White Season. Drama (1989)

FINLANDS TV
6.30 Kätkäläinen Part 2. Finnish film

LIFESTYLE
7.00 Sally Jessy Raphael

MTV
6.00 Hit List UK

NORWEGIAN TV
7.00 Today's Review

ONE WORLD CHANNEL
(Only broadcasts 8.30 a.m. – 9.00 a.m.

RTL PLUS
6.45 RTL Current Affairs
7.15 Explosive

SAT 1
7.00 Sport

SCREENSPORT
6.30 Basketball: Trophée Legrand. Yellow Jackets of Georgia Tech. – CAI Sargasse

SUPER CHANNEL
6.30 Bonanza
7.30 Serie Noire

TV 5 (French)
7.00 Carré Vert

TV 1000
7.00 The TV–1000 Hour (uncoded)

WORLDNET
(Only broadcasts between 12 a.m. and 3.p.m)

TV-STOCKHOLM
7.00 Film, Art and Theatre

Z-TV
7.00 Spirit of Adventure

Most television viewing takes place between 6 and 10 o'clock in the evening on an ordinary weekday. Families that have cable television can choose from some 30 channels.

Many people watch television alone and the wide range of programmes every day means that they can watch something at all hours of the day and night.

Young People's Sports

Various associations within the popular movements provide extensive sports programmes for and among children and young people, at virtually every place in Sweden. These are activities that may be categorised as "organised leisure". What is characteristic of activities within this group is that they are carried out under the supervision of specially appointed leaders and that they are organised at certain, usually fixed times, often once or twice a week. Sports usually offer more training periods per week, and they are normally part of a larger organisational framework. This part of organised leisure time activities plays a significant role in the way the young people involved organise their time. It also affects the way the whole family uses its time.

The list of the clubs and societies in an ordinary municipality shows the wide range of activities that active youngsters can choose from. During the past few decades there has been a tendency for clubs to become more and more specialised.

The present general opinion is that organised leisure time within the framework of clubs is beneficial for society, so there is an extensive range of grants for such activities, even though it may vary from municipality to municipality. The feature common to almost all of them is that the clubs are given some sort of activity grant. These grants are designed so that each meeting with children and young people aged 5 to 25 that meets certain requirements gets a grant partly in the form of a State grant and partly as a municipal grant.

The way in which the authorities make their grants has to some extent led to the specialisation mentioned above. Every club wants to expand. The more meetings that can be reported, the larger the public grants will be to the club.

Thus the number of possible leisure time activities is constantly on the increase. This in turn leads to keen competition for members, particularly active members. Alongside this form of organised leisure time there is a large group of young people who are not involved. It is this group that has on occasions been called "the unorganised youth".

The existence of organised leisure time activities affects all those who are involved. This is particularly true of families with sporty children, but families with active adult sportsmen also find their use of time controlled by the parents' activities.

YOUNG PEOPLE'S SPORTS — A TRANSPORT PROBLEM

Many of the activities in clubs and municipalities require the active support of parents in one way or another. This is particularly true of their efforts to solve what might be called the logistical problems of sport. How can children and young people be transported to their activities in the simplest possible way? The better the transports are organised, the more active participants there will be.

The competition among clubs and their specialisation has resulted in their activities taking place more and more frequently at some distance

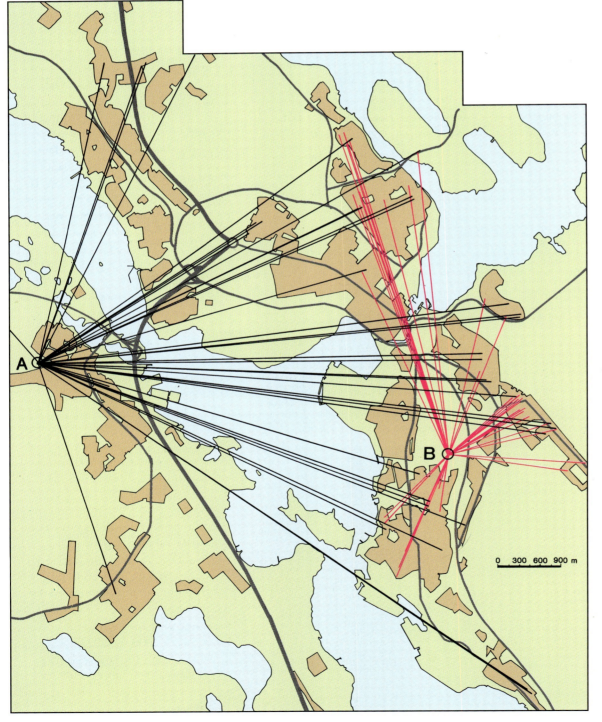

This map of the centre of Piteå shows where the young people who regularly take part in Strömnäs GIF's skiing activities live and train. In winter the youngest members train twice a week on one of the illuminated slopes (B) in the town. The somewhat older members meet at other places, depending on what they are practising. Here you can see the older group training ski-skating at (A). (K50)

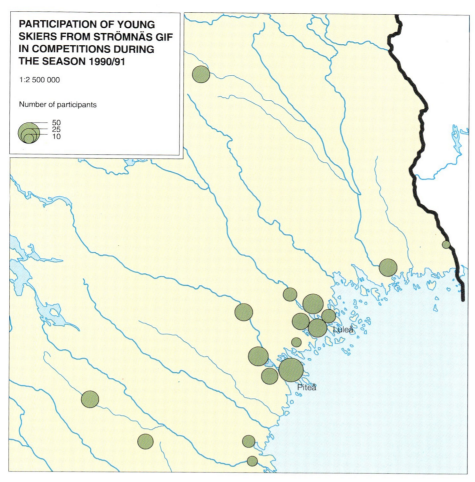

PARTICIPATION OF YOUNG SKIERS FROM STRÖMNÄS GIF IN COMPETITIONS DURING THE SEASON 1990/91

1:2 500 000

Number of participants
- 50
- 25
- 10

There are plenty of sports competitions for young people in which many parents are involved. Many Saturdays and Sundays are spent driving children to competitions and watching them compete. (K51)

Boys and girls have different leisure time interests. Riding is mostly a girls' activity.

from their members' homes. The extreme consequence of this development could be that young people who live near each other do not meet because they are always away from home taking part in some organised activity in another place. Sometimes they take part in the same kind of activity, but organised by different clubs at different places in the town. These varied activities and the consequent driving to and fro demands a considerable amount of time and money from the parents. Taking part in sports requires transportation two to four times a week, in addition to possible journeys to competitions on Saturdays or Sundays during the "season". The schedule is not quite so tight for "idealistic" clubs. Of course transportation is needed in all kinds of club life, but sports and in particular young people who play sports that require a lot of equipment rely heavily on being driven around by their parents.

A parent who drives his or her child to training sessions or matches gives up about 3 x 1.5 – 2 hours on weekday evenings, plus most of Saturdays and Sundays for at least a quarter of the season's weeks.

A comparison with television, the largest leisure time "activity", which costs a Swede 12–14 hours a week, shows that a week of training and competing costs the parent of a sporty boy or girl as much or more time during the week.

Journeys during a 40-week season plus 10 journeys to competitions in a season correspond to one sixth of a normal driver's annual mileage!

In Piteå, with 40,000 inhabitants, there are some 130 clubs and societies that report meetings eligible for grants. In the past few years the total number of meetings which have received grants has been about 40,000. One meeting produces (1992) a municipal grant of 47 kronor (a sum total of about 1,880,000 kronor). In addition there is the State grant, which varies at present according to the organisation concerned.

If only two parents are normally involved in driving children to each of these activities, and the normal distance driven is taken to be as little as 5 km one way, we arrive at a total of 2 x 2 x 5 x 40,000 = 800,000 km. Travelling costs for young people's sports would then amount to something like one million kronor in this medium-sized municipality.

Hunting and Fishing

Hunting and fishing have always been important in country districts. In the agrarian society they were a means of livelihood. Access to good fishing waters was important for food supplies.

Nowadays the importance of hunting and fishing for people's livelihoods has more or less vanished. Patterns of living have changed and only in exceptional cases are hunting and fishing necessary for making a living. Yet the interest lives on. What was previously a necessity of life has now become one of the leisure activities of today's urbanised society.

Only 0.65 per cent of total leisure time is on average used for hunting and fishing. The amount of time women devote to hunting and fishing is hardly measurable.

HUNTING

Despite the minor importance of hunting in terms of time, more than 350,000 people have a hunting licence. Everyone who wishes to hunt must have a hunter's diploma, access to hunting grounds and a gun licence, as well as a hunting licence which is renewable every year. In brief one might say that anyone who has a hunting licence is a sort of "authorised" hunter.

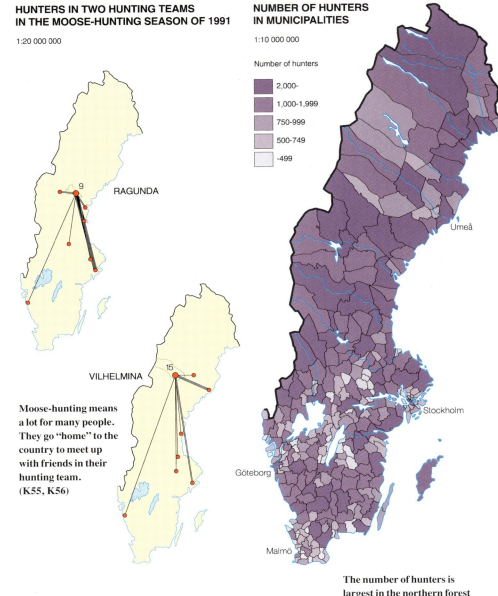

HUNTERS IN TWO HUNTING TEAMS IN THE MOOSE-HUNTING SEASON OF 1991
1:20 000 000

RAGUNDA

VILHELMINA

Moose-hunting means a lot for many people. They go "home" to the country to meet up with friends in their hunting team. (K55, K56)

NUMBER OF HUNTERS IN MUNICIPALITIES
1:10 000 000

Number of hunters
- 2,000-
- 1,000-1,999
- 750-999
- 500-749
- -499

The number of hunters is largest in the northern forest districts. (K57)

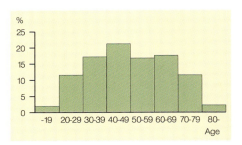

AGE DISTRIBUTION AMONGST HUNTERS IN THE 15 MUNICIPALITIES WITH THE HIGHEST MEAN AGE

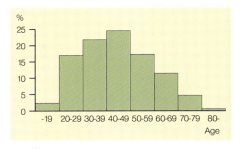

AGE DISTRIBUTION AMONGST HUNTERS IN THE 15 MUNICIPALITIES WITH THE LOWEST MEAN AGE

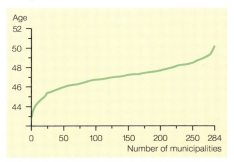

AVERAGE AGE OF HUNTERS BY MUNICIPALITY

In approximately 80 per cent of all municipalities the average age of hunters lies between 46 and 49.

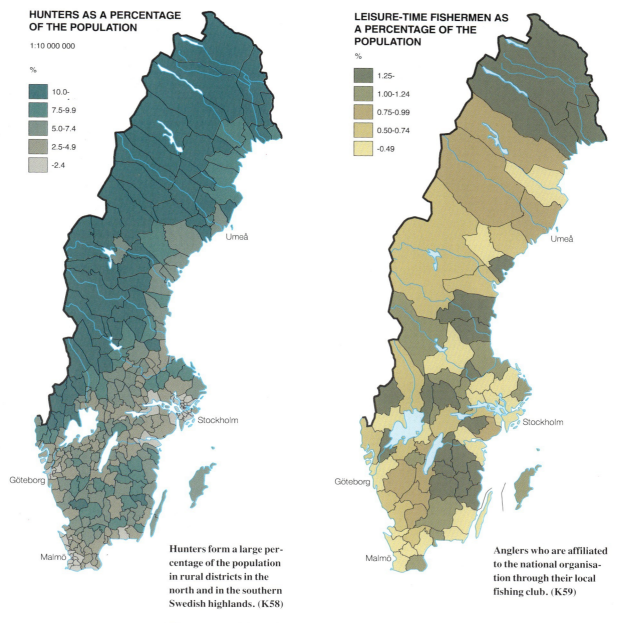

HUNTERS AS A PERCENTAGE OF THE POPULATION
1:10 000 000

%
- 10.0–
- 7.5–9.9
- 5.0–7.4
- 2.5–4.9
- –2.4

LEISURE-TIME FISHERMEN AS A PERCENTAGE OF THE POPULATION

%
- 1.25–
- 1.00–1.24
- 0.75–0.99
- 0.50–0.74
- –0.49

Hunters form a large percentage of the population in rural districts in the north and in the southern Swedish highlands. (K58)

Anglers who are affiliated to the national organisation through their local fishing club. (K59)

The geographical distribution of hunters reveals two tendencies. In areas north of the Norrland border and in the Småland highlands a large percentage of the population are hunters. This agrees with the fact that hunting was a traditional livelihood in country districts. The figures may indicate that hunting is still of some economic importance for hunters in these areas. The picture is quite different if one looks at the municipalities that have a large absolute number of hunters. What is evident above all, and perhaps somewhat surprisingly, is that there are a good many hunters in the major urban areas.

These "big-town" hunters reflect the population migration that has taken place in Sweden over the past few decades. Many migrants have remained members of their old hunting team, often together with retaining shares in their old farmstead, to keep a link with the community they have left. Thus the geographical distribution in hunting teams in country districts is often large. This means that most members of a hunting club can only take part in big, organised hunts. Moose hunting is the most important of these, and for many hunters the only season in which they hunt. This is particularly true of the "big-town" hunters who live far from the hunting grounds. It is quite usual for members of hunting teams to take some of their holiday during the moose-hunting season.

The average age of a hunter varies between 42.5 and just over 50 years. In about 10 per cent of the municipalities the average age is noticeably lower. An equally large group has a noticeably higher average age. The areas with "young" hunters are spread throughout the country, with a certain preponderance in the far north of Norrland, whereas the areas with "old" hunters are mainly to be found inland in central Norrland and in the areas 80–250 km north-west of Stockholm. In comparison with the population as a whole the upper age groups are over-represented. Hunting is the sport of middle-aged and elderly gentlemen!

FISHING

Compared with hunting, which is strictly controlled, it is more difficult to estimate the extent and geographical distribution of fishing.

Anglers are made up of all kinds of persons, from young teenage boys fishing for perch in a creek near home to the groups that go on fishing safaris in helicopters to the Lappland mountains or fish for salmon in Canada or Alaska. Some anglers also form clubs that put out game fish in their own or leased waters.

The Swedes' habitual ability to get themselves organised helps us to get a picture of the distribution of anglers in the country. Without providing a complete and exhaustive survey the distribution of the members of Anglers Associations may indicate how interest in angling is regionally distributed. At the time of the survey, 1 January 1991, there were just over 103,000 registered members, about 71,000 of whom were in local clubs. As with the hunters, the percentage of organised anglers is largest in the forest districts. The picture is not quite so clear, however, as it is for the hunters. The main centres of interest are in Småland, Bergslagen and northernmost Norrland, while the picture in the other forest districts is rather less clear.

The counties of Stockholm and Norrbotten are dominant with regard to absolute figures, having together some 20 per cent of the members. It is difficult to establish the age and sex of those who are interested in fishing, but as with hunters middle-aged men are probably in the majority.

Many people fish in their leisure time without being members of a club.

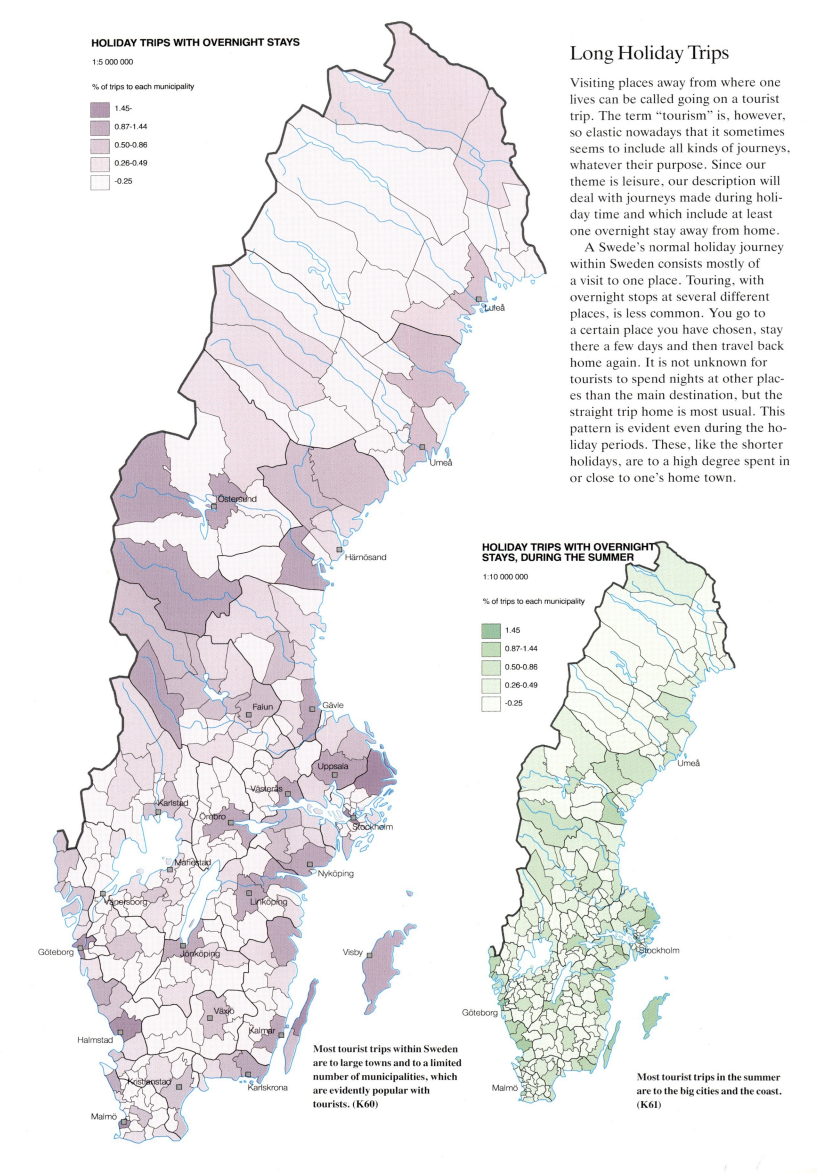

Long Holiday Trips

Visiting places away from where one lives can be called going on a tourist trip. The term "tourism" is, however, so elastic nowadays that it sometimes seems to include all kinds of journeys, whatever their purpose. Since our theme is leisure, our description will deal with journeys made during holiday time and which include at least one overnight stay away from home.

A Swede's normal holiday journey within Sweden consists mostly of a visit to one place. Touring, with overnight stops at several different places, is less common. You go to a certain place you have chosen, stay there a few days and then travel back home again. It is not unknown for tourists to spend nights at other places than the main destination, but the straight trip home is most usual. This pattern is evident even during the holiday periods. These, like the shorter holidays, are to a high degree spent in or close to one's home town.

Most tourist trips within Sweden are to large towns and to a limited number of municipalities, which are evidently popular with tourists. (K60)

Most tourist trips in the summer are to the big cities and the coast. (K61)

HOLIDAY TRIPS TO STOCKHOLM
The 50 municipalities that have most people travelling to Stockholm

1:5 000 000

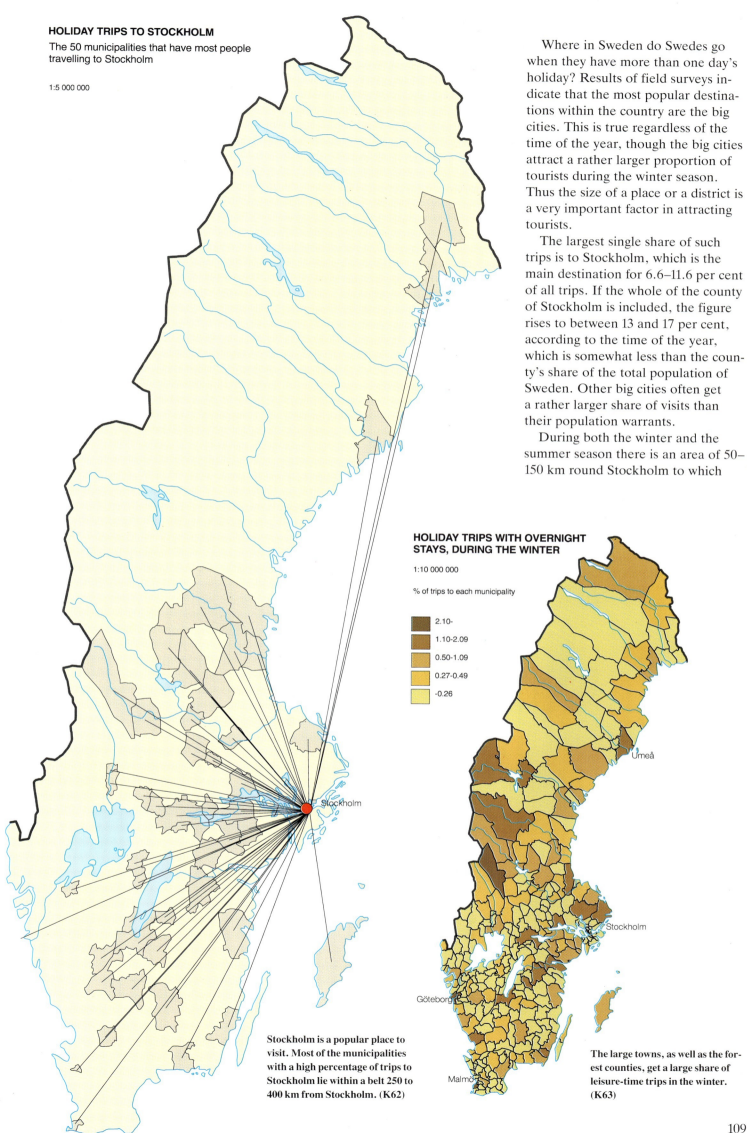

Where in Sweden do Swedes go when they have more than one day's holiday? Results of field surveys indicate that the most popular destinations within the country are the big cities. This is true regardless of the time of the year, though the big cities attract a rather larger proportion of tourists during the winter season. Thus the size of a place or a district is a very important factor in attracting tourists.

The largest single share of such trips is to Stockholm, which is the main destination for 6.6–11.6 per cent of all trips. If the whole of the county of Stockholm is included, the figure rises to between 13 and 17 per cent, according to the time of the year, which is somewhat less than the county's share of the total population of Sweden. Other big cities often get a rather larger share of visits than their population warrants.

During both the winter and the summer season there is an area of 50–150 km round Stockholm to which

HOLIDAY TRIPS WITH OVERNIGHT STAYS, DURING THE WINTER

1:10 000 000

% of trips to each municipality

- 2.10-
- 1.10-2.09
- 0.50-1.09
- 0.27-0.49
- -0.26

Stockholm is a popular place to visit. Most of the municipalities with a high percentage of trips to Stockholm lie within a belt 250 to 400 km from Stockholm. (K62)

The large towns, as well as the forest counties, get a large share of leisure-time trips in the winter. (K63)

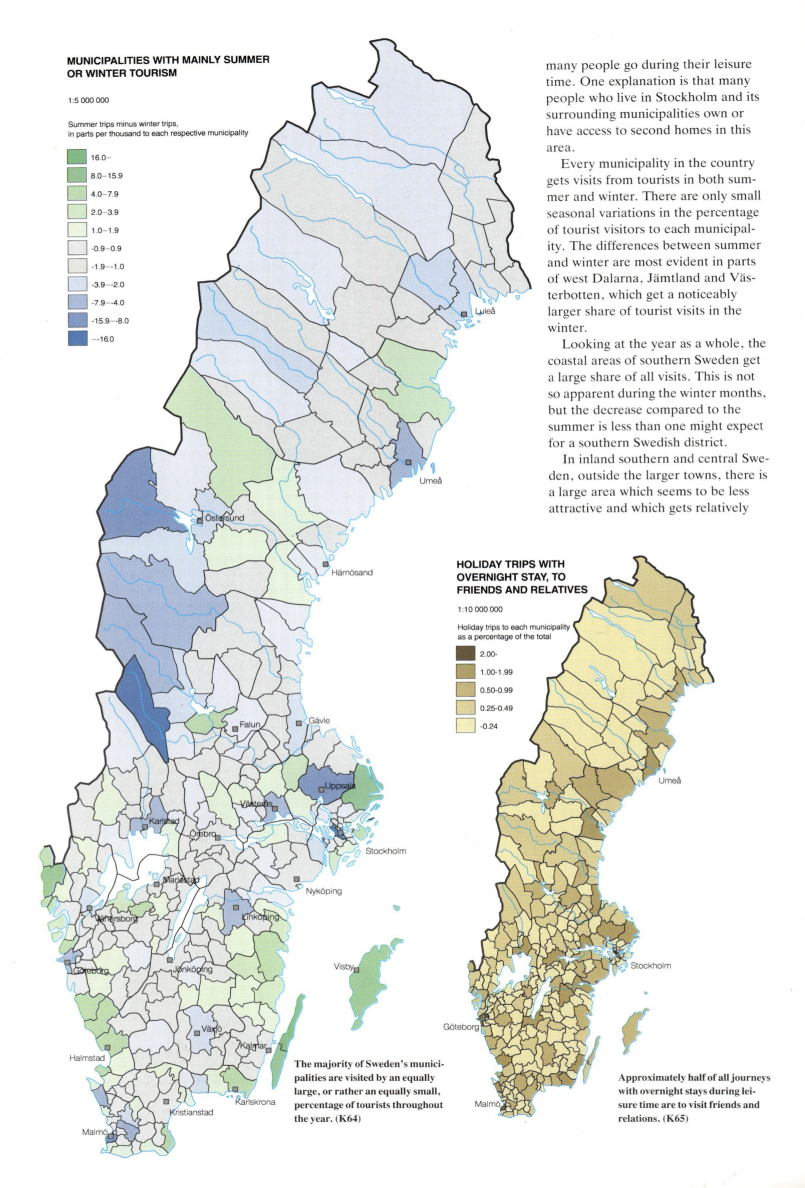

MUNICIPALITIES WITH MAINLY SUMMER OR WINTER TOURISM

1:5 000 000

Summer trips minus winter trips, in parts per thousand to each respective municipality

- 16.0–
- 8.0–15.9
- 4.0–7.9
- 2.0–3.9
- 1.0–1.9
- -0.9–0.9
- -1.9–-1.0
- -3.9–-2.0
- -7.9–-4.0
- -15.9–-8.0
- –-16.0

many people go during their leisure time. One explanation is that many people who live in Stockholm and its surrounding municipalities own or have access to second homes in this area.

Every municipality in the country gets visits from tourists in both summer and winter. There are only small seasonal variations in the percentage of tourist visitors to each municipality. The differences between summer and winter are most evident in parts of west Dalarna, Jämtland and Västerbotten, which get a noticeably larger share of tourist visits in the winter.

Looking at the year as a whole, the coastal areas of southern Sweden get a large share of all visits. This is not so apparent during the winter months, but the decrease compared to the summer is less than one might expect for a southern Swedish district.

In inland southern and central Sweden, outside the larger towns, there is a large area which seems to be less attractive and which gets relatively

HOLIDAY TRIPS WITH OVERNIGHT STAY, TO FRIENDS AND RELATIVES

1:10 000 000

Holiday trips to each municipality as a percentage of the total

- 2.00–
- 1.00–1.99
- 0.50–0.99
- 0.25–0.49
- –0.24

The majority of Sweden's municipalities are visited by an equally large, or rather an equally small, percentage of tourists throughout the year. (K64)

Approximately half of all journeys with overnight stays during leisure time are to visit friends and relations. (K65)

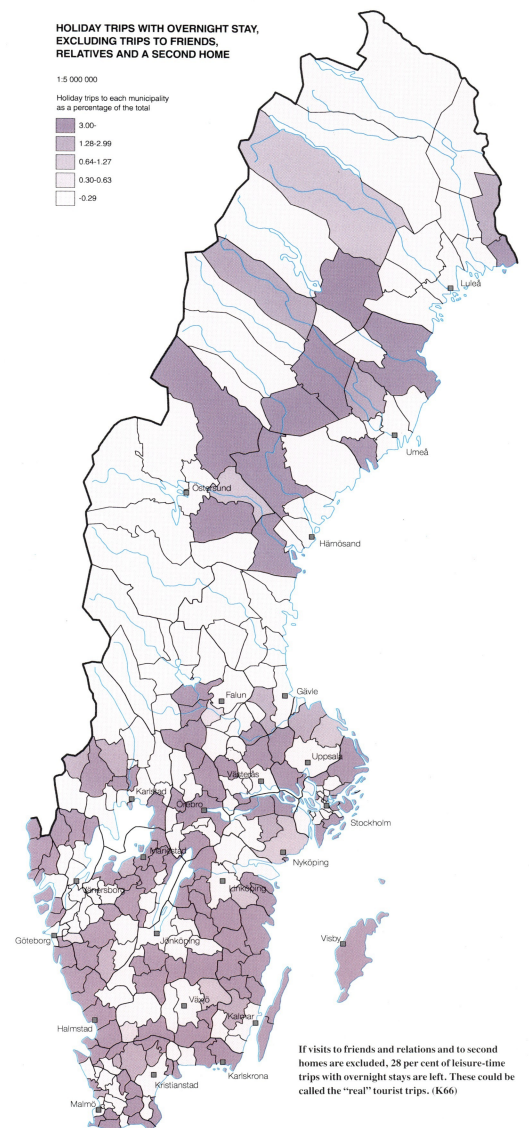

HOLIDAY TRIPS WITH OVERNIGHT STAY, EXCLUDING TRIPS TO FRIENDS, RELATIVES AND A SECOND HOME

1:5 000 000

Holiday trips to each municipality as a percentage of the total

- 3.00-
- 1.28-2.99
- 0.64-1.27
- 0.30-0.63
- -0.29

If visits to friends and relations and to second homes are excluded, 28 per cent of leisure-time trips with overnight stays are left. These could be called the "real" tourist trips. (K66)

fewer visits. This area is comparable to large areas in the interior of Norrbotten and Västerbotten.

FRIENDS AND RELATIONS

The term holiday trip conjures up visions of beautiful scenery, mountain walks, beach life, or visits to museums and so-called tourist attractions. But this picture does not really apply to the average Swedish tourist. The most usual reason for going on a long holiday journey is to visit friends or relations.

The Swedish Tourist Board's figures show that about 48 per cent of all long holiday trips are made principally to visit friends and relations.

Considering the large-scale migrations that have taken place in Sweden in the last few decades, it would be reasonable to expect that a good number of people's summer holiday trips would be back to the old home district, to see the friends and relations who still live there. It seems, however, that the regional distribution of this category of journeys is more or less the same, regardless of the time of the year. In fact the big cities are the most important destination for this type of journey as well. Possibly it is even more usual for those who "stayed behind" to visit their relatives and friends in the towns.

If one chooses to study the 52 per cent or so of trips which are not to visit friends and relatives, a different pattern emerges. The coast becomes more dominant. The same is true of a large area which stretches, with a few minor interruptions, north from Värmland all the way up to the interior of Västerbotten. The patterns of the most usual destinations for holiday trips have, however, a number of features in common, regardless of the type of destination the traveller has.

The above-mentioned 52 per cent of trips which were not to see friends and relatives include certain journeys to a second home in another municipality. Such trips give high tourist figures for the municipalities that are within "second-home distance" of Sweden's largest cities.

If one takes away trips to second homes, 28 per cent of the journeys remain. Journeys with a personal connection are thus out of the picture, and the remainder might well be called real tourist trips. The map now shows a very strong concentration of journeys to the big cities and the well-known tourist attractions.

CINEMA-GOING, 1991

1:10 000 000

Number of cinema-going/inhabitant
- 3.0–
- 2.0–2.9
- 1.0–1.9
- 0.5–0.9
- –0.4

Cinema, Theatre and Sports Events

The cinema, together with the theatre, concerts and visits to sports events etc. occupy on average only just over one per cent of leisure time. So certain groups of people must give clearly different priorities to time for various other activities. One example is the members of sports supporters clubs.

CINEMA

The regional distribution of cinema visits shows that people are most inclined to go to the cinema in the big cities, while certain rural districts have very few visits per inhabitant and year. This distribution pattern may be due to the fact that towns attract visitors from outlying smaller places. Stockholm provides a good example of this. The reduced population basis in rural districts means that there are few performances and thus small audiences. A large population basis means large audiences, which means a wider range of film programmes. In order to provide an even wider range of films, cinema owners in many towns have converted their cinemas into multi-screen theatres offering several parallel performances.

THEATRE

Theatre visits show the same pattern in principle as cinema visits, but on another scale. Even though the National Touring Theatre and the regional theatres have performances in many towns, it is the big cities that have most theatres and most theatrical performances.

Apart from the people who live in the capital, thousands of theatre-goers travel by coach every weekend from the whole of central Sweden, lower and central Norrland to go to the theatre in Stockholm. Most of these trips are to popular performances at the private theatres. Similar trips are arranged to Göteborg and Malmö, but not on the same scale.

SPORTS EVENTS

It is the team sports that attract the big numbers. Their supporters live at a comfortable evening trip's distance from the towns where the various big teams compete in the top divisions. Numbers decrease greatly, the lower down the league the teams are.

Sports spectators are mostly men, and this may be the reason why men devote more time to leisure journeys during normal weeks.

Home-Loving Swedes Make Many Journeys

TRAVELLING IN LEISURE TIME

Approximately seven per cent of leisure time is devoted to travelling. These journeys in leisure time have been estimated in travel surveys to amount to somewhat more than 50 per cent of all the journeys made in Sweden. In the same way a little more than 50 per cent of both travelling time and distance is in leisure time. This share of travelling has grown slowly but steadily. Travel to and from work is generally speaking longer than leisure time travelling, while that which is connected with running the home is shorter. These observations show that leisure travelling is of much greater significance for physical planning than is normally thought. Traffic and transportation planning is, however, mainly aimed at organising systems for work travel.

Leisure-time travelling is clearly a dominantly male activity. This is especially true of Saturdays and Sundays. This distribution is quite natural if one takes into account the distribu-

In most municipalities outside the big cities the number of visits to cinemas per inhabitant and year is very low. People also go to the cinema a lot in university towns like Lund, Uppsala, Linköping and Umeå. (K67)

Spectators at a football match at Ullevi in Göteborg. The top teams in the major sports attract large numbers of spectators, but on the whole there about as many sports spectators as there are churchgoers.

Every weekend large groups of people travel from the provinces into the big cities to go to the theatre. These groups are very important for many bus companies and travel agencies, as well as the theatres.

tion of activities. Men are dominant in those activities which more naturally take place away from the home's immediate surroundings. It also seems to be the case that it is more often men that drive children to and from the activities that to an increasing extent are being organised away from home.

The number of journeys made is to some extent dependent on organised leisure. Public halls and sports centres are, generally speaking, located so that people who utilise them have to travel short distances. Jokingly one might say that the typical leisure traveller is a young man on his way from home to the sports centre.

TRIPS DURING LEISURE TIME

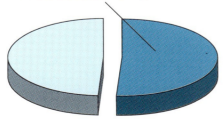

PERCENTAGE OF LEISURE TIME SPENT AT HOME

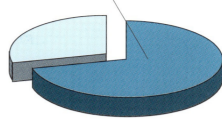

HOME-BASED LEISURE

The use of leisure time in Sweden in the early 1990s is home-based in the sense that more than 70 per cent of all time during a normal week is devoted to activities carried out in the home or nearby. Trends in consumption, meaning that one retires to one's home in an effort to gain control of one's daily life, have been observed in this period. Should these trends become further established in Sweden, the "home share" of life will increase somewhat during the next decade.

Of the remaining 29 per cent of the time, just over one third is used for social intercourse outside the home, and for activities not dependent on special facilities.

Holidays—something to save up

HOLIDAY LAWS

The law on holidays (Autumn 1992) gives every employee the right to 27 days of holiday with pay per year, provided one has been employed during that year. For shorter periods of employment paid holidays are shorter according to the time of employment, but one also has the right to add unpaid days up to a total of 27 days of holiday.

Paid holidays also vary in length depending on one's job; this is determined by collective agreements.

What applies to everyone is that the law on holidays allows one to save up unused holidays from one year to the next. The law entitles one to save up to five days per year for up to five years. Thus a maximum of 25 days of holiday may be saved. According to various agreements certain groups of employees are able to save more than the law allows. Thus municipal employees may use 20 days of their holiday per year and save the rest until they have reached a maximum of 40 saved days.

THE EXTENT OF HOLIDAY SAVING

It seems as if, at least in the municipalities, employees do not utilise all their holiday rights. On the other hand they do save days of holiday for future years.

It is not unusual for employees in medium-sized municipalities to have an accumulated total of 30,000–40,000 saved days of holiday, and the number of saved days is increasing, although the number of personnel is unchanged.

These savings rules have existed for so long that one might expect that there would now be a balance between savings and withdrawals, but this is not yet the case.

THE FUTURE

If the trend of the last few years continues, the number of days of holiday taken in the coming years will be somewhat less than what is allowable according to the law and agreements. If holiday saving continues at the present rate, it will reach a peak of about four times the present volume. If holiday time is increased, saving may also increase more rapidly. In the future more and more people will have approached their maximum. When the ceiling is reached, so to speak, one of two possible effects will arise. Either people will quite slowly and undramatically increase their annual withdrawal of days of holiday up to the number permitted, or quite new patterns of holiday time will arise, with long periods of holiday. Where and how such periodical long holidays will be spent is at present very unclear.

Not all possible leisure time is used. For example, many people save part of their holidays for a later date. An example from a municipality chosen at random shows how the number of saved holidays increases even if the number of work years is constant or decreases.

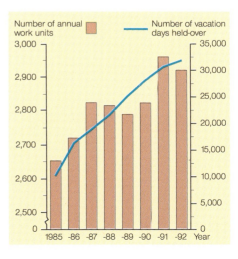

Recreational Areas

The next few pages are devoted to describing the ways in which six recreational areas are used, from the Arjeplog mountains in the north to the Torup Castle forests near Malmö in the south. The landscape/countryside is used in some cases, as at Ytterboda and Torup, mainly by the local population. The landscape may be used intensively, as at Ekerum's Golf Course on Öland, or only in specific parts, as along the Finnskogen Trail in northern Värmland. Or you can just pick wild berries and mushrooms in the forest surrounding your cottage in Småland. The recreational landscape round Ytterbodafjärden is a water landscape, whose open nature may be compared to the snowmobile landscape at Vuoggatjålme.

Snowmobiling in the Mountains

During late winter and early spring, around Easter and up to May lst, there is great activity in those parts of the mountain districts that do not have a ban on snowmobiles at that time. The central stretch of the Silver Way in Arjeplog, past Sädvajaure up to the Norwegian border, is open for snowmobiling. Even in the early winter many caravan owners drive up to the parking grounds between Jäkkvik and the Norwegian border. From March onwards they spend the nights in their caravans, especially at the weekends, in many cases as early as in the February skiing holiday week.

The pattern of driving snowmobiles in the mountain landscape presented here is based on a questionnaire given to all caravan owners in the area during Easter, 1981; it illustrates the holiday traffic starting from Vuoggatjålmejaure and Tjaktjaure west of Jäkkvik. During Easter, 1981, 600 caravans were parked along this road, mainly in 25 places. People from the same home town often keep together—one caravan "park" is called "Arvidsjaurville", in another everybody comes from Piteå. Some 2,000 drivers accounted for the total snowmobile traffic in the area during Easter.

Most of these caravan-owning families have one or two snowmobiles, which are used for both short and long excursions to fishing lakes in the mountains. Journeys of up to 20 or 30 kilometres a day are not uncommon. To some extent the snowmobiles follow special routes, often along valleys and lakes, but some people drive straight across the mountains. Some of the family may sit in a sledge behind the snowmobile. They dig a shelter in the snow high up on a mountain side facing south, drape it with reindeer skins, bring out the coffee thermos and a reindeer meat sandwich and enjoy the magnificent views across a wide-open landscape.

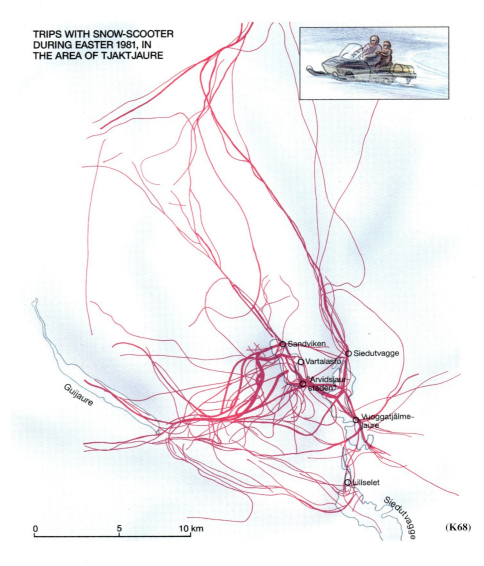

TRIPS WITH SNOW-SCOOTER DURING EASTER 1981, IN THE AREA OF TJAKTJAURE

Leisure Time on the Norrland Coast

The Västerbotten coast, and above all the area behind the Holmö islands, provides a wonderful setting for country cottages and recreation. The coastline is characterised by drumlins, a moraine landscape consisting of long, low spruce-clad ridges which follow the line of the last inland ice movement, here in a north-south direction. Drumlins vary in size, but here they are often one km long and 150–200 m wide. They rise only a few metres above the water, making an unusual shoreline consisting of long headlands separated by fjords a few hundred metres across, with narrow skerries a little further out to sea. The drumlins are ideal for country cottages, as it is easy to run a road along the moraine ridge, in principle giving everyone a piece of land bordered by the sea. Everyone has a boat of their own, most people have their own jetty and the landscape of narrow, sheltered fjords along the coast and more and more open sea the further out one goes is admirable for both winter and summer recreation. But the people there do not come from far away—about 70 per cent of the cottage owners live in Umeå and 20 per cent in Sävar and Holmsund. This means that they can make use of their cottages very often. Some families travel out every other weekend throughout the winter, many live there the whole summer from May to August/September, commuting to work in the towns, Umeå in particular.

A SPRING DAY

You can only really enjoy the inner parts of the fjords on a beautiful early spring day, when the ice is still lying thick between the islands. You go for walks, ride the snowmobile, or ski if the snow is still on the ground, out to some sunny shore. You fish, have coffee and visit friends. A certain geographical pattern is evident: while the people from Bådagrundet mostly keep to the fjords behind Diskgrundet, the Öllerögern families make their way out to the sea. The large group of people on Diskgrundet enjoy a broader area running south and east—but not to the north or to Bådagrundet.

SUMMER EXCURSIONS

The activities that are presented here for the summer require at least one whole week out at your cottage. The activity area covered by a boat is of course larger than in the winter—not everybody has a snowmobile—but for the people on Öllerögern it stretches only as far as the inner skerries. This means distances that seldom exceed a few nautical miles. Those living on Bådagrundet, who have a "one-sided" landscape as they only have one shore, mostly use the narrow waters behind Diskgrundet, but also those along Skeppsviksudden and further out to the island of Bjuren. Many people mention this particular island as the place they go to for an excursion, which means a boat ride of some ten nautical miles, mostly, however, in sheltered waters along the mainland and a large island to the west.

Drumlin landscape at Skeppsvik, Ytterbodafjärden, east of Umeå. Extract from the Quaternary Geological Map, 1:100,000.

Summer holiday landscape on the left and enjoying the ice on a beautiful late winter's day to the right. (K69, K70)

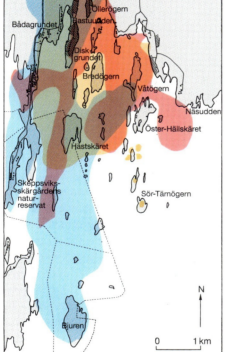
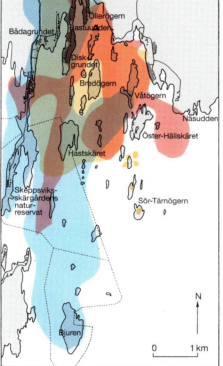

- Public road
- Private road
- Longer paths
- Shorter path
- Brook
- Lake
- Marsh
- Forest

5 min walking distance
m 0 200 400 600

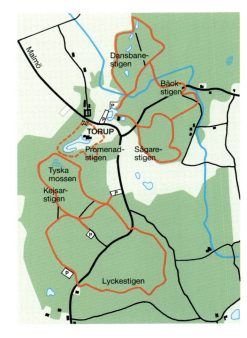

(K71)

Torup — Recreation for Townsfolk

The county of Malmöhus has by far the smallest area of common land, only 800 m² per person, of all the counties in Sweden, and the urban population has only 50–200 m² per person within walking and cycling distance. The municipalities there try to offer their inhabitants not only parks but also more natural landscapes to walk in.

Torup Castle and the surrounding beech forests, about 10 km east of Malmö, have been a favourite place for an outing for the people of Malmö ever since the end of the last century. In those days people went there by train, nowadays it is by bike, car or bus. The Torup Recreation Park, 365 hectares in area, was bought by the Malmö council in 1970, and has been designed and equipped for physical exercise and enjoyable walks in a variety of ways. The area is part of a "primary recreation area" at the national level, but in fact mainly meets the needs for recreation of those living close by in the city of Malmö.

THE BEECH FOREST AND TORUP CASTLE — AT THE TURN OF THE CENTURY

The first castle at Torup was built in the 13th century, but this building was destroyed in the 1530s during the Grevefejden conflicts. The castle was restored in 1630, and in 1970 the castle and its surrounding land was bought by the Malmö council.

Torup's history as an entertainments and recreation centre began in the early 19th century when the owner at that time, Gustaf Coyet, opened his forests to the people of Malmö and built an open-air dance pavilion in the beech forest. The dance floor was of beaten earth. Torup Forest had its heyday as a place for outings for Malmö people after the Malmö-Genarp railway opened in 1894 and up to the 1920s. The railway went past the forest and after a summer restaurant had been opened, a branch line was built to it. At Whitsun, when the beech forest stood in all its verdant splendour, twenty or so special trains, with 25 carriages in each, carried about 15,000 people from Malmö to the Beech Forest. They came with their rugs and picnic baskets, the women in dark skirts and white blouses, the men in cheviot suits, waistcoats and straw hats, the children in sailor suits. A brass band played, the children played on see-saws and roundabouts and elderly gentlemen drank coffee and cold punsch and smoked their cigars on the restaurant veranda.

The railway closed down in 1948 — the growing popularity of beach life had put the Beech Forest out of fashion. In 1970 a cycle track was built from Malmö to Torup, along the old Genarp railway track, which opened a new era in the history of the castle forests.

– AND TODAY

What do we expect nowadays of a recreational landscape close to town? Studies have shown that important criteria are the quality of the landscape, facilities and accessibility. The "natural" quality of a landscape includes aesthetic values, opportunities to enjoy plants, flowers and bird song and a pleasant mixture of culture and unspoilt nature. Opportunities for activities are to a certain extent dependent on the natural conditions: hills, streams etc. — but a great deal can be created with a little good will. Accessibility includes being close to town, but also a lack of obstacles and availability of roads and public transport.

How far does Torup meet these requirements? The landscape-quality criteria are certainly fulfilled. The gently rolling countryside and the magnificent beech trees of all ages, blended with groves of oak, lime and ash, give the best possible background. In the spring white anemones, oxlips and wood violets flower under a canopy of light green leaves. There is a fine old cultural monument to visit — and the castle park is open to all.

An open-air recreation centre with showers and a sauna has been housed in an old granite barn. From it lead several jogging tracks between two and ten kilometres long, two of them illuminated at night. There are walks with names like Dance Pavilion Walk and Emperor Way for less energetic strolls. If you want to go on a longer hike, there is the Skåne Trail and the trails to Svedala and Sturup (14 km) nearby.

Cottages and crofts in the parish of Långasjö, Emmaboda, with a sample of village names. (K72)

A decorated cottage with climbing roses, a rock garden, a terrace and a sun veranda – a long way from the monotony of everyday life.

Summer Cottages in Småland

The little red cottage by the lake with a few birch trees and a wooden fence, a meadow full of wild flowers and a dark fir forest in the background: that is one of the most Swedish of landscapes. A scene to long for for millions of Swedes, and in recent years even for town dwellers south of the Sound.

The red paint on the cottage walls, now so common, does not have a long history. Cottages used to be grey, just like everyday life beneath the low ceilings. The preservative paint from the copper mines in Falun has given Sweden a national colour. The ethnologist Orvar Löfgren speaks of the red cottage as "a magic territory, peopled by dreams, longings and associations. It is a concept blended from nostalgia and love."

The cottage by the lake has become a part of our national heritage. The reality behind the facade—life in the grey cottage which has now been given colour and a romantic veil—was, of course, quite a different one when the old crofter's wife lived there. To literally hack one's livelihood out of the stony Småland soil was no leisure-time occupation.

"Kleiner Bauernhof in schöner frier Lage, mit Erdkeller. DM 30.000"

The red cottage with the white corner timbers in darkest Småland was a very much sought-after property in the 1960s and early 1970s. There was a wave of interest among Stockholmers, for whom country cottages were reasonable priced by big-city standards. Petrol was cheap, so distance was not important. In the late 1970s many cottages were sold to Danes; people who live in Copenhagen have only one third of the way to drive to southern Småland. From the early 1980s buyers from Hamburg entered the scene. Better roads, new bridges and soon Småland was within weekend driving distance from the EC market. And Swedish cottages are cheap when priced in D marks.

DAILY LIFE IN COTTAGES AND CROFTS

Out in the Småland forests, often far from a public highway, there grew up over the past couple of centuries a cottage society. Right up to the 18th century the peasants who owned no property worked in villages in the country, as farmworkers and servants on farms. But after the rapid increase in population in the 19th century, there was no longer work for everyone, so people had to seek their livelihood outside the village.

Soldier's cottages were built as part of the military service system at the end of the 17th century, but the peasant cottage system came into being in the 18th century, reaching its peak in the 19th century. The crofter period did not entirely come to an end until the 1940s.

The crofters' smallholdings had poorer land and were less accessible than the peasants' smallholdings—that was part of the system. A croft should lie outside the village—on a stony slope, in a marsh or generally on infertile land.

Today most of these crofts and cottages have disappeared. Only the foundations and a few fruit trees bear witness to a bygone era. But the few cottages that have been preserved, many in a ramshackle state, have found a new life as second homes.

Roam along the Finnskogen Trail—Country Traditions along the Border.

*"Welcome to Finnskogen!
Visit Finnskogen and meet old cultural traditions and a beautiful landscape. It can also be a meeting with yourself in peace and quiet along the old trails."*

The Finnskogen Trail, inaugurated in 1992, zig-zags up the Swedish-Norwegian border. From Morokulien in the south to Sore Osen in Trysil in the north, 240 kilometres of old tracks and trails pass through nine municipalities. The Trail follows forest-clad ridges, great lakes, rivers and rivulets. You can walk the whole length of the Trail, divided into 15 stages, or join it at parking places on both sides of the border. There are already several places where you can make overnight stays, either in old cottages along the Trail or at some distance from it.

When you walk along the Trail you not only see Nature at its most beautiful, you also have many chances to enjoy the special cultural traditions of Finnskogen in their proper setting. This border country between Solor and Värmland, between the river Glomma and the river Klarälven, is the main area to which Finns immigrated from Savolaks from the middle of the 17th century onwards. The Finns were experts at burn-beating cultivation, and the great untouched fir forests gave them an opportunity to settle and cultivate in their own way these wild and desolate regions that no one else had been able to tame. The cleared land could then be used for building cottages and more traditional farming. The old farmsteads in Finnskogen often lie on high ground, where the rye crop ripened best.

The Finns kept to their old traditions when they built their homes, too. The smoking shed, the drying shed and the sauna house are preserved on many farms.

But today most of the farms have long been abandoned and the fields overgrown. Official bodies and private person are working to preserve this cultural landscape which has been "deep-frozen" at a stage which most inhabited districts passed long ago.

SEVEN COTTAGES IN SEVEN KILOMETRES

If you want to get some idea of the Finnskogen cottage atmosphere in a concentrated form, you should go on a day's outing to Södra Lekvattnet. It's best to start from Lomstorp at the northern end of Lake Lomsen, walk through Österby and Lebiko on the Norwegian side and end your tour at Ritamäki with a cup of coffee.

Finntorp in South Lekvattnet is on the Finnskog Trail. (K73)

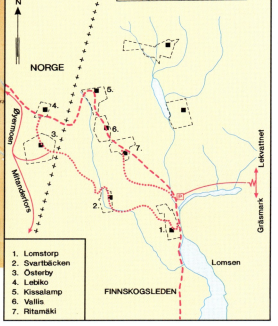

1. Lomstorp
2. Svartbäcken
3. Österby
4. Lebiko
5. Kissalamp
6. Vallis
7. Ritamäki

118

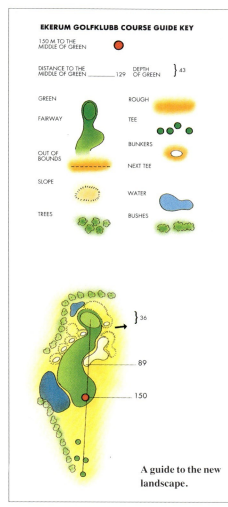

1990 there were some 300 golf courses and in a few years there may be yet another 200. Almost 50,000 people are on waiting lists to join a golf club. (K74)

A guide to the new landscape.

Landscape, with Kalmar Sound in the background, from the terrace of the 18th hole.

Bunkers, Rough and Greens—Our New Landscape on Öland

Ekerum Golf Course, 12 km south of Borgholm on Öland and next door to the Halltorp Meadows Nature Reserve, represents the latest kind of Swedish recreational landscape. Thousands of Swedes are on waiting lists for golf clubs today, but there are a limited number of places and the membership fees lie between SEK 20,000 and 40,000 (USD 3–6,000). This sport and its landscape is faced with many prejudiced opinions. Many people see the course as a protected "green" in the community, to which only the privileged few have access. Outside lies "the rough"—definitely to be avoided. Mowed, rolled, watered, fertilised, shining in the sun, hedged in by a multitude of rules—is this the ideal picture of the Swedish landscape at the turn of the next century?

THE LANDSCAPE AS IT WAS

"The road ran through the most beautiful groves one has ever seen, far exceeding all other places in Sweden and matching the best in Europe. They were of lime, hazel and oak trees growing on smooth, green-clad earth free of stones or moss. Here and there lay the most wonderful meadows and fields. He who has grown tired of this troubled world and seeks to withdraw from its vanities into a quiet obscurity can never find a more agreeable retreat." From Carl von Linné's (Linnaeus) "Journey to Öland" in May, 1741.

The loose debris deposited at the foot of the limestone cliffs on western Öland, when the inland ices melted, swelled up when the land was elevated to form shore lines. The raised terraces on the golf course mark the shores of the ancient Lake Ancylus and the Littorina Sea. The latter is about 7,000 years old. There were settlements on the slopes below the coastal cliffs in the Stone Age. Place names ending in -rum, meaning an open space in an oak forest, appeared in the late Viking era. The farms in the area later became part of the Royal Farm system. When Ekerum was made a farm of its own in 1804, it had 50 acres of cultivated fields, four crofts, one windmill and a lime kiln.

In 1939 the farm was bought by the Agricultural Society and in the 1980s the farm returned to private ownership, farming declined and parts of the landscape became scrubland.

SCOTLAND ON ÖLAND

Nowadays farming is not profitable on Öland, "the island of winds and the sun". The old agricultural landscape at Ekerum has been turned into a Scottish golf links, a course by the sea which is blown by the wind and tough to play. Much of the old landscape has been preserved; today many of the old wooden fences and stone walls between the fields make natural boundaries between the holes. But many fields have been grassed over, hollows have been dug and some of them have been filled with sand to make bunkers. In the Scottish landscape the sheep had to dig down into the ground to protect themselves from the wind and driving rain, which is the origin of the bunkers.

It takes more than 4 1/2 hours to play the first 18 holes on the Ekerum course, and how much of the landscape do you enjoy during that time?

The Future

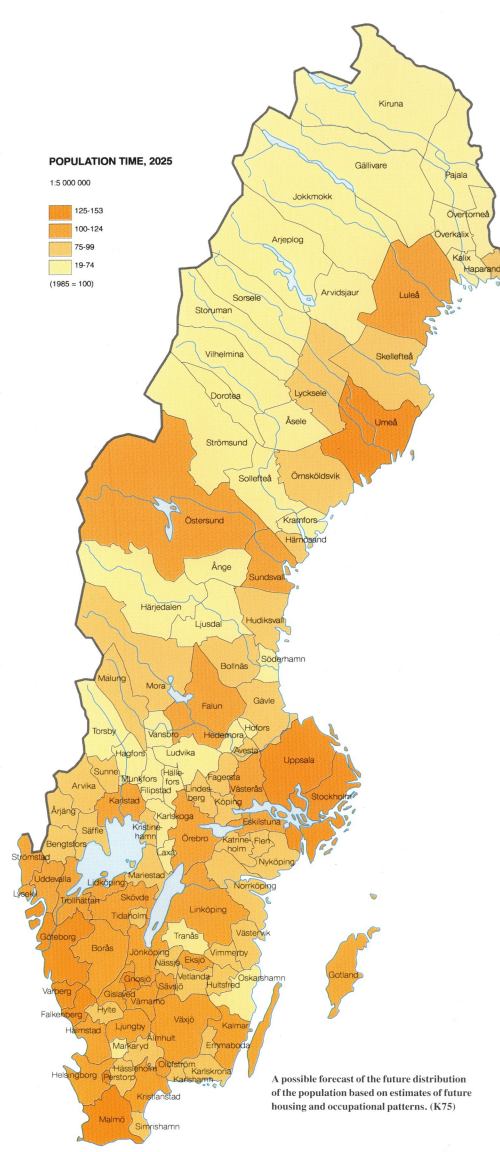

POPULATION TIME, 2025

1:5 000 000

- 125-153
- 100-124
- 75-99
- 19-74

(1985 = 100)

Even short-term forecasts for regional employment and housing can prove to be quite inaccurate. Nevertheless it may be of interest to predict the possible consequences of certain trends by means of projections into the future.

Where shall we spend our working and leisure hours in the future? The home is where we spend most of our time, yet we are at other places for one third of our time. We do this to work or to take part in various leisure activities and to cover the ever-increasing distances between our various activities by travelling. We get a comprehensive picture of where the population spends its time in Sweden by putting together the time each person spends at these various places.

The population time in one region during a year is the total time spent in the region by all the persons who were there at some time during the year. For example, a person who spends three-quarters of his time in his home town contributes 0.75 person years to the population's total time in that town and 0.25 person years to the time in all the other towns—and abroad.

The map illustrates how the distribution in Sweden of the total personal time of the whole population may change between 1985 and 2025. On average 76 per cent of all persons gainfully employed in a municipality in 1990 worked in the same municipality as they lived in, 18 per cent worked in a different municipality within the same county and 6 per cent in a different county. People spend their leisure time to an even greater extent at home and within their home municipality. The average person of working age spends at least 92 per cent of his or her time in the municipality where he or she lives. The municipalities on the map and in the calculations have been gathered together into 111 local labour-market regions, according to Statistics Sweden's division. These regions are defined by commuting criteria. Common destinations outside one's home municipality often lie within people's commuting region.

The distribution of the population among the commuting regions resembles therefore, to a high degree, the

A possible forecast of the future distribution of the population based on estimates of future housing and occupational patterns. (K75)

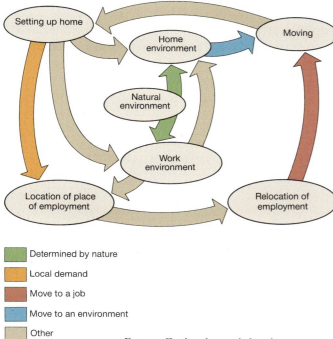

Factors affecting changes in housing patterns.

distribution of dwellings, but what affects the distribution of dwellings? The classic, natural-deterministic answer is that the location of natural resources such as agricultural land, minerals, energy sources, waterways and climate determine where the population can make a living and hence where they live. If these conditions change, we adapt by moving to new jobs. The future distribution of population time will be entirely determined by the ways in which the production environment and employment develop.

These conditions apply, roughly speaking, to hunting, collecting and primitive farming cultures. But specialisation and trade arise very early in human societies. Part of the work in the family/tribe separates out and is replaced by specialised services carried out by priests, midwives, warriors and later millers, blacksmiths, bakers, teachers, grocers and civil servants.

Most services are produced locally even today, and they exist because there is a demand for them from the local population. This localisation is dependent on where the population lives and not vice versa. Yet the localisation of both the population and service occupations is ultimately shaped, in this hypothetical model, by the localisation conditions for other local occupations. The supply of natural resources, transportation and markets determine what can be produced locally—both for direct local use and for "export" to pay for "imports" from outside.

A radically different approach leads to the simple observation that buying and transportation of natural resources accounts for an increasingly small share of costs in the production of goods and services, that transport conditions are as much a matter of "just in time" as distance, and that the market is often equally far away from every place in the country. Such work places are "foot-loose and fancy-free", their localisation in the country is not affected very much by the above-mentioned localisation factors. There are, however, several other factors which do affect the localisation of work places. The largest single cost for most companies is labour costs. The production value that can be got out of labour costs varies and depends on pay levels and how the workforce's training and experience—their competence—matches the needs for current and future production.

According to this theory the localisation of new workplaces adapts mostly to where it is easy to get hold of the "right" workforce—within or outside the country's frontiers. In the commuter regions in which these people choose to live one will find growth in the production which has a market at other places in the country and the world. It is to these regions, too, that the local service occupations and the rest of the population will gravitate. How the living environment is evaluated will directly and indirectly steer the localisation of both housing and workplaces.

There are many theories as to how the values placed on dwelling and production environments by different population groups develop. The emphasis can be placed on the way places are more or less suitable for rural and urban life styles and for different generations. A pleasant climate, beautiful countryside, closeness to open water, the chance of living in the country are common wishes, especially among people who still have experience of the primary agricultural sector from childhood, via the family, relatives or neighbours. The absence of personal security in certain environments, and the wish to live in housing areas that are socio-economically homogenous are gaining in importance when choosing where to live in Sweden. Many people feel that the intense rhythm and the multiplicity of opportunities for work, leisure, education, and personal contact in towns are very attractive factors. A growing minority see the whole world as their arena.

These wishes are often contradictory, varying with age, education and position in life. Many people look for multiple solutions. The "green wave", which concentrated people to small towns, suburbs and the countryside within commuting distance from the labour markets of the major cities, is one example. The "urbanised countryside" is a name for the same tendency round medium-sized and small places. An even later tendency is for certain professions to locate the base station of their work in areas whose attractiveness lies in the fact that it is not possible to commute daily from them to the big cities.

On the other hand, as far as what is produced in Sweden is concerned, the development of pay, competence and transportation costs is very significant. The previous advantage that the forest industries had in their proximity to their raw material is reduced, for example when recycled paper forms a larger proportion of the raw material and when the product is more highly processed and customised—that is to say, distance to the market increases in importance. As in the rest of industry, employment has decreased rapidly in recent years. Previous comparative advantages in education, competence, research and development have been reduced. The growth of the public sector has stagnated. Many experts predict that it will shrink fairly rapidly during the rest of the 1990s, above all because of the need to balance the budget in Sweden but also in order to adapt to conditions in a more integrated Europe. The State's own activities have become a major industry in many places. Some of these "State towns" may well be the crisis points of the 1990s.

The dream of a post-industrial development of the knowledge and service sector has not materialised as far as exports are concerned. The proportion of services in Swedish exports is still small. Even though new high-tech and "knowledge-intensive" products to a large extent involve sales of special services, these need to be dressed up in physical products to become saleable on the world market. So the catchword today is re-industrialisation. The means are investment in the infrastructure, education, research and development work. Even if it succeeds, it is not self-evident that the new workplaces will be where the old

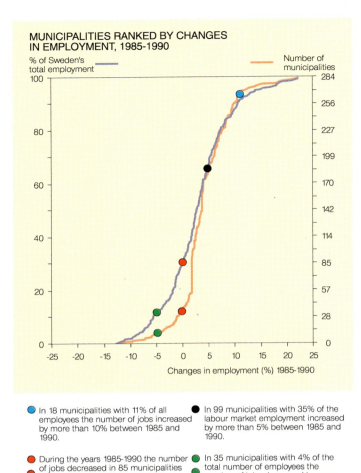

The curve on the right shows how many municipalities had increasing and decreasing levels of employment, 1985–90. The curve on the left shows what part of Sweden's total employment was in municipalities with increasing and decreasing levels of employment. What can be read from the diagram at the marked points is listed above.

There is some relationship between changes in employment and population in the municipalities.

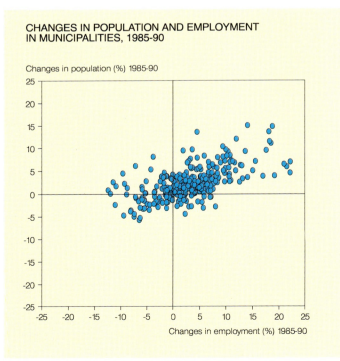

industrial workplaces were. The new ones may well develop better in an environment that is not too heavily burdened with old production traditions.

Re-industrialisation may succeed or fail in various business sectors, the public sector may be reduced more or less drastically, immigration may affect the distribution of population considerably, the extent and destinations of work and leisure travel may change markedly. Likewise there may be changes in different population groups' evaluations of rural versus urban lifestyles, and warmer or colder climates at varying distances from large towns within and outside the country; and the infrastructure can be expanded to eliminate obvious bottlenecks in and round towns or to link up the whole country more efficiently, etc.

Instead of attempting to weigh up speculations in all these areas to reach a "forecast", we present here as an example the consequences of a few simple hypotheses: the housing wishes of well-educated people will in the long term affect both the localisation of workplaces and housing for the whole population; employment to a considerable extent follows the population and well-educated persons are partly to be found where the state's resources for universities, research and development are localised. The significance of the interdependence between the development of housing for the whole population as well as for the well-educated section, the localisation of jobs and the allocation of resources for universities, research and development has been estimated on the basis of data from the 1980s.

Of equal importance for our conclusions are the inertia and variations in the pace of change between municipalities and commuter regions. Population and employment seldom change by more than one or two per cent a year in a municipality. Less than five per cent of those gainfully employed live in municipalities where employment decreased by more than five per cent between 1985 and 1990, ten per cent live in municipalities where employment rose by more than ten per cent. The direct, short-term connection between changes in employment and population in municipalities is relatively weak.

The most decisive localisation factor is that there are and have for a long time been people and activity at a place. As far as employment is concerned, it has been assumed that public sector activities will decrease by ten per cent except for employment funded by grants to universities and R&D (research and development). It has also been assumed that part of the current high level of unemployment will gradually develop into a relative decrease in the workforce, i.e. the percentage of those economically active will fall somewhat. Work in the home and informal work will increase correspondingly. The total population development for the whole country corresponds to Statistics Sweden's latest national population projection. The results at every point in time are balanced out to form an estimated total population time in each commuter region. For the whole of Sweden the sum total of the population time is identical with the total number of inhabitants in that year.

Applying these assumptions to a model that in other respects mainly extends observed tendencies and relations leads to the following result:

Population time (i.e. population and employment) will grow in most medium-sized and large towns. The highest rate of growth will be in Gnosjö, according to these calculations, during the 40 years between 1985 and 2025, followed by Umeå, Stockholm and Uppsala. On the west coast, apart from Göteborg, both Varberg and Falkenberg will show fast rates of growth. Malmö and Perstorp are also expected to show a rate of growth exceeding 25 per cent. The population of Sweden spent altogether 41 per cent of their time in these eight local labour markets in 1985. This may also be expressed by saying that at an average point in time during the year 41 per cent of the country's population was in one of these places. Five years later, in 1990, the percentage had risen to 42 per cent and according to calculations the percentage will continue to rise to almost 50 per cent in 2025. A glance at the map will show that this half of population time is mainly concentrated in four connected districts in and round Stockholm, Göteborg, Malmö and Umeå. Much of the green wave's housing is to be found on the outskirts of these districts.

Another few local labour markets, including Karlstad, Luleå, Jönköping, Halmstad, Linköping, Falun, Helsingborg, Växjö and Östersund, will grow at a faster rate than the national aver-

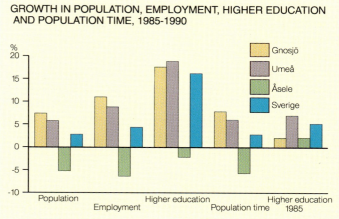

GROWTH IN POPULATION, EMPLOYMENT, HIGHER EDUCATION AND POPULATION TIME, 1985-1990

Gnosjö, which is shown by the calculations to have the fastest rate of increase in population time up to the year 2025, grew more rapidly than Umeå, for example, between 1985 and 1990 as well. The same is true of the growth in population and employment. The number of highly-educated persons increased nearly as rapidly in Gnosjö as in Umeå, but the starting level was as low as in Åsele.

age, i.e. by more than 13 per cent between 1985 and 2025. The diagram here shows the individual rates of development in each of these regions.

Of the 111 regions, 39 in all with a joint total of 76 per cent of the population in 1985 are expected to increase their population time by 2025, when they will account for 83 per cent of population time in Sweden. The other 72 local labour market areas are expected to decrease their population time, more or less rapidly. Altogether in 1985 there were just over two million person years in these regions, i.e. 24 per cent of the total population time. Forty years later this share will have decreased to 17 per cent according to our calculations. In the interior of Norrland, in parts of central and southern Sweden's forest belts and in parts of south-east Sweden the population and level of employment will decrease, thereby reducing population time both relatively and absolutely, but at a fairly slow rate. The use of our national territory for work and leisure will become more concentrated but will not show any fundamental changes in the coming decades. But new conditions, events and priorities within and outside Sweden may alter the pace of the process and the results for individual regions, but hardly the general direction of change.

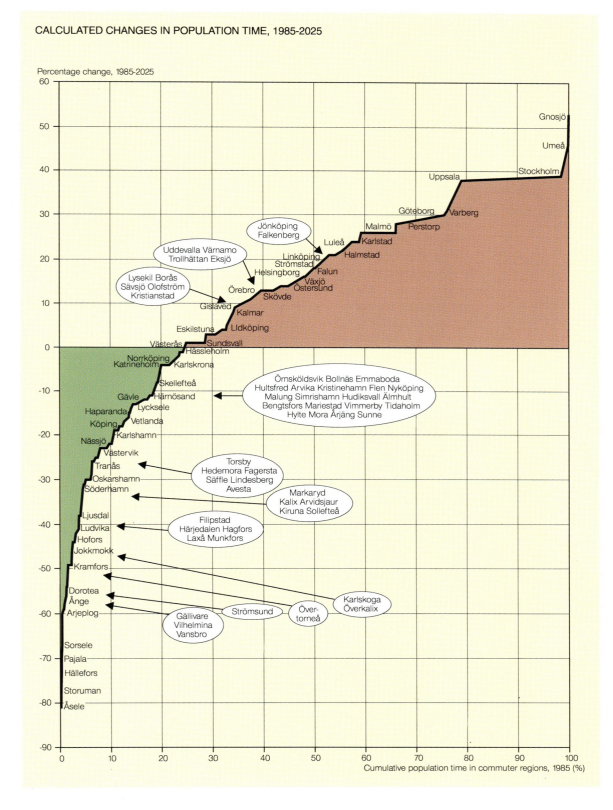

CALCULATED CHANGES IN POPULATION TIME, 1985-2025

The municipalities of Sweden ranked from the one with the greatest decrease up to the one with the greatest increase in estimated population time, 1985–2025, based on the model. The scale below shows what part of Sweden's total population time the various groups of municipalities comprised in 1985.

Literature and references

Aldskogius, G., 1992: *Svensk regionalpolitik. Utveckling och framtid.* Allmänna förlaget, Stockholm.

AKU, *Arbetskraftsundersökningarna 1970 till 1993.* Statistiska meddelanden, Ser. AM, SCB.

Arell, N., 1983: *Arbete och liv i Vittangi-Karesuando-området—om mark-användning och näringsmässiga relationer under äldre och nyare tid.* Umeå.

Braudel, F.,1982: *Vardagslivets strukturer. Det möjligas gränser.* Civilisation och kapitalism 1400–1800. Part 1. Stockholm.

Ellegård, K. och Lenntorp, B., 1980: *Teknisk förändring och produktionsstruktur—en ansats till analys med exempel från mejerihanteringen.* Svensk Geografisk Årsbok, Annual volume 56, pp. 75–88.

Ellegård, K., 1983: *Människa – produktion. Tidsbilder av ett produktionssystem.* Meddelanden från Göteborgs universitet, Department of Geography, Ser. B, no. 72.

Ellegård, K., 1987: *Vardagslivets arbetstid—och livets. Arbetstidens del av befolkningstiden.* Bidrag till en essäsamling från Arbetsmiljöfonden. "Kunskapsutveckling för arbetstidspolitik".

Fransson, U., 1991: *Flytta eller pendla. Aspekter på hushållens rörlighet.* Council for Building Research, SB:39.

Gatenheim, E. W., 1977: *Studiecirkeln 75 år.* Sober Förlags AB.

Heimer, O., 1979: *Bilder från Södermalm 1895–1916.* Compiled by Torsten Palmér. Stockholm.

Hellspong, M. och Löfgren, O., 1976: *Land och stad. Svenska samhällstyper och livsformer från medeltid till nutid.* Liber.

Holm, E. och Tapper, H., 1990: *Geografin i den ekonomiska politiken.* Ds 1990:74, Ministry of Industry.

Hägerstrand, T. och Lenntorp, B., 1974: *Samhällsorganisation i ett tidsgeografiskt perspektiv.* I Ortssystem och levnadsvillkor. SOU 1974:2, pp. 221–232.

Häggström, N., Borgegård, L-E. och Rosengren, A., 1990: *När finländarna kom. Migrationen Finland-Sverige efter andra världskriget.* Council for Building Research.

Ingelstam, L., 1980: *Arbetets värde och tidens bruk—en framtidsstudie.* Liber.

Johannisson, B., Persson, L-O. och Wiberg, U., 1989: *Urbaniserad glesbygd, verklighet och vision.* Ds 1989:22, Stockholm.

Johansson, M. och Persson, L-O., 1991: *Regioner för generationer.* Publica.

Kvinnors arbetsmarknad. 1990-talet—återtågets årtionde? Arbetsmarknadsdepartementet Ds 1993:8.

Nilsson, J-E., 1991: *90-talets regionalpolitik—populära läsningar eller målinriktade åtgärder.* Nordrevy no. 4.

Nordström, B. och Svedberg, P., 1991: *SR Publik- och programforskning: TV-tittandet 1990.*

Olsson, J., 1990: *70-talisternas värderingar. Delredovisningar 1–3. Ungdomars etablering på arbetsmarknaden.* Institute for Futures Studies.

Sanne, C., 1991: *Mer eller mindre arbete?—löntagarnas arbetstidsönskemål.* SCB, Levnadsförhållanden, Report 70.

SCB, SOS, 1991: *Tema invandrare.* Levnadsförhållanden, Report 69.

SCB, SOS: *Så använder vi tiden.* Preliminär rapport från tidsanvändningsundersökningen. Levnadsförhållanden, Report 59.

SCB, SOS, 1989: *Arbetstiden—omfattning och förläggning.* Information om arbetsmarknaden 1989:2.

SCB, *Hälsan i Sverige.* Hälsostatistisk årsbok 1991/92.

SCB, 1990: *Offentliga sektorn. Utveckling och nuläge.* Second edition.

SCB, *Arbetsförhållanden, ohälsa och sjukfrånvaro 1975–1989.* Levnadsförhållanden, Report 78.

Straarup, J., 1992: *Svenska kyrkans statistik per stift 1991.* Tro & Tanke 1992:10. Church of Sweden Research Department, Uppsala.

SOU, 1992:27: *Årsarbetstid.* Ny lag om arbetstid och semester. Framtider no. 1, 1992: Kaos i livets trappa.

Vilhemson, B., 1988: *Befolkningens resvanor i tidsperspektiv. Livscykel- och generationsaspekter perioden 1978–1985.* School of Economics at Göteborg University. CHOROS 1988:1. Göteborg.

Vilhelmson, B., 1990: *Vår dagliga rörlighet. Om resandets utveckling, fördelning och gränser.* School of Economics at Göteborg University. CHOROS 1990:3. Göteborg.

Authors

Abrahamsson, Kurt Viking, 1934, Ph. D., Department of Geography, Umeå University

Arell, Nils, 1938, Ph. D., Department of Geography, Umeå University

Borgegård, Lars-Erik, 1941, Ph. D., Department of Geography, Umeå University

Ellegård, Kajsa, 1951, Ph. D., Department of Human and Economic Geography, Göteborg University

Fransson, Urban, 1948, Researcher, National Institute for Building Research, Gävle

Holm, Einar, 1942, Professor, Department of Geography, Umeå University

Jansson, Bruno, 1942, F. L., Department of Geography, Umeå University

Lenntorp, Bo, 1938, Ph. D., Department of Social and Economic Geography, Lund University

Lundin, Lars, 1943, Researcher, National Institute for Building Research, Gävle

Many persons have in different ways contibuted to our work. We would in particular like to mention Marita Andersson, Ann-Mari Eriksson and Jessica Rydberg, at the National Institute for Building Research in Gävle, Håkan Appelblad, Erik Bylund and Johan Håkansson, at the Department of Geography in Umeå, and Ulf Wiberg, at Centre for Regional Science in Umeå.

Thematic Maps

MAP	SCALE	THEME	PAGE
K1		A letter to Venice	11
K2		Important industries and investment projects in the 19th century	16
K3	1:20M	Dairies 1985	30
K4	1:20M	Dairies 1930	32
K5	1:10M	Higher education, born in the thirties	44
K6	1:10M	Higher education, born in the forties	44
K7	1:10M	Higher education, born in the fifties	44
K8	1:5M	Years of education	45
K9	1:20M	University students	45
K10	1:5M	Active workforce	46
K11	1:2,5M	Work 1989	48–49
K12	1:5M	Women in the workforce	50
K13	1:5M	Women at work	51
K14	1:10M	Part-time work	52
K15	1:10M	Distribution of working hours	52
K16	1:5M	Men at work, aged 55–64 years	53
K17	1:5M	Persons working in manufacturing	54
K18	1:5M	Persons working in the public sector	55
K19	1:2,5M	Public and private employment	56–57
K20	1:5M	Persons working in the service sector	58
K21	1:10M	Knowledge-intensive occupations	58
K22	1:10M	Research and higher education	58
K23	1:10M	Cultural activities	59
K24	1:10M	Banking and finance	59
K25	1:10M	Persons working in business services	59
K26	1:1,25M	Journeys to work	62–69
K27	1:5M	Commuting to work	68
K28		Local labour markets, 1970	70
K29		Local labour markets, 1980	70
K30	1:10M	Commuters	71
K31-K32		The work force at home and at work in Gävle	74–75
K33	1:5M	Migration into three municipalities	77
K34	1:10M	Foreign-born persons	79
K35	1:20M	Unemployment 1981	80
K36	1:20M	Unemployment 1988	80
K37	1:20M	Unemployment 1992	80
K38	1:5M	Unemployment, Jönköping county 1992	80
K39	1:5M	Unemployment, Norrbotten county 1992	80
K40	1:10	Disability pensions among men, aged 50–64 years	81
K41	1:10M	Absence from work due to illness	82
K42	1:5M	Earned income per employed	85
K43	1:10M	Development areas 1972	91
K44	1:10M	Development areas 1990	91
K45	1:10M	Duration of regional development support	91
K46	1:10M	Relocated employment	92
K47	1:10M	Regional distribution of state subsidies	93
K48		Development areas within EC	93
K49	1:10M	Book loans from public libraries, 1989	99
K50		Where the young people who regularly take part in Strömnäs GIF's skiing activities live and train	102
K51	1:2,5M	Participation of young skiers from Strömnäs GIF in competitions, 1990/91	103
K52	1:10M	Study-circle hours 1990	104
K53	1:10M	Attendances at services in the church of Sweden, 1991	105
K54	1:10M	Members of free churches in Sweden, 1990	105
K55	1:20M	Hunters in a moose-hunting team, Ragunda 1991	106
K56	1:20M	Hunters in a moose-hunting team, Vilhelmina 1991	106
K57	1:10M	Number of hunters in municipalities	106
K58	1:10M	Hunters as a percentage of the population	107
K59	1:10M	Leisure-time fishermen as a percentage of the population	107
K60	1:5M	Holiday trips with overnight stays	108
K61	1:10M	Holiday trips with overnight stays, during the summer	108
K62	1:5M	Holiday trips to Stockholm	109
K63	1:10M	Holiday trips with overnight stays, during the winter	109
K64	1:5M	Municipalities with mainly summer or winter tourism	110
K65	1:10M	Holiday trips with overnight stays, to friends and relatives	110
K66	1:5M	Holiday trips with overnight stays, excluding trips to friends, relatives and a second home	111
K67	1:10M	Cinema-going, 1991	112
K68		Snowmobiling around the lake Tjaktjaure	114
K69		Recreational areas during the summer	115
K70		Recreational areas a spring day	115
K71		Torup recreation area	116
K72		Cottages and crofts in the parish of Långasjö socken, Småland	117
K73		The Finnskogen Trail	118
K74	1:20M	Golf courses, 1990	119
K75	1:5M	Population time, 2025	120

Acknowledgements for Illustrations

B = Bildhuset AB
LMV = Lantmäteriverket (National Land Survey of Sweden)
N = Naturfotografernas bildbyrå (Agency of Nature Photographers/Sweden)
NM = Nordiska museet (The Nordic Museum)
RFV = Riksförsäkringsverket (National Social Insurance Board)
SCB = Statistiska centralbyrån (Statistics Sweden)
SGU = Sveriges geologiska undersökning (Geological Survey of Sweden)
SNA = Sveriges Nationalatlas (National Atlas of Sweden)
SSM = Stockholms Stadsmuseum (The City Museum of Stockholm)
TDB = Turist och resedatabasen, Sveriges turistråd (Tourist and Travelling Data Base, Swedish Tourist Board)
Tio = Tiofoto AB

Page
2 Drawing Nils Forshed
6 Drawing Nils Forshed
7 Diagram SNA, data SCB
8 Diagram top SNA, data SCB
Diagram bottom Hans Sjögren, data Svensk kärnbränslehantering/Swedish Nuclear Fuel and Waist Management CO
9 Drawing Nils Forshed
10 Drawings Nils Forshed
11 Maps SNA, data Braudel
Drawings Hans Sjögren
12 Photo top Réunion des Musées Nationaux, Paris
Photo bottom NM
13 Photo SSM
14 Drawing Nils Forshed
15 Maps Hans Sjögren, data Arell
Diagram Hans Sjögren, data Arell
16 Map top Nils Forshed
Map bottom Hans Sjögren, data NM
17 Photos SSM
Diagram Bokstaven, data Borgegård and others
18 Photos NM
19 Photo top SSM
Photo bottom NM
Diagram Hans Sjögren
20 Photos SSM
21 Photo top private
Photo bottom SSM
22 Diagram SNA, data SCB
Drawings Nils Forshed
23 Diagram top SNA, data SCB
Diagram bottom Hans Sjögren, from Ellegård
Drawings Nils Forshed
24 Diagram top Hans Sjögren, from Ellegård
Diagram bottom SNA, data SCB
Drawing Nils Forshed
25 Drawing Nils Forshed and Hans Sjögren, from Ellegård
26 Drawing Nils Forshed, data Ellegård
27 Diagram SNA, data SCB
28 Drawing Hans Sjögren, data Ellegård
29 Diagram SNA, data SCB
Drawing Hans Sjögren, data Ellegård
30 Map and diagram SNA, data SCB
Drawings Nils Forshed
31 Diagram left SNA, data SCB
Diagram right SNA, from Ellegård
Drawings Nils Forshed
32 Map and diagram SNA, data SCB
Photo Arla
Drawings Nils Forshed
33 Diagram left and bottom right SNA, data SCB
Diagram top right SNA, from Ellegård
Drawing Nils Forshed
34 Diagram SNA, data SCB
Drawings Nils Forshed
35 Diagram SNA, from Ellegård
Drawing top Hans Sjögren
Drawing bottom Nils Forshed
36 Drawing Nils Forshed
37 Drawing Nils Forshed, from Ellegård
38–39 Drawing Nils Forshed
40 Diagram Hans Sjögren, from Borgegård
Photo Hans Pettersson
Drawing Nils Forshed
41 Diagram SNA, data SCB
Photo Västerbotten

125

	museum, Harald Österberg		Diagram right SNA, data SCB		Forshed Drawing bottom Herr Sandberg	114	Tio Map top left SNA Map top right Hans Sjögren, from Abrahamsson Drawing Nils Forshed
42	Diagram Bokstaven, data SCB Photo Anders Kratz	74	Map SNA, data SCB Photo Sundberg and Olsson/Skoindustrimuseet	95	Drawing top OA Drawing bottom Nils Forshed Photo Heine Pedersen/B	115	Map top SGU Soilmap AK5, Umeå/Holmön, scale 1:100 000 Map bottom Hans Sjögren, from Abrahamsson Drawing Nils Forshed
43	Diagram SNA, data SCB	75	Map top SNA Map bottom SNA, data SCB Diagram Hans Sjögren, data SCB Photo LMV	96	Drawing Hans Sjögren Photo Ulf Risberg/N		
44	Photo Lidingö School Administration Maps SNA, data SCB			97	Drawing left Martin Lamm Drawing and diagram right Hans Sjögren, data Sveriges Radio and Närradionämnden		
45	Maps SNA, data SCB Diagram SNA, data SCB	76	Diagram SNA, data SCB			116	Map Hans Sjögren Drawing Nils Forshed
46	Map SNA, data SCB Diagram SNA, data SCB	77	Map SNA, data SCB			117	Map Abrahamsson Photo K V Abrahamsson Drawing Nils Forshed
47	Drawings Nils Forshed	78	Photo top Tommy Landberg/Ateljé J-berg Photo bottom Tommy Olofsson/Mira	98	Diagram SNA, data		
48–49	Map SNA, data SCB			99	Map SNA, data SCB Photo left Hans Wretling/Tio Photo top right Nils Johan Norenlind/Tio Photo bottom right Hans Wretling/Tio	118	Map left Lars Norrby Map right Hans Sjögren, from Abrahamsson Drawing Nils Forshed
50	Map SNA, data SCB Diagram SNA, data SCB	79	Map SNA, data SCB Diagram SNA, data Regionplane- och trafikkontoret/Office of Regional Planning and Urban Transportation				
51	Map SNA, data SCB Diagram SNA, data SCB					119	Map SNA, data Svenska golfförbundet Photo K V Abrahamsson Drawing Nils Forshed
52	Maps SNA, data SCB Diagram SNA, data SCB			100	Diagram SNA, data SCB Photo Sveriges Radios Bildarkiv		
53	Map SNA, data SCB Diagram SNA, data SCB Photo Hans Pettersson	80	Maps SNA, data SCB Diagram SNA, data SCB	101	Diagram SNA, data Sveriges Radio AB Photo Hans Pettersson Drawing Hans Sjögren	120	Map SNA, data SCB
						121	Diagram Hans Sjögren data SCB
54	Map SNA, data SCB Photo Karin Larsson	81	Map SNA, data SCB Diagram top SNA, data RFV Diagram bottom Hans Sjögren, data SCB Photo Eva Hedling/Tio			122	Diagram SNA, data SCB
55	Map SNA, data SCB Photo Felix Oppenheim/B			102	Map SNA, data Jansson	123	Diagram SNA, data SCB
				103	Map SNA, data Jansson Photo Torbjörn Lilja/N		
56	Diagram SNA, data SCB	82	Map SNA, data RFV Diagram SNA, data RFV Photo Staffan Arvegård/N				
56–57	Map SNA, data SCB			104	Map SNA, data SCB Photo top private Photo bottom Jan Rietz/Tio		
58	Maps SNA, data SCB Photo Per Lindström						
59	Maps SNA, data SCB	83	Diagram Hans Sjögren, data SCB Photo Pär Domeij/Great Shots	105	Maps and diagram SNA, data Svenska kyrkans forskningsråd/Church of Sweden Research Department Photo Folke Hårrskog/N		
60	Photo Lars Berglund Drawing Hans Sjögren						
61	Diagram SNA, data SCB Photo top Sveriges järnvägsmuseum/The Railroad Museum Photo centre Örebro County Museum Photo bottom Jan Töve J:son/N Drawing Hans Sjögren	84	Diagram SNA, data SCB				
		85	Map SNA, data SCB Photo S-E Banken				
		86	Diagram SNA, data SCB				
		87	Diagram SNA, data SCB Photo top Lena Paterson/Tio Photo bottom Bo Brännhagen/N	106	Maps and diagram SNA, data Svenska jägarförbundet/Swedish Hunters Association Photo Hilding Mickelsson/N		
62–69	Map SNA, data SCB						
64	Photo Klas Rune/N						
67	Diagram SNA, data SCB	88	Photo Kramfors kommun				
68	Map SNA, data SCB	89	Diagram Hans Sjögren, data SCB Photo top Georg Sessler/B Photo bottom John Wahlbjärg/Bureau 21 AB	107	Map left SNA, data Svenska jägarförbundet Map right SNA, data Fritidsfiskarna Photo Tor Lundberg/N		
69	Map SNA, data SMHI						
70	Maps Hans Sjögren, data SCB						
71	Map SNA, data SCB Photo top Hans Wretling/Tio Photo bottom Nils Johan Norenlind/Tio			108	Maps SNA, data TDB		
		90	Photo top Hilding Mickelsson/N Photo bottom Bo Rosén	109	Maps SNA, data TDB		
				110	Maps SNA, data TDB		
72	Diagram top Hans Sjögren, data SCB Diagram bottom SNA, data SCB Photo top John Björklund/Kulturförvaltningens arkiv, Fagersta Photo centre Planand byggkontoret, Eksjö Photo bottom Per Lindström	91	Maps SNA, data Svensk författningssamling/Code of Statutes Photo Valmet	111	Map SNA, data TDB		
				112	Map SNA, data Svenska Filminstitutet/Swedish Film Institute Photo Bengt Olof Olsson/B		
		92	Map SNA, data SCB Photo Stefan Kalm/Bild-punkten AB				
		93	Map left SNA, data SCB Map right SNA Drawing Gunnel Eriksson/Typoform, data SCB	113	Diagram top and bottom left SNA, data SCB Diagram bottom right SNA, data Jansson Photo Lena Paterson/		
73	Diagram left Hans Sjögren, data SCB						
		94	Drawing top Nils				

Index

Attendances at services **105** (K53)

Banking and finance **59** (K24)
Book loans **99** (K49)
Braudel, Fernand 10
Business services **59** (K25)

Careerist 47
Church of Sweden 105
Cinema 112, **112** (K67)
Coastal population 18
Commuting 61, 62–69 (K26), 68 (K27), 71 (K30)
Constraints on everyday life 37
Cottages and crofts **117** (K72)
Cultural activities **59** (K23)

Dairies **30** (K3), **32** (K4)
Development areas **91** (K43–45)
Development areas within EC **93** (K48)
Disability pensions **81** (K40)

EC **93** (K48)
Early retirement 81
Earned income **85** (K42)
Economic activity 50
Education 44, **44** (K5, K6, K7), **45** (K8), **58** (K22), 77
Eksjö 72
Employee 46
Employment 23, 122
Everyday resources 38

Fagersta 72
Family in a smalltown 26
Family in the big city 24
Finnskogen Trail 118, **118** (K73)
Fishing 106
Foreign-born persons **79** (K34)
Free churches 105, **105** (K54)
Full-time 52

Gainful employment 46, 55
Gnosjö 72, 123
Golf courses **119** (K74)
Gävle 74

Hobbies 99
Holiday trips 108, **108** (K60, K61), **109** (K62, K63), 110 (K64, K65), **111** (K66), 112
Holidays 113
Household 27
Household work 86
Housing patterns 121
Hunting 106, **106** (K55-K57), **107** (K58) (K57, K58)

Illness 82, **82** (K41)
Immigration 78
Ingot steel process 19
Intensiveness of economic activity 52

Jönköping county 70, **80** (K38)

Labour markets 60, 70, **70** (K28, K29)
Labour Movement's 89
Labour organisations 88
Lancashire method 19
Legislation 89
Leisure 94
Leisure-time fishermen **107** (K59)
Life phases 28
Life's stages 12, 40

MTM method 19
Manufacturing 19, 54, **54** (K17)
Men **53** (K16)
Migration **77** (K33)
Migrational work 16

Norrbotten county **80** (K39)

Olsson, Oscar 104
Opportunities in everyday life 36

Part-time work 52, **52** (K14)
Participation in competitions **102** (K50), **103** (K51)
Pay 13, 84
Perceptions of time 10
Population pyramids 22
Population time 120, **120** (K75), 123
Private employment **57** (K19)
Producticity 9
Public employment **57** (K19)
Public sector 54, **55** (K18)

Radio 97, 101
Reading 99
Recreational areas 114, **115** (K69, K70)
Regional policies 90
Reindeer farming year 15
Reindeer nomadism 14
Religious activities 105
Relocated employment **92** (K46)
Relocation policy 91
Research **58** (K22)

Service sector **58** (K20), 59
Småland 117
Snapshots in time 30
Snowmobiling **114** (K68)
Social intercourse 99
Social life 20
Sports 102, 112
State subsidies **93** (K47)
Stockholm, trips to **109** (K62)
Study circles 104, **104** (K52)

Television 97, 100
Theatre 112
Torup 116, **116** (K71)
Transport routes for milk 30–35

Unemployment 80, **80** (K35-K39)
University students **45** (K9)
Use of time 7, 23

Venice 11, **11** (K1)
Video 101

Women **50** (K12), **51** (K13)
Work 40, **48–49** (K11)
Work specialisation 42
Workforce **46** (K10)
Working environments 83
Working hours 29, **52** (K15)
Working year 17

Öland 119

National Atlas of Sweden

A geographical description of the landscape, society and culture of Sweden in 17 volumes

MAPS AND MAPPING
From historic maps of great cultural significance to modern mapping methods using the latest advanced technology. What you didn't already know about maps you can learn here. A unique place-name map (1:700,000) gives a bird's-eye view of Sweden. Editors: **Professor Ulf Sporrong, geographer, Stockholm University, and Hans-Fredrik Wennström, economist, National Land Survey, Gävle.**

THE FORESTS
Sweden has more forestland than almost any other country in Europe. This volume describes how the forests have developed and how forestry works: ecological cycles, climatic influences, its importance for the economy etc. One of many maps shows, on the scale of 1:1.25 million, the distribution of the forests today. Editor: **Professor Nils-Erik Nilsson, forester, National Board of Forestry, Jönköping.**

THE POPULATION
Will migration to the towns continue, or shall we see a new "green wave"? This volume highlights most sides of Swedish life: how Swedes live, education, health, family life, private economy etc. Political life, the population pyramid and immigration are given special attention. Editor: **Professor Sture Öberg, geographer, Uppsala University, and Senior Administrative Officer Peter Springfeldt, geographer, Statistics Sweden, Stockholm.**

THE ENVIRONMENT
More and more people are concerning themselves with environmental issues and nature conservancy. This book shows how Sweden is being affected by pollution, and what remedies are being applied. Maps of protected areas, future perspectives and international comparisons. Editors: **Dr Claes Bernes and Claes Grundsten, geographer, National Environment Protection Board, Stockholm.**

AGRICULTURE
From horse-drawn plough to the highly-mechanized production of foodstuffs. A volume devoted to the development of Swedish agriculture and its position today. Facts about the parameters of farming, what is cultivated where, the workforce, financial aspects etc. Editor: **Birger Granström, state agronomist, and Åke Clason, managing director of Research Information Centre, Swedish University of Agricultural Sciences, Uppsala.**

The work of producing the National Atlas of Sweden is spread throughout the country.

THE INFRASTRUCTURE
Sweden's welfare is dependent on an efficient infrastructure, everything from roads and railways to energy production and public administration. If you are professionally involved, this book will provide you with a coherent survey of Sweden's infrastructure. Other readers will find a broad explanation of how Swedish society is built up and how it functions. Editor: **Dr Reinhold Castensson, geographer, Linköping University.**

SEA AND COAST
The Swedes have a deep-rooted love for the sea and the coast. This volume describes the waters which surround Sweden and how they have changed with the evolution of the Baltic. Facts about types of coastline, oceanography, marine geology and ecology, including comparisons with the oceans of the world. Editor: **Björn Sjöberg, oceanographer, Swedish Meteorological and Hydrological Institute, Göteborg.**

CULTURAL LIFE, RECREATION AND TOURISM
An amateur drama production in Hässleholm or a new play at the Royal Dramatic Theatre in Stockholm? Both fill an important function. This volume describes the wide variety of culture activities available in Sweden (museums, cinemas, libraries etc), sports and the various tourist areas in Sweden. Editor: **Dr Hans Aldskogius, geographer, Uppsala University.**

SWEDEN IN THE WORLD
Sweden is the home of many successful export companies. But Sweden has many other relations with the rest of the world. Cultural and scientific interchange, foreign investment, aid to the Third World, tourism etc. are described in a historical perspective. Editor: **Professor Gunnar Törnqvist, geographer, Lund University.**

WORK AND LEISURE
Describes how Swedes divide their time between work and play, with regional, social and age-group variations. The authors show who does what, the role of income, etc, and make some predictions about the future. Editor: **Dr Kurt V Abrahamsson, geographer, Umeå University.**

CULTURAL HERITAGE AND PRESERVATION
Sweden is rich in prehistoric monuments and historical buildings, which are presented here on maps. What is being done to preserve our cultural heritage? This volume reviews modern cultural heritage policies. Editor: **Dr Klas-Göran Selinge, archeologist, Central Board of National Antiquities, Stockholm. Ass. Editor: Dr Marit Åhlén, runologist, Central Board of National Antiquities, Stockholm.**

GEOLOGY
Maps are used to present Sweden's geology — the bedrock, soils, land forms, ground water. How and where are Sweden's natural geological resources utilised? Editor: **Curt Fredén, state geologist, Geological Survey of Sweden, Uppsala.**

LANDSCAPE AND SETTLEMENTS
How has the Swedish landscape evolved over the centuries? What traces of old landscapes can still be seen? What regional differences are there? This volume also treats the present landscape, settlements, towns and cities, as well as urban and regional planning. Editor: **Professor Staffan Helmfrid, geographer, Stockholm University.**

CLIMATE, LAKES AND RIVERS
What causes the climate to change? Why does Sweden have fewer natural disasters than other countries? This volume deals with the natural cycle of water and with Sweden's many lakes and rivers. Climatic variations are also presented in map form. Editors: **Birgitta Raab, state hydrologist, and Haldo Vedin, state meteorologist, Swedish Meteorological and Hydrological Institute, Norrköping.**

MANUFACTURING, SERVICES AND TRADE
Heavy industry is traditionally located in certain parts of Sweden, while other types of industry are spread all over the country. This volume contains a geographical description of Swedish manufacturing and service industries and foreign trade. Editor: **Dr Claes Göran Alvstam, geographer, Göteborg University.**

GEOGRAPHY OF PLANTS AND ANIMALS
Climatic and geographical variations in Sweden create great geographical differences in plant and animal life. This volume presents the geographical distribution of Sweden's fauna and explains how and why they have changed over the years. There is a special section on game hunting. Editors: **Professor Ingemar Ahlén and Dr Lena Gustafsson, Swedish University of Agricultural Sciences, Uppsala.**

THE GEOGRAPHY OF SWEDEN
A comprehensive picture of the geography of Sweden, containing excerpts from other volumes but also completely new, summarizing articles. The most important maps in the whole series are included. Indispensable for educational purposes. Editors: **The editorial board of the National Atlas of Sweden, Stockholm.**